A MOB INTENT ON DEATH

Richard C. Cortner

A MOB INTENT ON DEATH
The NAACP and the Arkansas Riot Cases

Wesleyan University Press
Middletown, Connecticut

All inquiries and permissions requests should be addressed to
the Publisher, Wesleyan University Press, 110 Mt. Vernon
Street, Middletown, Connecticut 06457

LIBRARY OF CONGRESS CATALOGING-IN-PUBLICATION
DATA
Cortner, Richard C.
  A mob intent on death.

  Bibliography: p.
  Includes index.
    1. Riots—Arkansas—Phillips County—History.
2. Phillips County (Ark.)—History. 3. National
Association for the Advancement of Colored People.
4. Afro-Americans—Arkansas—Phillips County—
History.
5. Phillips County (Ark.)—Race relations—History.
I. Title.
F417.P45c67   1988   976.7'88052   85-29511
ISBN 0-8195-5161-9 (alk. paper)

Manufactured in the United States of America

First Edition

For David Fellman,
who pointed the way

Preface

I first became interested in exploring the litigation in *Moore* v. *Dempsey* while engaged in research on an earlier work dealing with the application of most of the rights in the Bill of Rights as restrictions upon the powers of the states via the Due Process Clause of the Fourteenth Amendment.[1] Much attention had been devoted to the U.S. Supreme Court's decision in *Gitlow* v. *New York* in 1925, in which the Court assumed that freedom of speech and freedom of the press are guaranteed against state action by the Due Process Clause.[2] It occurred to me that much less attention had been given to its decision in *Moore* v. *Dempsey*, which marked the beginning of the Court's strengthening of the requirements the Due Process Clause imposes on the conduct of state criminal trials. The *Moore* case, I believe, is as important to the law of criminal procedure under the Constitution as the *Gitlow* case is to the nationalization of First Amendment rights. And as my research on the *Moore* litigation progressed, I was pleased to discover that this important milestone in constitutional development also involved an especially intriguing story of constitutional litigation. Indeed, like many other decisions of the Supreme Court, the *Moore* decision proved to be rather like the tip of an iceberg; underlying the decision were more than five years of litigation in state and federal courts that illuminated the nature of the judicial process.

Since undertaking my research on the litigation that produced *Moore* v. *Dempsey,* I have incurred numerous debts of gratitude to both individuals and organizations for help and cooperation extended to me. I therefore express my appreciation to the Manuscript Division of the Library of Congress, the Wisconsin State Historical Society, the University of Arizona Library, and the members of the staffs of those institutions for cooperating in my search for information and archival materials related to the *Moore* litigation. My manuscript has also had the benefit of comment and criticism from my colleagues in the Department of Political Science at the University of Arizona, Professors Clifford M. Lytle, Vine Deloria, Jr., and John E. Crow. I have in addition had the good fortune to have received similar comments and criticism of the manuscript from Professor, Emeritus, David Fellman of the Department of Political Science at the University of Wisconsin-Madison, Professor Karen O'Connor of the Department of Political Science at Emory University, and the late Professor Clement E. Vose of the Department of Political Science at Wesleyan University. The dedication of this book, I hope, adequately expresses my gratitude to David Fellman especially, not only for his help on this project but also for his unfailing support and guidance throughout my professional career.

While I have benefited greatly from the comments of my colleagues on my manuscript, I confer upon them the traditional absolution for any sins of omission or commission that follow. That responsibility, unfortunately, cannot be shared, but must be mine alone.

R. C. C.

Contents

x   Contents

List of Illustrations

Arkansas Governor Charles H. Brough
The New York Sun, October 7, 1919
John F. Miller, prosecutor in the Helena trials
J. S. Utley, Arkansas attorney general, a prosecutor in the riot cases
John D. Arbuckle, Arkansas attorney general
Robert L. Hill, union leader arrested in Kansas
Henry J. Allen, governor of Kansas
E. H. Dempsey, keeper of the Arkansas State Penitentiary
The Chicago Defender, September 3, 1921
News stories about Robert T. Kerlin, Virginia Military Institute profes-
    sor who protested death sentences
Arkansas Democrat, January 9, 1923
Judge Jacob Trieber of Arkansas U.S. District Court
Judge John E. Martineau of the Pulaski Chancery Court

following p. 178
Walter F. White, NAACP assistant secretary who investigated the riot
Article by Walter White, *Chicago Daily News*, October 18, 1919
Mary White Ovington of New York, NAACP board member
James Weldon Johnson, first black secretary of the NAACP
Article by Walter White, *The Nation*, December 6, 1919
Colonel George Murphy, former Confederate officer and
    defense attorney
Scipio Africanus Jones, ex-slave and prominent black defense attorney
E. L. McHaney, white defense attorney
George B. Rose, white Little Rock defense attorney
Editorial in black paper, *The Cleveland Gazette*
Moorfield Storey, Boston aristocrat and NAACP president,
    who presented case to U.S. Supreme Court
Storey's obituary, October 25, 1929, in *The Boston Herald*
Justice Charles Evans Hughes, whose dissent with Justice Holmes in
    the Leo Frank case set precedent for the Arkansas cases
Arkansas Democrat, January 3, 1923
Arkansas Democrat, January 10, 1923
Members of U.S. Supreme Court, whose 1923 decision was a landmark
    of due process

A MOB INTENT ON DEATH

. . . it is our duty . . . to declare lynch law as little
valid when practiced by a regularly drawn jury as
when administered by one elected by a mob
intent on death.

—JUSTICE OLIVER WENDELL HOLMES, JR.,
  dissenting in *Frank* v. *Mangum*

Introduction

The U.S. Supreme Court's decision in *Moore* v. *Dempsey* is a landmark decision under the Due Process Clause of the Fourteenth Amendment. It paved the way for federal constitutional restrictions on the conduct of state criminal trials that are regarded today as commonplace.[1] In addition, the *Moore* case was an important episode in the development of interest-group litigation. It reached the Court through the efforts of a fledgling organization dedicated to justice for black Americans—the National Association for the Advancement of Colored People (NAACP).

Under contemporary principles of constitutional law, it is common practice for the Supreme Court to reverse state criminal convictions it believes violate the Due Process Clause. During the 1960s the Court interpreted the Due Process Clause as embracing almost all of the criminal procedure provisions of the Bill of Rights, imposing those provisions upon the state courts in the conduct of criminal trials and adding significantly to the bases upon which criminal convictions may be overturned on appeal. This "revolution in criminal procedure" made the Due Process Clause a potent instrument for federal judicial supervision of state criminal proceedings.[2]

The origin of this transformation is the 1923 decision of the Court in *Moore* v. *Dempsey*.[3] Before that decision the Court had interpreted due process as allowing the states to conduct criminal trials largely as they saw fit—an interpretation epitomized by the Court's refusal to reverse Leo Frank's conviction in *Frank*

1

v. *Mangum* in 1915, despite evidence that his Georgia trial seemed to have been dominated by a mob.[4] Eight years later, in *Moore* v. *Dempsey,* similar issues of mob domination of a state trial were raised, but this time the Court looked behind the mere forms of proceedings in the state courts and inquired under the Due Process Clause whether the states had, in fact, given criminal defendants fair trials. And writing for the majority in the *Moore* case, Justice Oliver Wendell Holmes, Jr., announced the Court's shift in philosophy in classic language. If "the case is that the whole proceeding [in the state court] is a mask,—that counsel, jury, and judge were swept to the fatal end by an irresistible wave of public passion, and that the state courts failed to correct the wrong,—," Holmes said, "neither perfection in the machinery for correction nor the possibility that the trial court and counsel saw no other way of avoiding an immediate outbreak of the mob can prevent this court from securing to the petitioners their constitutional rights."[5]

The litigation that produced *Moore* v. *Dempsey* began with a racial clash between whites and blacks in Phillips County in eastern Arkansas in October 1919. In the wake of the "Elaine" or "Phillips County" "race riot," sixty-seven blacks were sentenced to prison and twelve other blacks, all men, were condemned to death for the murders of whites. Still only ten years old, the NAACP intervened in defense of the Phillips County blacks and embarked upon what became the Association's most extensive involvement in constitutional litigation up to that time. Retaining as counsel in Arkansas a white attorney who was an ex-Confederate officer and a black attorney who was an ex-slave, the NAACP fought out the litigation until the skill and eloquence of its president, Boston aristocrat Moorfield Storey, won for it the ultimate victory with the Supreme Court's decision in *Moore* v. *Dempsey.* By 1925 the NAACP had succeeded not only in freeing all of the Phillips County blacks sentenced to prison but had, with some compromise, gained the release of the twelve men who had been condemned to death. The NAACP was therefore finally victorious in what it called "one of the most spectacular and bitterly fought contests ever waged for justice in America."[6]

The litigation activities of the NAACP have since been recognized for their expansion of the constitutional right of equality in the United States. The NAACP's contributions to U.S. Supreme Court decisions broadening the right of equality in the fields of voting rights, housing, and, most notably, public education in *Brown* v. *Board of Education,* have been the subjects of much scholarly inquiry and are widely known. The Association's victories in the school desegregation cases in 1954 have come to be recognized as the central achievement of the NAACP in the development of the interpretation of constitutional rights.[7] But largely unknown is the fact that the most complex and time-consuming litigation the NAACP undertook in its early years was not concerned with the constitutional right of equality as such but rather with the criminal procedure requirements of the Due Process Clause and the right not to be deprived of life and liberty without a fair trial.

This is the story of the litigation in *Moore* v. *Dempsey*—a story that began with tragedy and hopelessness but which, after more than five years of protracted litigation, ended with victory and freedom. Most important, however, it is the story of how the U.S. Supreme Court came to make a landmark decision that contributed significantly to an enhanced protection for liberty under the Constitution.

1 Autumn 1919: The Phillips County Riot

The postwar euphoria of victory in the United States in 1919 was soon replaced by disillusionment with the war and with domestic discontent—a growing hysteria about the alien, foreign-born and native radical elements in its midst, increased racial conflict and bitterness between whites and blacks, and an antiradical mood, fed in part by the Bolshevik Revolution. Widespread persecution of such radical groups as the Industrial Workers of the World (IWW) and those who were participating in the new communist movement were a consequence; so were deportations of aliens charged with harboring radical sentiments.[1]

The war had encouraged the migration of thousands of blacks from the South to the labor-short industrial centers of the North in search of a better way of life. Competition between whites and blacks for jobs intensified, and racial tensions in the North increased; so did tensions between the races in the South, where whites viewed with alarm the loss of the cheap supply of black agricultural labor. Blacks had been drafted into the army during the war, where their military service had awakened a dormant resentment of the second-class citizenship to which they had been consigned since Reconstruction. The East St. Louis race riot erupted in the spring of 1917, followed by race riots and other violence in Washington, D.C.; Chicago; Omaha; Knoxville; and Indianapolis during the summer and fall of 1919.[2]

5

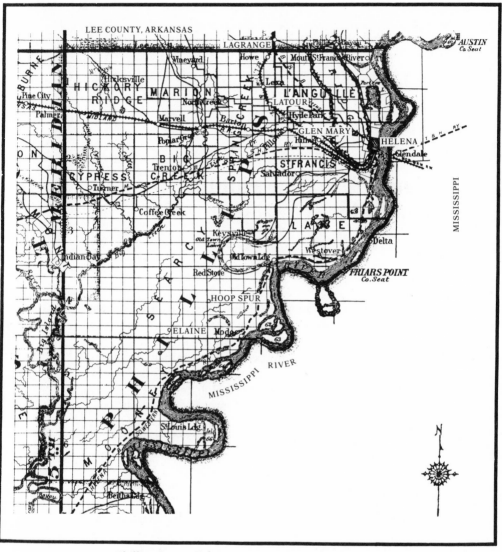

Phillips County, Arkansas. *Courtesy of the Library of Congress*

The racial violence in these urban centers seemed far re-moved from quiet and isolated, primarily rural Phillips County in Arkansas. Phillips County is in the eastern part of Arkansas, its eastern boundary the Mississippi River. Across the river is the state of Mississippi; the Arkansas state capital, Little Rock, is almost one hundred miles to the west. In 1919 the principal industries in the county were logging and large-scale cotton farming. There were 44,530 persons in the county—11,601 of them white; 32,929 black.[3]

Signs that there might be trouble between whites and blacks in Phillips County had apparently begun to surface during the late summer. Rumors that blacks in the county were organizing a union had come to the attention of several influential whites, and white leaders formed a committee to investigate these dis-turbing rumors. In early September 1919 Sebastian Straub, a leading merchant of the county seat at Helena, hired a black detective agency from Chicago which sent an agent into Phillips County to investigate what blacks were planning. The agent, a black man, is said to have reported that several black share-croppers and tenant farmers had organized a union and were plotting the assassination of several white planters. The mur-ders were scheduled to take place in early October in the vicin-ity of Elaine, about twenty-five miles south of Helena. There were reports also that unusually large quantities of firearms and ammunition had been purchased from Helena hardware stores during September. Meetings between white and black leaders in Helena discussed the prevention of interracial vio-lence. The telephone operator in Helena was instructed to notify members of the American Legion post if she heard any report of trouble near Elaine.[4]

On October 1, Governor Charles H. Brough of Arkansas re-ceived a telegram from the town of Elaine signed by a C. W. L. Armour and a Sid Steaks. Their dispatch said that there were "race riots here in Elaine and [we] need some soldiers at once. Several white men and negroes killed last night and this morn-ing." Another telegram from Helena said that "circuit and county judges, sheriff, mayor and leading private citizens ur-gently request immediate dispatch of 500 troops with machine guns to Elaine. Situation tense. One hundred seventy-five negro prisoners are expected to arrive at any moment among white men. Two dead and from 5 to 25 wounded." A subsequent telegram from Phillips County advised that the situation "continues very serious. One hundred prisoners. Five or six wounded, two of Phillips county dead. Posse numbering at least 500 will be in Elaine neighborhood before 6 p.m. Considering situation it is absolutely necessary federal troops be at Elaine at earliest possible moment." Banner headlines in the *Arkansas Gazette,* published in Little Rock, reported "Desperate Fighting Between Whites and Negroes" on October 1, a "Race War" had broken out at Elaine: "Elaine at midnight was quiet after a day of fighting between organized negroes armed with high-powered rifles and sheriff's posses in the streets of that town and in the country near by." White women and children from Elaine and its vicinity, it was reported, were being sent to Helena via a special train to protect their safety.[5]

The underlying cause of the riot was initially unclear, and, indeed, the causes cited by authorities changed considerably over the next several days. The earliest reports indicated that on the night of September 30, Phillips County Deputy Sheriff Charles W. Pratt; W. A. Adkins, a special agent of the Missouri-Pacific Railroad Co.; and "Kidd" Collins, a black trusty at the Phillips County jail, had been en route by car to Elaine to arrest a bootlegger, reported to be drunk and on a "rampage." Because of car trouble, the trio had stopped outside of a black church at Hoop Spur, some three miles north of Elaine. They were fired upon by armed blacks guarding the church. Adkins was killed and Pratt was wounded; Collins escaped and telephoned a report of the shootings to the authorities. A sheriff's posse dispatched to the scene was driven off by the gunfire of blacks who had converged in the vicinity of Elaine.[6]

There were later reports that, during the day of October 1, "between 1,000 and 1,500 negroes had assembled in the vicinity of Elaine and were armed with high-powered rifles. A girl telephone operator, between screams, [said that] fighting was in progress in the streets [of Elaine]. Messages followed in quick succession urging additional reinforcements, guns and ammunition. Every available man was sent to Elaine." Among the white men engaged in fighting the blacks was a detachment of members of the Helena American Legion post. Armed whites were also reported to have arrived from Clarendon, Marianna, and Marvell, Arkansas; and from Lulu, Tunica, Friars Point and Clarksdale, Mississippi, as news of the trouble spread. In the fighting between whites and blacks in Phillips County, three

white men, Clinton Lee and James A. Tappan, Helena legionnaires, and Orley R. Lilly were killed on October 1, and seven
black deaths were also reported.[7]

Orley R. Lilly, a widely known real estate agent and member
of the Helena city council, was said to have been killed by Dr.
D. A. E. Johnson, a black dentist of Helena, who had been taken
into custody along with his three brothers by Lilly and deputy
sheriffs. Dr. Johnson, it was reported, had seized Lilly's gun from
him and killed him, whereupon the deputies fired on and killed
all four of the Johnson brothers, including Dr. Louis Johnson, a
physician from Oklahoma who had been visiting in Helena.[8]
The Johnson brothers were reported in the press to have been
"ringleaders of the rioting." Dr. Johnson's dental office was
searched, and it was reported that "a dozen high-powered rifles
and hundreds of rounds of ammunition were confiscated." Later
press reports said that the discovery of high-powered rifles and
"several cases of ammunition in the headquarters of the Johnson brothers at Helena . . . show plainly that an insurrection
was planned, and that only an accident, the tragedy at Hoop
Spur . . . prevented a much more serious situation from arising
sooner or later."[9]

Early reports from Phillips County also attributed the riot to
the activities of a white, O. S. Bratton. O. S. Bratton was the
son of U. S. Bratton, an Arkansas native and a former postmaster. The elder Bratton had been an assistant U.S. attorney for
twelve years and practiced law in Little Rock. He was to become a key figure in the defense of the blacks convicted in the
wake of the Phillips County riot. O. S. Bratton and several
blacks were arrested at Ratio, approximately five miles south
of Elaine. The press said it was "alleged that Bratton has
been connected with activities of propagandists in [Phillips]
County who have been preaching the doctrine of social equality
to the negroes. It is charged that he was present [on September 30] with the negroes who shot [W. A.] Adkins from am-
bush near Hoop Spur." Bratton was jailed in Helena on October 1.[10]

On October 3 U. S. Bratton released a statement to the press
denying that his son had had anything to do with the violence.
O. S. Bratton had been in Phillips County on legitimate business
for his father's law firm, Bratton, Bratton and Casey. About
sixty-five blacks of the county, U. S. Bratton said, had retained
his law firm to represent them in obtaining a fair price for their

cotton crops from the owners of the plantation on which they were tenant farmers. The tenant farmers also wanted the Bratton firm to get itemized accounts of the sums they owed the plantation owner for supplies and necessities. U. S. Bratton said that his son had left Little Rock on the evening of September 30 by train and had arrived at Ratio by way of McGehee at nine o'clock on the morning of October 1.[11]

"The purpose of his going was to get from the negroes a statement of their contention and also to collect the balance of the fee," U. S. Bratton said. "After he had made these arrangements it was his plan to go to the manager of the plantation, who represented the Northern owner, and see if some settlement could not be effected. The trouble which started in that locality, started on Tuesday evening, while my son was on the train en route to McGehee from Little Rock. There is absolutely no foundation for any statement that he was connected with the trouble in any way." "It has been reported that he had been in that locality for several weeks, circulating propaganda," Bratton continued. "The truth is that neither he nor any member of our family or firm has been in that locality at all for the last several months." "I challenge the world to show that I or any member of my family have encouraged, directly or indirectly, social equality of the races. I have always advised the negroes to be lawabiding citizens. The best citizens of Little Rock will bear me out that on all moral issues waged in this community I have used my best efforts to induce the negroes to take the higher side of moral issues."[12]

Despite this statement, Bratton's son remained in custody in Helena, and it was reported that additional evidence had been uncovered by Phillips County authorities that the riot had been "due to agitation by a white man . . . among the negroes to fight for their 'rights'. The white man . . . had obtained numerous powers of attorney from the negroes to represent them in legal actions against the planters employing them." Local Helena officials declared their belief that the white man in question was O. S. Bratton.[13]

Governor Charles H. Brough was faced with deciding what action the state should take. He had been governor since 1916. A Mississippian by birth, he had been graduated from Mississippi College and had received a doctorate from Johns Hopkins

University in 1898. He was said to be one of the youngest persons to receive such a degree up to that time. After receiving a law degree from the University of Mississippi, he had moved to Arkansas in 1903 and taught economics at the University of Arkansas. He saw himself as a symbol for lawful, orderly process.[14] Brough now asked for a detachment of U.S. troops from Camp Pike, a U.S. Army base near Little Rock. Major General S. D. Sturgis, the commander of Camp Pike, refused to order troops into the county without orders from the War Department. But after the intervention of both the U.S. senators from Arkansas, the War Department sent orders, and shortly after midnight on October 2, 583 officers and men from the Third Division and the 57th Infantry, accompanied by Governor Brough, left Little Rock by train; they arrived at Elaine at 8:15 A.M., under the command of Colonel Isaac C. Jenks.[15]

Colonel Jenks ordered all civilians, white and black, disarmed, while a company of the Third Division was dispatched to Helena, armed with two machine guns to prevent the lynching of O. S. Bratton and the black prisoners held there.[16] The troops in the Elaine area proceeded to arrest large numbers of blacks, confining them in the basement of the public school. Blacks were not permitted to move about in public without passes signed by the military authorities, and no military passes were issued to blacks unless they were vouched for by whites.[17] One of the troops was killed, one was wounded, and one soldier accidentally shot himself in the foot. Governor Brough was fired at three times, but was unscathed.[18]

After the intervention of U.S. troops, the cause of the riot attributed in news accounts began to shift to a secretly organized union of blacks called the Progressive Farmers and Householders Union of America. The Progressive Farmers Union, it was reported, had been organized to get higher wages for black cotton pickers and higher prices for the cotton grown by black tenant farmers. With the encouragement of the union's leaders, blacks had been urged to arm themselves for their own protection and to be prepared to respond to attacks from the whites.[19]

On October 4 it was reported that the law office maintained by U. S. Bratton at Helena had been raided and quantities of Progressive Farmers Union literature, as well as socialist literature, had been discovered. Bratton issued a statement denying any knowledge of this literature and pointed out that G. R.

Casey was the representative of his law firm in Helena. "The firm is Bratton, Bratton & Casey, and Mr. G. R. Casey is the representative [in Helena]," Bratton said. "No member of my family has been to Helena for some time. I attended Circuit Court there about a year ago, and was there again two months ago taking some depositions. The boy [O. S. Bratton] they have arrested is not even a lawyer and had no connection with the office. He has not been to Helena at all until taken there by officers."[20]

The reports of a secret organization among the black population led to some signs of panic among Arkansas authorities. Sales of guns and ammunition were banned in Jefferson, Lincoln, Arkansas, and Desha counties,[21] and there were published rumors that the Phillips County trouble was the result of a Communist plot.[22] When ammunition and rifles were discovered at a black school, the Branch Normal College at Pine Bluff, this was said to indicate that "the contemplated uprising was of more than a local nature, possibly planned for the entire South."[23] The ammunition and weapons found at Branch Normal College, it turned out, were there legitimately, for the use of the college's ROTC unit. Army officials nonetheless removed the ammunition and the bolts from the rifles. The officer in charge reported to the commanding general of Camp Pike that he "found no excitement in Pine Bluff that would indicate that race rioting is liable to break out, but I did find uneasiness on the part of the constituted authorities with these rifles and ball ammunition in the hands of this colored institution. This uneasiness entirely disappeared when it was learned of the action taken."[24]

The commander of Camp Pike had strengthened the guard at Little Rock and had the movements of blacks carefully monitored, and he had organized two additional provisional companies of troops at Camp Pike. While "there were quite large gatherings of negroes in Little Rock, with rumors of brewing trouble," he reported, "there were no incendiary speeches, and nothing developed that required any action."[25]

As the role of the Progressive Farmers Union was elaborated upon and the union's purposes came to be increasingly portrayed in the public reports of the causes of the riot as sinister, the role of "white agitators", in general, and O. S. Bratton, in particular, was downplayed. O. S. Bratton was indicted by the

Phillips County grand jury for barratry (that is, "soliciting un-necessary litigation"). He was, however, released later without trial after thirty days in the Helena county jail and surrepti-tiously escorted out of Helena in the middle of the night.[26] The authorities in Helena subsequently admitted that the shooting at Hoop Spur which had precipitated the riot had occurred be-fore O. S. Bratton had arrived at Ratio and was unrelated to his activities there.[27]

In Helena, a Committee of Seven was formed with the ap-proval of Governor Brough to investigate the riot and determine its cause. Its seven members were H. D. Moore, the county judge; F. F. Kitchens, the sheriff; J. C. Knight, the mayor of Helena; E. M. Allen, president of the Helena Business Men's League; Sebastian Straub; E. C. Hornor; and T. W. Keesee. The committee interrogated the blacks who had been rounded up by the military and held in Elaine and in the Helena county jail. As a result of these interrogations and an examination of the literature of the Progressive Farmers Union, the Committee of Seven reported their conclusion about the cause of the Phillips County trouble.[28] The leaders of the Progressive Farmers Union, the committee said, had led the members of the union to believe that the federal government would back them up in demanding high prices for their cotton and in seizing the land of white plantation owners. The black union members in the County armed themselves and drilled in secret, so it was said, in prep-aration for an insurrection against whites. Twenty-one white landowners and merchants were to be killed immediately at the beginning of the insurrection, scheduled for October 6. The shooting of Adkins and Pratt at Hoop Spur on the night of Sep-tember 30 had prematurely set off the insurrection, according to the Committee of Seven, with the result that the authorities were able to suppress what would otherwise have been a black massacre of the white population of Phillips County.[29]

E. M. Allen, chief spokesman for the Committee of Seven, an-nounced the results of the committee's investigation to the press. Allen was a real-estate broker and owned the townsite at Elaine; he was also treasurer of the Gerard B. Lambert Com-pany of St. Louis, which owned a twenty-one-thousand-acre cot-ton plantation near Elaine that employed 750 black sharecrop-pers. "The present trouble with the negroes of Phillips County is not a race riot," Allen informed the press. "It is a deliberately planned insurrection of the negroes against the whites, directed by an organization known as the 'Progressive Farmers' and 'Household Union of America,' established for the purpose of banding negroes together for the killing of white people. . . . The fight at Hoop Spur was unpremeditated as far as the negroes were concerned as they were organizing their forces Wednesday morning to attack and capture Elaine but when runners informed the leaders that white men were entering the woods at Hoop Spur they decided to go up and wipe out the little gang that was reported to be there, before entering upon the more serious task of capturing Elaine. They underestimated the size of the force from Helena and the battle ensued. . . . Every negro who joined these [union] lodges was given to kill white people. Unquestionably the time for the attack had been set but plans had not been entirely perfected and the shooting of the officers [at Hoop Spur] brought on the insurrection ahead of schedule."[30]

The leader of the Progressive Farmers Union, Allen reported, was Robert L. Hill, a thirty-year-old black from Winchester, Arkansas, "who saw in it a opportunity of making easy money" by collecting dues from the blacks of Phillips County. Hill had "simply played upon the ignorance and superstition of a race of children—most of whom neither read nor write." "I have cross-examined and talked to at least one hundred prisoners at Elaine," Allen claimed. "They belong to different lodges in that section. The stories they tell are almost identical as to the promises and representations made by Hill. . . . A remarkable thing about the developments is that some of the ringleaders were found to be the oldest and most reliable of the negroes whom we have known for the past fifteen years. . . . As far as oppression is concerned, many of the negroes involved own mules, horses, cattle and automobiles and clear money every year on their crops, after expenses are paid."[31]

Other leaders of the union were identified from among Phillips County blacks: brothers Ed and Frank Hicks, Frank Moore, and Ed Ware. All except Ed Ware were taken into custody during or immediately after the riot; Ware managed to escape to New Orleans, but he was arrested there in early November and returned to Phillips County.[32] An associate of Robert Hill, V. E. Powell, also regarded as a key leader of the union, was arrested in Arkansas City and sent to the Helena jail on October 5.[33] Hill himself successfully eluded the Arkansas authorities, although he was said by them to have been the mastermind of the insurrection plot.[34]

With most of the "leaders" of the riot in custody, along with hundreds of other blacks, Phillips County officials announced to the press on October 4 that they believed the situation was under control and that the racial trouble was at an end.[35] On October 7, the Committee of Seven issued a proclamation to the black population of the county, admonishing them to "Stop talking; stay at home; go to work; don't worry. Soldiers now here to preserve order will return to Little Rock within a short time."[36] On October 9 the U.S. troops, who had named themselves the "Phillips County Expeditionary Forces,"[37] began to return to Camp Pike, leaving behind a detachment to guard the jail at Helena.[38] The Committee of Seven telegraphed to Governor Brough also on October 9 that with the troops leaving the county the committee felt "the absolute need of providing means of preserving peace in event of trouble." They asked the governor to "kindly go to the War Department and requisition or bring our community 100 regulation army rifles with 25,000 rounds of ammunition and six Browning rifles with 5,000 rounds of ammunition. Our committee has given this matter most serious consideration and believes that no other course will give us the protection required." "The arms will be in charge of the sheriff and used only in event of a riot," the committee assured the governor. "Our county has never permitted mob violence to exist and we intend in [the] future to maintain the proud record of our past, just as we have done in this insurrection." The War Department had indicated that it had no authority to sell or loan army weapons to civilians, but Congressman Thaddeus H. Caraway intervened and secured the promise of the Chief of the Bureau of Militia that the weapons would be forthcoming.[39]

During the last part of October and early November, the Phillips County grand jury began to return indictments against those alleged to have taken part in the riot. Ultimately 122 blacks were indicted by the grand jury on charges growing out of the riot, seventy-three charged with murder.[40] No whites were indicted. The press reported that it was "not expected that much time will be lost in trying these cases. It is believed that the selection of juries will be accomplished without much legal sparring, and the taking of evidence will occupy more time than any other feature of the trials. It is also believed that the arguments will be considerably curtailed. For these reasons the preliminaries are expected to be short and the trials will proceed without waste of time."[41]

On November 2, just over one month after the riot, the trials of the indicted blacks began in the Circuit Court of Phillips County, presided over by Judge J. M. Jackson. "No disorder" was reported in Helena, but "as a precautionary measure one company of troops was assigned to aid in guarding the city."[42] Since most of the defendants were indigent, Judge Jackson appointed counsel for them. It was reported that practically "every attorney in Helena has been appointed to defend one or more of the accused negroes."[43] But no defense lawyer made a motion for a continuance of the cases because of the short time that had elapsed since the riot; no motions were filed requesting a change of venue because of the possible prejudice against the defendants in Phillips County; and no challenge was made to the grand jury that indicted the defendants or the petit juries at the trials on the ground that blacks were systematically excluded from service on grand and petit juries in Phillips County.[44]

Frank Moore, Ed and Frank Hicks, J. E. Knox, Paul Hall, and Ed Coleman were tried on November 2 for the murder of Clinton Lee, who had been shot under the left arm while riding in a car during the riot and died almost immediately. First, Frank Hicks was tried alone, since he had been indicted for firing the shots that killed Lee. Prosecuting attorney John E. Miller represented the state. The jury convicted Hicks of first-degree murder after only eight minutes of deliberation. Then, Frank Moore, Ed Hicks, J. E. Knox, Paul Hall, and Ed Coleman were tried together as accessories to the murder of Lee; the state contended that they had been with Frank Hicks when he killed Lee and had aided and abetted him in that crime. Moore, Ed Hicks, Knox, Hall, and Coleman were represented at their trial by two white, court-appointed lawyers, John I. Moore and Greenfield Quarles, with John E. Miller once again prosecuting for the state. A white witness testified that he had been with Clinton Lee when he was shot but had no idea who had shot him. A white physician testified that Lee had died of a gunshot wound, and another white witness testified that he had seen a group of blacks, one of whom had fired shots at whites, but he could identify none of the defendants as having been among that group of blacks. On the other hand, two black witnesses, John Jefferson and Walter Ward, testified that they had been with Frank Hicks and other blacks when Hicks had killed Clinton Lee. J. Graham Burke, the municipal court judge of Helena, testified that Ed Coleman, J. E. Knox, and Ed Hicks had admitted to him that they had been present when Lee was killed. Under cross-examination, Burke denied having knowledge that Hicks, Knox, and Coleman had been coerced to elicit these confessions. After deliberating seven minutes, the jury convicted all five men of first-degree murder.

"The law today called to an accounting the first six of the negroes who sought to secure the property of others by insurrection and went to the length of taking human life in the effort to realize their ambitions," the *Arkansas Gazette* said of the trials. And "unless the unexpected and improbable occurs, they will meet their death in the electric chair at Little Rock on a date to be fixed by Judge J. M. Jackson."[45]

On November 4 Albert Giles and Joe Fox were tried for the murder of James A. Tappan; and John Martin; Alf Banks, Jr.; and Will Wordlow were tried for the murder of W. D. Adkins. Will Wordlow's case was severed from the other cases on motion of defense counsel, and he was convicted, after nine minutes of jury deliberations. Albert Giles and Joe Fox were convicted by a jury after it deliberated for six minutes.[46] On November 11 Judge Jackson sentenced all eleven of the blacks convicted of first-degree murder to death in the electric chair. Judge Jackson told Frank Moore, the first to be sentenced to death, that he had "been declared guilty by a jury of your own choosing of murder in the first degree, and it is the judgment of the court that you be delivered to the sheriff, who shall deliver you to the keeper of the penitentiary, who shall cause you to be put to death by electrocution between the hours of sunrise and sunset on the 27th of December, 1919." "The court is more lenient with you than you were to your victims . . . ," Judge Jackson continued, "for you sent them to their death without warning and without time in which to make preparation for meeting their Maker." The other ten convicted blacks received the same sentences, to be carried out on December 27, 1919, and January 2, 1920.[47]

Ed Ware, who had initially escaped to New Orleans but had

been captured and returned to Helena, was tried November 18 for the murder of Adkins. He was represented by L. A. Semmes, a white Helena lawyer, as defense counsel in a trial that lasted slightly more than two hours. Testifying in his own defense, Ware acknowledged that he was the secretary of the Progressive Farmers Union but denied firing any shots at Hoop Spur. The jury deliberated in his case for four minutes before returning a verdict of guilty.[48] On November 19 Ware was sentenced by Judge Jackson to die in the electric chair on January 2, 1920. He became the twelfth black to be sentenced to die as a result of the Phillips County trouble.[49]

After the trials and death sentences, the prosecution accepted pleas of guilty from many of the other blacks who had been indicted for offenses said to have been committed during the riot. Those who pleaded guilty to various offenses from murder to nightriding were sentenced by Judge Jackson to prison terms ranging from one year to twenty-one years. In addition to the twelve men condemned to death, sixty-seven other blacks were sent to prison.[50]

V. E. Powell, who was reputed to be one of the two principal officers of the Progressive Farmers Union, was indicted by a federal grand jury for impersonating a federal officer with intent to defraud and was arraigned on November 7 and held in jail pending trial.[51] Hill himself continued to elude the Arkansas authorities, but otherwise it was clear by mid-November that the legal proceedings growing out of the Phillips County riot were nearly over. All the proceedings that decided the fate of the twelve blacks condemned to death had been completed in less than two weeks.

A reporter who interviewed these twelve men described them as "shaggy, slovenly creatures," "ignorant cotton field negroes . . . not far removed from the primitive days of savagery." He said that one "is impressed by the deplorable condition to which their state of ignorance has brought them." "They will become sacrifices on the altar of ignorance," the reporter continued, "but the man who brewed the devil's stew [Robert L. Hill] . . . so far has saved his own skin."[52] "No appeals have been taken in any of the cases [of the condemned men]," it was also reported, "and so far as is known no effort has been made to appeal or obtain a new trial. The convicted men have apparently accepted their fate philosophically and without protest."[53]

The press and the authorities in Arkansas generally congratulated themselves on the manner in which the Phillips County trouble had been handled. The *Arkansas Gazette*, the state's leading newspaper, deplored the riot: "all the people of the state keenly regret this terrible business, both as a moral misfortune for Arkansas and on account of the grievous loss of life among men who had answered the call of duty in time of public danger in their community." Noting rumors of secret black organizations and "mischievous propaganda" being spread among the blacks immediately following the riot, the *Gazette* called for a thorough investigation of the cause of the riot. "Knowing the Southern white man as we do," the *Gazette* said, "we feel sure that if the negro has anywhere been misled the whites can be depended upon to bring him to an understanding of his best interests, which, needless to say, are bound up with peace and order and friendly relations between the races."[54]

The *Gazette* initially expressed some doubts about the reports that the riot was the result of a prematurely started planned insurrection by the Phillips County blacks: "even if an insurrection had been thought of it never would have been actually attempted." The blacks undoubtedly had been misled by propaganda, but even their possession of arms was not entirely sinister.

The Phillips County negroes may have been told that to support their rights they must be armed. The possession of a high-powered rifle would give a negro a feeling that he was in a position of strength and advantage. He would look on it as sort of a grim protecting deity presiding over his house—albeit this deity was the terrible undoing of many of its worshippers. . . . Can it be believed that D. A. E. Johnson, for example, the dentist, could have let himself believe that the negroes could put down the whites by armed insurrection and take over the land for themselves? A negro of Johnson's intelligence must have known that for negroes to hold control of a certain region through the force of arms was a thing inconceivable and that an insurrection could only have one result.[55]

Despite these editorial doubts, the *Gazette* expressed confidence that the true cause of the trouble would be discovered by the people of Phillips County, who were "not surpassed by any others in the state for general high character." "The men are the breed of men that won the battle of King's Mountain and the battle of Buena Vista, the battle of Chickamauga and the battle of the Argonne Forest. They will go to the bottom of the business. They will guarantee peace and order and they will restore that good relation between the races which is happily the normal condition in Arkansas."[56] The initial doubts of the *Gazette* that a planned insurrection had been the source of the riot were later abandoned, and the newspaper wholly accepted the report of the Committee of Seven in Helena as embodying the underlying facts. By mid-November the *Gazette* was stating editorially that the trouble "was not a race riot but an insurrection in which ignorant negroes, led by vicious and designing members of their own race, organized an insurrection the purpose of which was to murder the white planters and confiscate their property."[57]

The *Gazette* thus became a forceful and adamant defender not only of the planned insurrection theory but also of the manner in which the suppression of the riot and the resultant legal proceedings had been conducted. The newspaper repeatedly pointed out that the riot had been handled entirely within the law, and that no lynching or mob violence had occurred. The Phillips County authorities' reaction to the riot should, therefore, be a source of pride for Arkansas, the *Gazette* said, and the record of the state in dealing with racial conflict could be compared favorably to the manner in which the riots in northern urban areas, such as Chicago and Washington, D.C., had been handled. "The newspapers the length and breadth of the United States, and especially north of the Mason and Dixon line, should not fail to remark [on] this outstanding feature of the trouble in Phillips County, that through it all the law, as represented by local authorities and by federal troops, was in control. There was no bursting of all restraints and no uncontrollable disorder like that disorder which reigned in Washington and Omaha and Chicago."[58] "The Phillips County trouble has been put down and put down within the law," the *Gazette* pointed out. "Those northern newspapers that are decently fair will call attention to this fact and will compare the legal methods used in Phillips County with the murderous lawlessness in Washington, Chicago and Omaha."[59]

The *Gazette* attributed part of the blame for the racial tensions in Arkansas and in the South generally to propaganda spread by northern blacks. Northern manufacturers were luring southern blacks to the industrial centers of the North, the *Gazette* noted, but prior to the war "[the] South had attempted to stop the exodus by reasoning with the negroes." The northern manufacturers and "certain Northern Republican politicians," however, had financed propaganda published by northern blacks which had "for its purpose the inflaming of Southern negroes against the whites and against conditions in the South."[60] "Unless something is done there will be other outbreaks in the South," the *Gazette* warned.

Each outbreak will mean more decided action against the negroes until finally an outbreak will mean annihilation of the negroes in the infected district. . . . [Northern blacks are] paving the way for ignorant Southern negroes to go to their graves. The manufacturers and the politicians have given aid in this dirty business. These are not palatable facts but they are facts that both white and negro leaders should look squarely in the face. Steps toward correcting the trouble should be taken at once. The correction lies largely with negro leaders, and the sooner they begin work the better. Any change in the condition of the negro will come by evolution and not by revolution. To those who have lived in the South this truth must be apparent.[61]

Governor Brough, who had marched at the head of the troops when they entered Helena,[62] returned to Little Rock on October 4 after order had been restored. He was quoted as assuring the public the situation "has been well handled and is absolutely under control," and there "is no danger of any lynchings. The saying is current among the white citizens that Phillips County has never had a lynching and would not have one even in this crisis."[63] The governor was in turn praised for his actions during the riot by U.S. Senator Joseph T. Robinson, who said that the "race riot situation in Phillips County was handled with promptness and skill, and I congratulate you and the good people of Phillips County on the sound judgment exemplified in dealing with the subject."[64]

Governor Brough fully accepted the report of the Helena Committee of Seven on the cause of the riot, and consistently praised the Phillips County authorities.[65] Although the governor referred to the riot as a "damnable insurrection," he took pains to express his sympathy for Arkansas blacks and to denounce lynching and mob violence.[66] The Phillips County difficulty, the governor nonetheless asserted, "was the direct result of a conspiracy on the part of an organized group of negroes to enforce certain demands from the farmers. . . . The uprising failed because it was started prematurely, and I was able to reach

Elaine and Helena with federal troops in time to prevent a clash which, had it occurred, undoubtedly would have cost the lives of many, both whites and blacks."[67]

The version of the riot reported by the Committee of Seven and so strongly endorsed by the *Arkansas Gazette* and by Governor Brough was corroborated also by Reverend A. C. Millar, a white Methodist minister and the editor of the *Arkansas Methodist*. Millar reported that he had investigated the riot, attended the court proceedings, examined the Progressive Farmers Union literature, and talked to many of the blacks arrested in connection with the trouble. "In Phillips County there was a deliberately planned insurrection of negroes, which, if it had not started prematurely, would have resulted in the wholesale slaughter of the whites in the vicinity of Elaine and an attempt to take possession of the property of the white owners," Millar reported. The "wholesale slaughter of the whites" had been the object of the Progressive Farmers Union, Millar said. In organizing the union, Robert L. Hill and Dr. D. A. E. Johnson had represented themselves as agents of the federal government and had misled Phillips County blacks into believing that the whites' land was actually owned by the government and could be obtained cheaply. While "doubtless some comparatively innocent negroes were killed", he said, on the whole the situation had been handled admirably by the Committee of Seven and the Phillips County authorities.[68] Millar "saw many of [the blacks charged with participating in the riot] in the courtroom, and Sunday morning preached to [several of the] convicted men. The following information was readily given at that time: Fifteen can read, five only were originally from Arkansas, 15 from Mississippi, eight from Louisiana, two from Georgia, and one from Texas; 33 claimed to be Baptists, seven African Methodists and three were not church members." "They did not look vicious," Millar continued, "but seemed primitive and undeveloped. They responded freely, seemed deeply penitent, and readily admitted that they had been grossly deceived and misled by their own crafty leaders."[69]

Robert Hill and the other leaders of the union "sought first financial gain and the glory of leadership," Millar believed. "They were probably shrewd enough to realize the futility of actual insurrection, but played upon the hopes and fears and patriotism and religious feelings of their weak and incredulous fellows so far that the movement got beyond control. The conditions were favorable. Most of the land in the vicinity of the insurrection had been cleared first by big mill companies, and then improved in recent years. Labor being scarce, many negroes from other states where there had been crop failures had come in and in order to hold the much-needed labor the owners had been remarkably lax in dealing with them."[70]

As a prominent man in Helena had told him, Millar said, "negroes are a race of children who need the oversight and management of the stronger race, and, if the average Southern manager is to blame, it is rather for being too easy in dealing with his labor." "While we could not claim that in this insurrection the white men of Phillips County were absolutely right and might not be justly criticized," he concluded, "still when all the circumstances are considered we hold that they are entitled to great credit for handling a very ugly situation in an admirable manner."[71]

The *Arkansas Gazette* responded that "Mr. Millar's standing with both whites and negroes is such that his statements concerning the insurrection will put to rest any doubt that may have existed in the minds of people who know him" regarding the facts behind the Phillips County trouble.[72]

Nonetheless, a very different version of the events in Phillips County was soon offered by the National Association for the Advancement of Colored People. The result would be not only a bitter war of words between the NAACP and Arkansas authorities over the facts but also a protracted legal battle for the life and freedom of the convicted Phillips County blacks—the battle the NAACP later called "one of the most spectacular and bitterly fought contests ever waged for justice in America."[73]

2 Walter White's Longest Train Ride: The NAACP Reacts

At the time of the Phillips County riot, the NAACP was suffering from financial woes and from ineffective leadership. In a comment on the trials of the blacks, the *St. Louis Argus,* a black newspaper, called the cases "a mockery of the law and a travesty on justice," and said, "We would appeal to the National Association for the Advancement of Colored People for aid, but the experience of its National Secretary, Hon. John R. Shillady, in Austin, Texas, recently, leads us to believe they will be a little fearful about sending a man from New York [to investigate the Arkansas situation]."[1]

In August 1919, when the national office of the NAACP in New York City had learned from its Austin branch that Texas authorities were attempting to oust the NAACP on the ground that the organization was not chartered to do business in the state, NAACP secretary John Shillady, a white social worker, had traveled to Austin in an attempt to see the governor and attorney general and explain the purposes of the NAACP. He was unable to see either official. Instead he was attacked and beaten unconscious by a group of men in Austin, a group that included a judge and a constable. The NAACP protested the attack in a telegram to Texas governor William P. Hobby demanding that the assailants be brought to justice. Shillady had been the offender, the governor responded, and he had already been punished. Austin police officials pointed out that Shillady had been

24

"received by red-blooded white men" who disliked having "Negro-loving white men" in the state. "We attend to our own affairs down here," the NAACP was told, "and suggest that you do the same up there."[2] Shillady never recovered either physically or mentally from the beating he had received in Austin. Although he resumed for a time his duties as secretary, he resigned in August 1920. "I am less confident than heretofore of the speedy success of the Association's full program," he said in his letter of resignation, "and of the probability of overcoming, within a reasonable period, the forces opposed to Negro equality by the means and methods which are within the Association's power to employ."[3]

Shillady was replaced as NAACP secretary by James Weldon Johnson, the first black to hold this position. Johnson had served as a United States consul in Venezuela and subsequently as an editor on the staff of the *New York Age*. The Association had suffered as a result of the effective hiatus in its leadership. In every month between October of 1919 and August of 1920, for example, the NAACP had deficits in its treasury, the total deficit by the time Johnson took over being almost nine thousand dollars.[4] As Walter White said later, "not only were we broke, we owed sizable debts for printing, rent, and other operating costs. Jim saw to it that the stenographers were paid, but he and I went without salary for as long as four months while we all worked desperately to place the Association on a sound financial basis."[5]

Despite its low fortunes, the NAACP had not neglected the tragedy in Arkansas. It had sent its young assistant secretary, Walter F. White, to investigate the situation. Immediately after the riot, White had informed Shillady that he believed the incident required "careful investigation." He said that he was "exceedingly anxious to make the investigation personally and I do so with full realization of the past, and am assuming complete responsibility for any personal consequences which may ... arise."[6]

White visited Little Rock and Helena in early October, almost immediately after the Phillips County riot. He had blue eyes, blond hair, and a fair skin and could easily "pass" for white, although he identified himself as a black. He had joined the NAACP as assistant secretary in 1918. He was then twenty-four, a graduate of Atlanta University; he had been an insurance agent before he took on the job of secretary of the Atlanta branch of the NAACP and then went to New York to join the national office.[7]

White got in touch with Dr. Charles E. Bentley of Chicago, who, in turn, arranged for Charles H. Dennis, the managing editor of the *Chicago Daily News*, to accredit White as a correspondent for his paper. "Had it not been for such a guise as this," White said later, "I do not think I would have been able to have secured the facts [in Arkansas] or to have gotten out safely, as it was the most dangerous situation in which I have been."[8] Posing as a *Daily News* correspondent, White was granted an interview with Governor Brough, who expressed his pleasure that "a Northern newspaper has sent so able and experienced a reporter"; his reports, the governor thought, could counter the distortions of the affair being published by the northern black press. Brough assured White that Phillips County whites had demonstrated remarkable restraint in suppressing the riot. "In a burst of warmth and Southern hospitality," White said later, "[Brough] gave me a letter of identification, in which he called me 'one of the most brilliant newspapermen he had ever met,' for me to use in Phillips County in case I ran into any difficulty there." The governor also gave White an autographed picture of himself.[9]

In Helena, Walter White interviewed some whites, but, alerted by a black man that his identity had been discovered and that a lynching party was being prepared for him. he boarded the first train out of Helena. "But you're leaving mister, just when the fun is going to start," the conductor on the train said. White inquired what the nature of the fun would be, and the conductor replied that there was "a damned yellow nigger down here passing for white and the boys are going to get him." "What'll they do with him?" White asked. "When they get through with him," the conductor replied, "he won't pass for white no more!" "No matter what the distance," White said later, "I shall never take as long a train ride as that one seemed to be."[10]

Of vastly greater importance than his visit to Helena and his interview with Governor Brough was White's meeting with U. S. Bratton in Little Rock. From Bratton, White and the NAACP first received what they came to regard as the truth about the Phillips County riot. Not only did he give his account of the episode to White but he also filed a lengthy report with the U.S. Department of Justice.

While an assistant U.S. Attorney, Bratton had prosecuted several eastern Arkansas planters for holding blacks in peonage and had secured guilty pleas and heavy fines from the planters. "This resulted in the breaking up of the open system of peonage," he said, "but another system followed in its wake." Planters in eastern Arkansas, Bratton charged, had devised a system by which the blacks whom they employed were dependent upon them for basic necessities. They were charged for these supplies the "most outrageous and exorbitant prices imaginable," with the result that they were perpetually in debt to the planters. In addition, the planters refused to supply to the black farmers itemized accounts of their indebtedness, but always claimed when their crops were sold at the end of each year that they remained in debt. The planters likewise furnished no accounting for the sale of crops owned by their black tenant farmers. And the planters agreed among themselves not to hire blacks employed by another planter as long as they were in debt to the planter employing them; household goods of blacks who attempted to leave were seized, or charges were trumped up against them.[11] The result of this system, Bratton told White, was that the blacks in eastern Arkansas, perpetually in debt to the planters, were compelled to submit to a system of peonage from which it was difficult to escape. "These conditions have resulted in the Negroes, in large numbers, coming to us in an effort to get relief, and we have attempted to obtain relief for them and have been able to obtain judgments in the courts in some of their cases," Bratton said. "It having been known that we did not hesitate to take their cases, they came to us from distant parts of the state, our office being located in Little Rock, more than one hundred miles from Phillips County, wherein are Helena, Elaine, and where the recent trouble, heralded as 'race riots' was had."[12]

In September of 1919, Bratton reported, blacks from the Ratio plantation in Phillips County contacted his law firm. They asked Bratton to represent them in getting fair settlements for their cotton crops and itemized statements of the amounts they owed to the planter on whose land they were tenants. Bratton's son, O. S. Bratton, had gone by train to Ratio to collect legal fees and to ascertain the facts. But "while he was talking with the Negroes out in the open in front of the store where the white manager, as I understand, had charge, [he] was swooped down upon by white persons and arrested on the theory that he was there inciting the Negroes to engage in a general race riot, when the facts are that he had not been in the county for at least six or seven years prior to this time, and had not been in the county except from the time that the train arrived that morning." U. S. Bratton immediately released a public statement detailing the reason his son was at Ratio, but he found "that public sentiment had been so aroused that it was a miracle that he was not lynched, on the theory that he was there inciting a race riot. . . . Notwithstanding the fact that he was not and had no connection with [the Phillips County trouble] whatever, he was kept in jail for one solid month, the Constitutional provisions as to examination, trial, and bail being absolutely ignored, and later on he was indicted for barratry, and stands indicted in Phillips County for the crime of barratry, when he is not an attorney. . . . An investigation will show that those things are all done for the sole purpose of deterring me and others from daring to take cases of the Negroes who are being systematically robbed of the fruits of their labor by the large plantation managers who operate in that country."[13]

A fair and impartial investigation would also show, Bratton said, that the claim that blacks had plotted insurrection was "merely made for the purpose of covering up the outrages that were committed against the Negroes for the purpose of deterring them from attempting to take any action in the county that would protect their legal rights." He believed, Bratton continued, that the blacks who had gathered at the church at Hoop Spur had heard that he was going to represent the Ratio blacks and were organizing for the purpose of obtaining Bratton's aid for themselves. Bratton believed that the whites, in turn, had learned of the blacks' meeting at Hoop Spur and had fired on the church. "It was probably not intended to kill anybody but merely to deter," he said, "but by reason of some of the Negroes being armed and fighting back, the white man was killed and thus the trouble originated."[14]

Walter White returned to New York determined to publicize the facts and counteract the official version of the trouble. "I personally investigated the Arkansas riot," he said later, "and I confess I have never felt so bitter, as I did on my return."[15] White was disappointed with the results of his efforts to publicize the NAACP version. "At the time of the outbreak," he said, "several newspapers of the country played up the alleged 'massacre,' devoting columns to the affair. On my return to New York, reporters from several of the New York papers were in the office and I presented absolute facts to them of the truthfulness of the statements which I made. Notwithstanding this, on the following morning only one of four newspapers carried the account, and that a very brief one."[16] Later White and the NAACP were able to get their version of what had happened rather fully publicized. White's article was published in the *Chicago Daily News* on October 18, appearing under his own name and attributed to an NAACP investigation. The trouble had occurred, the article said, because white planters had resisted the attempts of blacks to challenge the peonage system under which they were being forced to live. In Phillips County, the article reported, "thousands of negroes are held in the bonds of debt-slavery and peonage of the most flagrant sort." The Progressive Farmers Union had organized them and raised money for the purpose of challenging the peonage system in the courts, and the allegation that there had been a black plot to massacre whites was "only a figment of the imagination of Arkansas whites and not based on fact." The planned insurrection theory of the trouble was refuted by the fact that Robert L. Hill, "the negro who is supposed to be the prime mover in the organization [of the Progressive Farmers Union], is an ignorant, illiterate country farm hand, without brains enough to engineer so big a movement."[17]

Walter White's findings were published in other white- and black-owned newspapers, including the *Pittsburgh Dispatch*, the *Boston Chronicle*, the *Buffalo Express*, and the *Chicago Defender*.[18] White sent an article on the NAACP's version of the events to the *New Republic*, but the *New Republic* refused it. It was accepted and published by *The Nation* on December 6, 1919,[19] and a similar article was also published in the *Survey*.[20] The article in *The Nation* was republished in pamphlet form by the NAACP and more than a thousand copies were distributed by January 1920.[21]

White's articles again attributed the Phillips County riot to the white planters' resistance to blacks' efforts to attack the peonage system in the courts. "The cause of the Phillips County trouble, according to Governor Charles H. Brough, was the circulation of what he considers incendiary Negro publications like the *Crisis,* the official organ of the National Association for the Advancement of Colored People," White said in his *The Nation* article. "Having been a professor of economics for seventeen years before becoming Governor, it is incredible that he is ignorant of the exploitation of Negroes in his State." White charged that some of the blacks arrested in the aftermath of the Phillips County trouble had been placed in an electric chair and shocked until they made incriminating statements. Unless the death sentences of the twelve blacks convicted upon the basis of evidence secured in such a manner were reversed on appeal, he said, they would be electrocuted by the State of Arkansas, "additional victims of America's denial of rudimentary justice to 12,000,000 of its citizens because of their color."[22] There had been no planned insurrection by the blacks with the purpose of massacring the whites, White said in the *Survey* article; the turmoil had been caused by roving gangs of whites who had slaughtered innocent blacks after the shooting at the Hoop Spur church. At least twenty-five blacks had been killed, he said, although several "white men in Helena told me that more than one hundred Negroes were killed."[23]

White appears to have been conservatively estimating the number of blacks killed. The NAACP reported later that from two hundred to two hundred fifty had been killed by roving mobs of whites and by the federal troops. The NAACP said, "Mr. White reported that Negroes were being hunted and 250 shot-down like wild beasts, in the Arkansas cane brakes, because they had organized to employ a lawyer in an endeavor to obtain settlements and statements of account from the landlords under the share-cropping system."[24] "It is a most difficult matter to determine just how many of the colored people killed in Phillips County in October were killed by troops and how many by members of a mob," White said later. "A large number of colored people who were killed were put to death by troops who used machine guns to mow down colored people. Citizens' posses, however, murdered a great many more."[25]

In the two months following the riot, the NAACP also published its version of the Phillips County riot in its monthly magazine, the *Crisis.* The *Crisis* had 100,000 readers by 1919, and the key position of editor was filled by W. E. B. Du Bois, the leading black intellectual of the period.[26] On learning that the peonage system was going to be attacked by blacks in the courts, the white planters, the *Crisis* charged, had decided to intimidate the blacks, and after the shooting at Hoop Spur, the "white planters called their gangs together and a big 'nigger hunt' began. They rushed their women and children to Helena by auto and train. Train loads and auto loads of white men, armed to the teeth, came from Marianna and Forrest City, Ark., Memphis, Tenn., and Clarksdale, Miss." Five whites and from 25 to 50 blacks were killed, the *Crisis* said, and "the stench of dead bodies could be smelled two miles."[27] The four Johnson brothers, the *Crisis* charged, who were killed by sheriff's deputies and called "ringleaders" in the insurrection plot, had been completely innocent victims of the mob spirit that prevailed after the September 30 shooting. The brothers had been squirrel hunting when they were taken into custody by Orley Lilly and sheriff's deputies. Dr. D. A. E. Johnson had killed Lilly after wresting his gun from him because the brothers had feared that they were going to be lynched. The deputies had then gunned down all four of the Johnson brothers in what was perhaps the greatest tragedy of the Phillips County riot.[28] When the federal troops arrived in Phillips County, the article continued, more than a thousand black men and women were arrested and held in custody. They were released only when they were vouched for by white planters, and this only after they agreed to the planters' terms on working conditions and wages. Despite these injustices, the *Crisis* said, the "*Arkansas Gazette* has issued an editorial demanding that Negro leaders give their people 'proper advice,' and warning them that their race is in danger of annihilation unless Negroes cease to be led by the lure of Liberty and equal political rights and also warning them that the freedom of the Negro from bad economic conditions is not to be obtained by the methods which were resorted to by the Negroes of Phillips County."[29]

The publication of the NAACP's version produced angry reactions in Arkansas. On October 14, Governor Brough announced that he was taking action to suppress the distribution in Arkansas of both the *Crisis* and the black newspaper the *Chicago Defender*. "The last issue of 'The [Chicago] Defender' contained an erroneously and basely false account of the recent race riot at Elaine," Brough said, and "endeavored through its columns to leave the impression that the white people of Phillips County were responsible for the riot. I expect to obtain several copies of these incendiary organs and forward them to the postmaster general with the recommendation that they be suppressed" by barring them from the mail.[30] Brough duly sent a letter of complaint to the U.S. Post Office Department on October 17, and the department solicitor replied, thanking the governor "for informing [him] of the trouble the transmission of [publications like the *Chicago Defender* and the *Crisis*] in the mails to that section of the country is causing between the members of the white and black races, and beg[ging] to assure [him] that the matter will receive due consideration."[31] Nothing came of Governor Brough's complaint to the post office, but Arkansas authorities continued to oppose the distribution of what they considered to be incendiary publications. In February of 1920, for example, injunction proceedings were initiated against nineteen prominent blacks in Pine Bluff to prevent their distribution of the *Chicago Defender*. The newspaper, the authorities alleged, had contained untrue and seditious charges about the killing of a black man in Arkansas.[32]

The *Arkansas Gazette* played a leading role in the attempts to rebut the NAACP's version of the riot. When Shillady, then NAACP secretary, issued a press release on October 11 with Walter White's report on the riot, the *Gazette* telephoned the mayor of Helena and urged that a counter announcement be issued to offset the publicity being given to the NAACP version.[33] The Committee of Seven, in response, issued a statement denying that the riot had had anything to do with the economic exploitation of the Phillips County blacks. The committee pointed out that the shooting at the Hoop Spur church had occurred before O. S. Bratton had arrived at Ratio. "From the evidence we have secured the negroes at Ratio at that time knew nothing about the shooting at Hoop Spur and were not involved in that insurrection," the committee said, and "therefore it would be rather difficult to prove that the Hoop Spur shooting was caused by or had any relation to the settlements asked for by the negroes at Ratio. Our evidence clearly shows that the killing of the officers on Tuesday night, September 30, precipitated the insurrection which was to have begun on Monday, October 6, 1919." The *Gazette* reported the Committee of Seven's response to the NAACP's version of the riot on page 1, along with the report that considerable "indignation at the reported assertion of the unknown official of the organization mentioned was expressed here [in Helena], and the most frequent question asked was, 'Who supplied the information upon which the assertion was based?'"[34]

A *Gazette* editorial also vigorously attacked the NAACP for distorting the facts.

The "correspondent near the scene of the race riots in Arkansas," who supplied the National Association for the Advancement of Colored People with its information, utterly failed to explain why, when the negroes at Ratio had asked for settlements for their cotton, negroes at other places in Phillips County had armed themselves with high-powered rifles and had perfected a system of runners whereby their forces could be quickly concentrated. The authorities of Helena and of Phillips County should have a reckoning with the National Association for the Advancement of Colored People over this matter. The president of the association is Moorfield Storey of Boston. He should be asked to examine the evidence that has been brought out by the Committee of Seven at Helena.[35]

Moorfield Storey was a successful white Boston attorney who had served as the president of the American Bar Association in 1895. His ancestors had been among the first Puritan colonists in America, and after the Civil War he had been a clerk to the great champion of the rights of blacks, U.S. Senator Charles Sumner. Storey therefore served as a link between the NAACP and the earlier abolitionist movement. He had become president of the NAACP in 1910. This was one year after the founding of the NAACP by a small group of blacks and white civic leaders, such as John Haynes Holmes, Rabbi Stephen Wise, and Oswald Garrison Villard, who were concerned that a "new slavery" had been imposed upon American blacks through increasingly rigid racial segregation, disfranchisement of southern blacks, and lynching and mob violence. Storey served as NAACP president until his death in 1929. The program of the organization, as Storey described it, was to "create a public opinion which will frown upon discrimination against [blacks'] property rights," and to "endeavor to see that they get in the courts the same justice that is given to their white neighbors, and that they are not discriminated against as they are now all over the country." "We want to make race prejudice if we can as unfashionable as it is now fashionable," Storey said. "We want to arouse the better feelings of the white people, and broaden the sympathy which should be felt for the race to which we owe so much, and it seems to me that this is the field of our labor."[36] Storey had made significant contributions to the NAACP's objectives not only as president of the organization but also as counsel for the Association in the Oklahoma grandfather clause case, the Louisville segregation ordinance case, and other cases.[37] He would argue the Arkansas riot cases in the U.S. Supreme Court.

The publication in early October by the *New York Sun* of an article with Du Bois's analysis of the Arkansas riot from the NAACP's perspective was a source of further aggravation to the *Arkansas Gazette*. The *Gazette* charged that Du Bois

does not explain why negroes who had formed a labor union should have provided themselves with high-powered rifles and quantities of ammunition. . . . Helena and Phillips County should be on the job in the matter of publicity. That part of Arkansas is now the target of slings and arrows from many directions. There should be [an] organized and systematic effort to answer each and every publication that fails to give a true account of the recent troubles. . . . What we want to do is to point out the need for Helena, through its Committee of Seven or other body, [to see] to it that the country is rightly informed. . . . Helena can do this [monitor all newspapers in the United States and Canada] much better than the Gazette can do it because Helena is informed about all the facts and circumstances.[38]

It had become clear that the *Arkansas Gazette* believed a defense of the Committee of Seven's version of the Phillips County trouble was inseparable from a defense of the honor and integrity of the State of Arkansas and, to an extent, of the entire South. And as the NAACP's challenge to the official version of the events in Phillips County received more widespread publicity, the *Gazette's* editorials increasingly reflected a perception of Arkansas as the innocent victim of malicious propaganda in the northern and eastern press. By mid-November, the *Gazette* was complaining of the "many injustices done to Arkansas by some Northern newspapers and organizations since the trouble at Elaine":

When the insurrection came the Gazette and other newspapers sent reporters to the scene of the trouble. The accounts of every reporter agreed that the trouble was an organized and premeditated insurrection and not a sporadic race riot. This information was sent to the newspapers of the country through the Associated Press, but in the face of it many papers in the North editorially pooh-poohed the idea of insurrection and published a statement from a Northern organization, organized ostensibly to aid the negro in the South, that the trouble came because white planters were trying to defraud negroes in the annual settlements for the cotton crop.

At the trials of the negroes arrested the facts concerning the insurrection were brought out, but those papers and organizations in the main refused to give credence to the testimony produced at the trials and some of them suppressed the truth entirely. The fact that accused negroes admitted membership in the organization which brought on the insurrection, admitted taking part in the insurrection and pleaded guilty to the charges against them made no difference. These papers and organizations were determined to believe only what they wanted to believe.[39]

The war of words proved confusing to other parties who sought to discover the truth behind the affair. In mid-November, for example, William Anthony Aery of the Hampton Institute in Virginia, a respected educational institution for blacks, wrote to E. M. Allen, the principal spokesman of the Committee of Seven in Helena, pointing out that the committee's version of the riot was at variance with the report of White and the NAACP and requesting further information, since at "Hampton we are all eager to know the truth in this difficult situation."[40] Allen responded with a lengthy defense of the Committee of Seven's version, a response printed in full in the *Arkansas Gazette* in late November. It was a full reaffirmation of the planned insurrection theory. He had read White's report, Allen said, but upon inquiry the "leading negroes here who have co-operated with us in this matter state that neither White nor any other representative of his association has been to Helena since October 1." The White report was "false in many respects," Allen said, and it was "absurd to say that negro farmers as a class were being exploited by white planters. Too many proofs to the contrary are in evidence all over the South. There may have been individual cases of this sort, but not enough to condemn the white planters as a whole, any more than we should condemn all the negroes of the South because a few of them in this county deliberately violated the law."[41] The Phillips County riot was a "deliberately planned" insurrection set off prematurely by the shooting at Hoop Spur; Allen said that the "negroes killed during the trouble were shot while resisting United States soldiers and while firing upon United States soldiers." Allen argued that the convictions of blacks in the courts "were based entirely on voluntary confessions and upon evidence of those negroes who were involved. This evidence has been carefully transcribed and verified by the negroes themselves. No hearsay or circumstantial evidence was considered. No innocent negro was permitted to suffer." "There was not a hint of mob violence at any time," Allen continued. "Our people from the very beginning were determined to permit no lawlessness to exist, and assured the negroes here and in the county that none but the guilty would be apprehended."[42] "The statement sent to the Associated Press by the committee in charge in Helena details facts, all of which you can verify," Allen assured Aery. "The data, evidence and information forming the premises from which our conclusions were drawn can be examined in Helena by any committee or individual whom you may send here for that purpose. We invite investigations." "The negro papers in some instances have carried articles which were distorted and false from beginning to end," Allen concluded. "Their attitude has not helped this community in the slightest, and it is too bad that what we have endeavored to do here has not been recognized by those negro journals which are in a position to mould the sentiment of the members of the race."[43]

"It would be fortunate for Helena and Phillips County and for Arkansas and the whole South," the *Arkansas Gazette* said, "if the statement on the Elaine trouble prepared by E. M. Allen, president of the Helena Business Man's League, . . . could be published in every newspaper north of the Mason & Dixon line." In rebuttal to Allen's statement, however, Walter White supplied to William Aery the information that U. S. Bratton possessed about the riot. "I am sure that you realize the very grave danger of Mr. Bratton's being subjected to mob violence, and, perhaps, lynching, even though he is a white man, if it were known in Arkansas that he had made such a statement," White wrote Aery. He hoped Aery would appreciate after reviewing Bratton's story, White said, "the reasons for the vicious attacks on the statements we have made by those who profit directly from the policy of obscurantism."[44]

The Phillips County trouble was investigated also by Monroe N. Work of the Tuskegee Institute, another prominent black institution, during December of 1919 and early January of 1920. Work largely confirmed Walter White's findings. Upon receipt of Work's report, the NAACP noted that "Mr. Work interviewed a number of persons, including the twelve condemned men. He comes to conclusions similar to those reached by Mr. White . . . after his investigations, there being no material differences of fact."[45] Work's report discredited part of Allen's statement that his account of the trouble would be vouched for by Dr. E. C. Morris, a prominent black minister in Helena, and head of the Negro Baptist Association. "Dr. E. C. Morris of Helena," Allen had said in his statement to Aery, "will verify everything I have said in this letter to you if you care to take the matter up with him."[46] Work, however, had obtained a statement from Morris in which he refused to confirm this account. "I regard Mr. Allen as a splendid man, and yet I cannot see how he could have known the facts about the Elaine matter when he was fully eighteen miles from the scene of the riot," Morris said. "I have never believed that the Negroes at Elaine had planned to murder the white planters and take their lands."[47]

The success of the NAACP's publicity efforts in counteracting the "planned massacre of the whites" story that had initially gone largely unchallenged helped to alleviate the organization's financial problems. Many individuals responded with contributions for the legal defense of the Arkansas blacks. White's reports of the Phillips County trouble "created a gratifying sensation," he himself said later. "Our empty treasury began to be replenished by the contributions of both white and Negro Americans who were shocked by the story and wanted to aid."[48]

Its exposure of the peonage system in eastern Arkansas and its open challenge of the official Arkansas version of events were not without cost to the NAACP, however. For by becoming the most visible challenger of the official version of the riot, the NAACP brought down upon itself the almost universal condemnation of the Arkansas authorities and press. Arkansas Congressman Thaddeus Caraway, whose district included Phillips County, reflected the hostility the NAACP had aroused in the state in remarks delivered on the floor of the U.S. House of Representatives in November 1919. Defending the death sentences for the condemned blacks as entirely justified, Caraway noted that there was "in New York City an association called the National Association for the Advancement of Colored People." "I think," he added, "its correct title should be 'An association for the promotion of revolution and inciting to riots.'" Caraway denounced the NAACP for protesting the convictions and accused the Association of thriving "financially by falsehoods and antagonisms." "If people who know nothing of conditions would take time to ascertain the truth, societies like this would cease to exist," the congressman declared. "Its membership is composed of but two classes. One class is desirous of meddling with affairs of which it knows nothing—merely to be in the public eye—the other seeks advantages for itself, whatever harm may follow."[49]

As a consequence of such hostility, the NAACP was compelled to conceal, at least for a time, its efforts on behalf of the convicted blacks. But organization of an effective legal defense for the Arkansas blacks now became crucial to the NAACP's ultimate success in ensuring that justice was done. By 1919, the tenth anniversary of its founding, the NAACP had 220 branches scattered across the country and a total of 56,345 members. The organization had cut its teeth in litigation in defense of the rights of blacks, an activity which more than any other would bring it to public attention. It had scored early victories in the U.S. Supreme Court in 1915 and 1917 with its attacks upon the Oklahoma "grandfather clause," which excluded blacks from voting, and upon a Louisville, Kentucky zoning ordinance designed to segregate the races residentially. The Arkansas riot cases were the natural sequel.[50]

3 A Glimmer of Hope: The Organization of a Legal Defense

In early November, the attorney U. S. Bratton left Arkansas for New York City for a private meeting with the NAACP board of directors. He told them of his "knowledge of the underlying causes of the Arkansas situation, which were the economic exploitation of Negro sharecroppers and tenants, failure to give proper settlements [for the blacks' cotton crops], and the deliberate misrepresentation of their efforts for redress."[1] Bratton's contact with the NAACP was treated with secrecy, but he did address several "parlor meetings" organized by the Association in New York and Boston.[2] A social worker who had been one of the NAACP's founders and was now a member of the board of directors, Mary White Ovington, reported that "We were very favorably impressed with him," and she noted that the forums they organized were "very confidential, not inviting many people, but asking each one to bring a friend."[3] Bratton would marshal the legal defense for the Phillips County blacks. But first he concentrated on the fate of his son, O. S. Bratton, who had been jailed in Helena throughout October.

As mentioned earlier, O. S. Bratton told his father that he had arrived at Ratio at nine o'clock in the morning on October 1 to collect fees and obtain statements from the black tenant farmers who wanted the Bratton law firm to represent them. From twenty-five to fifty blacks met him there, but after they talked for about half an hour, six to eight heavily armed white men

39

arrived. "I guess you will have to adjourn your little meeting," one of the whites said to Bratton. "Yes, if you insist," he replied, "since you seem to be in the majority." The younger Bratton said later, "I of course had no suspicion of the gravity of the situation."[4] The armed men who took him into custody were trailed by five or six automobiles carrying thirty or so men. No one explained why he had been arrested. At Elaine, Bratton "was met by the citizens en masse, who appeared in a very inflamed state and some of them appeared exceedingly anxious to deal out 'summary justice'." They called him a "ring leader," chained him between two black men, and took them off to a brick store. "Shortly the report came that the Negroes were coming in on us," Bratton said, "and I was given a sack of flour and told by a deputy sheriff (and he was a real friend and worried to death for my life) to sit on it if the Negroes began shooting, as they might shoot me through the window."[5]

One of Bratton's guards at Elaine, he wrote, was "one of the leading men there apparently, and a devil incarnate, who though guarding me did all in his power to stir up the mob spirit by repeatedly remarking to each new-comer, 'There he is. Isn't he a pretty looking son-of-a-bitch; he's the ring leader.' The group searched Bratton and claimed to have turned up literature of the Industrial Workers of the World (IWW) and the Progressive Farmers Union. They told him, he said, "I had better tell it all before we break your neck. Several others advised me to get ready to die, that they would be after me in a few minutes."[6]

A group of men from Helena arrived at Elaine, including Judge J. M. Jackson, who assured Bratton that "they were going to protect [him] and take [him] to Helena." At the train station "all Hell-ena awaited the glorious spectacle—of seeing a white man chained to two Negroes." One or two individuals expressed a desire to "hang the son-of-a-bitch." With Bratton lodged in the Helena jail, a mob began forming to lynch him. But the federal troops arrived, locked the members of the mob in the county courthouse and warned that they would be machine-gunned if they attempted a lynching. Bratton's older brother, Guy, was his first outside visitor. Guy Bratton was also protected by soldiers when he left Helena.[7]

By mid-October, the Committee of Seven was admitting that Bratton had arrived at Ratio after the riot had begun and that "the negroes at Ratio at that time knew nothing about the shooting at Hoop Spur and were not involved in that insurrection, [and] therefore it would be rather difficult to prove that the Hoop Spur shooting was caused by or had any relation to the settlements asked for by the negroes at Ratio."[8] But despite this admission, Bratton continued to be held in the Helena jail. His father wrote the Committee of Seven on October 15, "I have contemplated asking for a full hearing on a writ of habeas corpus but have been informed by various persons, that such a course would be at the risk of the life of my son; that he would not be protected . . . and that he might be mobbed." He had also sought the release of his son through E. L. McHaney, another Little Rock lawyer, Bratton said, but the Committee of Seven had refused to guarantee his son's safe passage in leaving Phillips County.[9]

"As to my having committed any violations of the law or anything that could subject me to censure by fair-minded people," U. S. Bratton told the Committee of Seven, "I want to make this proposition to you; that I will waive all my Constitutional rights, the right of an indictment, the right of a jury trial, the right of a Circuit Court proceeding and allow you to submit anything that you have to the Supreme Court [of Arkansas] and give me an opportunity to answer it and to disprove anything, if such you have, and after I have finished my testimony, let the members of the Supreme Court say whether or not I have committed any offense known to the law." "If I have," Bratton continued, "I will then surrender myself to the proper official and take the punishment which the court says that I should have meted out to me. If your committee should feel that the fore-going proposition is not fair, then I will agree to submit the whole matter to the Governor, Attorney General and Secretary of State and be governed in the same manner and if this proposition is not acceptable, then I will agree for the Governor to appoint a Committee of five, made up of Circuit Judges of the State of Arkansas, one member of the five to be Judge Jimerson Jackson, Judge of the Circuit in which Phillips County is located."[10]

After a month in the Helena jail, the younger Bratton was released and secretly escorted out of Helena. In the courtroom in the county courthouse, he said, Judge Jackson explained "that I would be discharged on my own recognizance, and in a very friendly manner, as man to man, not Judge to prisoner, explained his plan for my leave taking." Bratton and his wife were to pack his belongings, and they were slipped out of the jail and lodged in a hotel until three o'clock in the morning, then put aboard a train leaving West Helena.[11]

Bratton; G. R. Casey, the representative of the Bratton firm in Helena; and U. S. Bratton himself were all indicted for barratry by the Phillips County grand jury.[12] When Guy Bratton conferred in early November with the Phillips County prosecutor, John E. Miller, he was promised that the barratry charge would not be prosecuted; Miller told Guy Bratton that "he did what he did to appease the mob, but that enough was enough."[13]

With his son out of danger, Bratton left for the New York City meetings with the NAACP, then traveled with Walter White to Washington, D.C., to confer with an official in the Department of Justice about the riot. The official "wired agents of the Department of Justice at Little Rock instructing them to proceed immediately to Helena and other points in Phillips County and investigate the alleged 'massacre' of whites and exploitation of Negroes. Investigation showed no grounds for belief that any massacre of whites was planned. The Progressive Farmers and Household Union of America sought through legal means to test the methods by which landowners, their agents and merchants exploited Negro sharecroppers and farmers."[14]

White and Bratton conferred with Congressman L. C. Dyer of Missouri and Senator Charles Curtis of Kansas, both of whom had introduced resolutions calling for congressional investigations of the riots of 1919 and the post-war wave of lynchings.[15] Senator Curtis asked Bratton to dictate a full statement on the Phillips County riot. Curtis also apparently agreed that Bratton should appear as a witness in support of his resolution on the 1919 race riots, should the Senate Judiciary Committee hold hearings on it. Walter White later forwarded Bratton's full statement to Senator Curtis and said that "it would be a splendid and valuable thing if it could be arranged for Senators Nelson and Dillingham, and perhaps Senators Kellogg and Walsh, to hear the statement made by this southern white man who is so very broad in his attitude."[16]

The NAACP hoped the hearings on the Curtis resolution would bring national publicity on the peonage conditions in Arkansas and on its version of the Phillips County trouble; it expected the hearings to have a beneficial effect on the legal defense of the

blacks who had been convicted.[17] But the hearings on the resolution were delayed until January 1920, and, although Bratton
testified then, they produced minimal publicity, at least in Arkansas.[18]

Of much greater help to the NAACP was Bratton's success in
recruiting Arkansas counsel to represent the convicted blacks.
On November 14 the Anti-Lynching Committee of the NAACP
met in Boston at the home of Moorfield Storey and "approved
of taking action to secure mitigation of the sentences and to do
all that was possible to bring the actual facts before the Governor of Arkansas and the general public concerning the alleged planned Negro uprising in Phillips County, Ark." The committee agreed that U. S. Bratton should attempt to secure
Arkansas counsel, subject to the approval of the board of directors.[19]

Bratton proceeded to negotiate with Colonel George W. Murphy, of the Little Rock law firm of Murphy, McHaney & Dunaway, hoping to win Murphy's consent to represent the imprisoned men. Colonel Murphy was regarded as one of the leading
criminal lawyers in Arkansas, and he could not have been a
more effective symbol for the defense. Murphy had been born in
Carroll County, Tennessee, in 1841 and had joined the Confederate army in 1861. Although he had been severely wounded at
the Battle of Shiloh, he joined Forrest's Cavalry in 1864, only to
be wounded again at Bryce's Crossroads and at Harrisburg.
When the Civil War ended, Murphy rode into Arkansas. He was
admitted to the practice of law in 1866 and moved his law practice to Little Rock in 1890. He was elected as attorney general
of Arkansas and served in that position from 1901 to 1905. Murphy was defeated as a Progressive Party candidate for governor
in 1912.[20]

Murphy did agree to undertake the defense, but insisted that
Bratton handle the financial arrangements with the NAACP
since he did not want to deal with an organization outside the
state of Arkansas.[21] A special meeting of the NAACP board of
directors was called on November 24 "to decide whether the
Association will employ Arkansas counsel in an effort to secure
commutation of sentences, new trials or other legal remedies"
in the cases of the Arkansas blacks.[22] At the meeting, the board
of directors approved an agreement which stipulated that "Colonel G. W. Murphy will represent the interests of all the colored

men who were defendants in the cases tried in November, 1919, in the Courts of Phillips County, Ark., growing out of the alleged uprising of Negroes in that County, and of any Negroes subsequently to be indicted and tried for offenses growing out of or related to this alleged uprising." Murphy was to try to secure new trials for the blacks or commutations of their sentences by the governor "and to appear in their behalf in all the courts of Phillips County, Ark., and the State of Arkansas, including all appeals to higher courts, up to but not including the Supreme Court of the United States, availing himself fully of all legal remedies afforded by law and the courts." The NAACP in turn agreed to pay Murphy three thousand dollars and additional incidental expenses.[23]

The NAACP also took steps to check on Murphy's actions. James Weldon Johnson wrote to Robert R. Church, a member of the NAACP's board of directors who lived in Memphis, to ask that Church look into Murphy's standing with and attitude toward blacks. And Johnson also requested that Church "undertake the task of keeping a check on Colonel Murphy as best you can. As you know, we are to pay him $3,000 for his services and what we want, of course, are action and results. We do not wish to write or communicate with Colonel Murphy in any way which would cause him to think that we did not have the fullest confidence in him."[24]

The Association also decided that its role in the defense should be concealed. Mary White Ovington noted that U. S. Bratton "has secured for us one of the most skillful attorneys in the state to take up the cases of the twelve men sentenced to be electrocuted, for whom he expects to get a new trial." The legal proceedings would be financed by the NAACP, Ovington continued, but "it is not possible for us to make a public appeal for this money. It would queer the case if a northern organization was known to be financing it, but we are asking for funds through the executive committees of our branches and from friends that we may meet the attorney's expenses which are sure to be heavy."[25] Walter White said of the need for secrecy, "We are defending all of the colored men involved [in the Arkansas cases], but because of the prejudice against the Association for exposing this system, it is necessary for us to remain in the back-ground until the cases are won."[26] Barred, therefore, from public appeals for funds, the NAACP was required to solicit funds privately, and wealthy contributors, who could be approached in confidence, became crucial to the success of the NAACP's legal defense efforts. James Weldon Johnson asked Julius Rosenwald of Sears & Roebuck for a legal defense contribution in December: "there is no case which has ever come to our attention which demands greater intervention on the part of fair-minded people. Unless definite action is taken the men under sentence will undoubtedly be executed."[27] "If it is necessary for us to take the cases to the Supreme Court of the United States it is not at all unlikely the total cost will probably be nearer $25,000 than $5,000, indeed it is our hope and intention to raise a 'defense fund' of $50,000," Johnson continued. "You will realize that while the lives of the twelve men now under sentence of death are very important, and we are very anxious to save them, we are making an equal effort for the correction of the evils which brought on the conflict of last October, not only in Arkansas, but in all other southern states where the system of exploitation exists."[28]

Julius Rosenwald agreed to contribute to the Arkansas defense fund five hundred dollars for every $4500 that the NAACP raised elsewhere,[29] and the Association was at least initially quite successful in its fund-raising efforts; $6,244.13 had been raised for the Arkansas defense fund by January 12.[30] One contribution of twenty dollars came to the NAACP from blacks in Tonapah, Nevada. Every "colored man in our town which are very few gave one dollar each without being coaxed," the accompanying letter said.[31] However, the secrecy surrounding the NAACP's role in the legal defense tended to confuse defense activities in Arkansas itself, since Arkansas blacks, unaware that another plan was underway, had created their own defense organization independently of the NAACP.

The first response of Arkansas black leaders to the Phillips County trouble, at least as reported in the white press, primarily involved reassurances that Arkansas blacks in the state had not embraced violence as a means of solving their problems. Reverend E. C. Morris, pastor of the Helena Centennial Baptist Church for thirty years and president of the American Baptist Association for twenty-five years, told whites that they had nothing to fear from the black population of the city. [32] And at meetings of blacks throughout Arkansas, resolutions were adopted condemning violence and pledging that the blacks of the state would be law-abiding citizens. In early October a meeting of blacks at Newport, organized by black ministers, passed resolutions condemning "the work of agitators and charged the Phillips County disturbance to the work of false leaders who sought to exploit the negroes for their own gains. A strong stand in favor of law enforcement was urged and the negroes were called upon to oppose any efforts by propagandists to promote disruption among the negroes."[33] A meeting of blacks in Arkadelphia adopted similar resolutions, denouncing "false agitators" and pledging not "to participate in any such organizations as were formed in east Arkansas, which led to race rioting." The Arkadelphia resolutions pointed out that since "there is no desire or ambition of the negro to dominate, supplant or overthrow the powers that be, for there is no power but that ordained by God, we, the negroes of Arkadelphia, deplore these conditions and hereby declare that there is no race hatred or friction such as has occurred in other places."[34] The blacks of Blytheville also subsequently pledged that "they would allow no one to establish any organization among them that might create trouble, and that the ministers would take the matter up and instruct their congregations against such organizations or doctrines."[35]

In mid-October, a letter was sent to Governor Brough complimenting him on his role in suppressing the riot; it was signed by Reverend J. P. Robinson, pastor of Little Rock's black Baptist church; Bishop J. M. Conner, of the African Methodist Episcopal (A.M.E.) church; J. M. Cox, president of Philander Smith College; and by Scipio Africanus Jones and John A. Hibbler, two black attorneys of Little Rock:

We are writing you this letter to assure you that we appreciate very keenly your prompt action in handling the very serious situation at Elaine, Phillips County, Arkansas. The very high standard which you have set as governor of the state of Arkansas in all matters which have come before you as governor during your incumbency has endeared you to us as one of Arkansas' best governors. You have set a worthy example for the governors who may come after you in this state, and one to be copied by the governors of the other states North, East, South and West. You went directly to the scene of trouble and danger with sufficient federal troops to marshal the situation. You put down the riot, you stopped the mob, you restored order, thus saving many lives in both races and much destruction of property. We are on the ground, we know what you have done, and wish to again assure you that the best colored people of the state of Arkansas endorse your stand and stand shoulder to shoulder in all things that tend to bring peace and good will between the races and for the uplift of Arkansas.[36]

In late November Governor Brough addressed the Negro Baptist state convention and reiterated his opposition to lynching and mob violence. He urged the fifteen hundred blacks in attendance to boycott publications like the *Chicago Defender* and expressed his appreciation to Arkansas black leaders "for the wise, conservative advice they have given their race in urging them to be law-abiding, peaceful and industrious."[37]

On November 22 the twelve blacks who had been sentenced to death in the trials following the Phillips County riot were brought to the state prison at Little Rock to await execution.[38] Two days later Governor Brough convened a meeting of blacks and whites for the reported purpose of promoting racial harmony and preventing any further trouble. The governor said that "it is probable steps will be taken by the conference to answer the attacks made in the newspapers of the North and East against the whites of the South."[39]

He again praised Phillips County authorities for the exemplary manner in which they had handled the riot. He noted that he had received several warning letters, threatening his assassination if the twelve men sentenced to death were executed, another threatening the burning of Helena. The governor announced at the conference the appointment of a commission to study race relations in Arkansas; it would be composed of nine whites and eight blacks. The *Gazette* did not carry the names of the white appointees, but listed the black commission members as E. J. Money, J. M. Cox (president of Philander Smith College), J. A. Booker (president of Arkansas Baptist College), S. L. Green, H. C. Yearger, J. M. Conner (Bishop of the A.M.E. church), Scott Bond, and E. C. Morris (pastor of the Centennial Baptist church in Helena).[40]

On a motion by Reverend Morris, the conference convened by Governor Brough passed a unanimous resolution "that it was the sense of the conference that the body expresses its willingness that the cases of the 12 condemned negroes be appealed to the Arkansas Supreme Court." Several speakers said the defendants had had a fair trial, but they agreed that the cases should be appealed to the state supreme court, since considerable "publicity [had] been given the fact that it required only a few minutes for the juries to reach verdicts in some of the cases, . . . and if the higher tribunal should affirm the verdicts, the newspapers of the North and East could no longer 'harp' on that point."[41]

J. M. Cox later said that the black members of the conference and of the Commission on Race Relations felt free to express their opinions honestly, and not "a Negro on the commission believes that the condemned men had a fair trial, not a Negro believes that [the Progressive Farmers Union] was organized for the purpose of killing white men and taking their property. In our meetings we have discussed the Elaine trouble again and again and the Negro members have expressed fearlessly their views concerning the whole affair."[42]

After the November 24 conference, Bishop Conner was quoted as saying, "The negroes of the state express themselves as absolutely satisfied that amicable conditions will result from the meeting. The negroes of the state express themselves as absolutely satisfied with the explanation of the governor regarding his position, and believe his position is safe and sound. They have expressed confidence in his leadership. Everything said at the conference leads me to believe that the whites and negroes will better understand each other in the future and that less friction is sure to follow." And Reverend E. C. Morris offered similar views, noting that he had also received threatening letters for condemning the Phillips County uprising. "The governor of Arkansas set the pace for all other Southern governors when he convened the interracial conference," Morris said. "The governor has, in real fact, made Arkansas a leader among the Southern states and a model for the states throughout the nation in the mutual handling of the delicate race question."[43]

With a resolution in hand approving an appeal of the cases to the state supreme court, the black leaders on the Commission on Race Relations took steps in December 1919, together with other prominent blacks, to organize a legal defense. Those principally responsible were Bishop Conner, Scipio Africanus Jones, Henry Avant, J. A. Hibbler, and J. A. Booker.[44] Indeed, Scipio Jones, and another black attorney, Thomas J. Price, had taken steps as early as November to save the twelve condemned blacks, apparently unaware of the NAACP's simultaneous intervention.

Thomas Price wrote Walter White in late November informing him that

Mr. Scipio A. Jones and myself are attempting to do what we can to
save those 12 unfortunate Negroes convicted at [Helena] from the chair
and to that end we are going to have the Arkansas Supreme Court
review the proceedings. . . . We plan to lay a foundation to carry the
cases to the United States Supreme Court if need be . . .[but the] work
is very expensive and we need money, as all this work must be done
rapidly in view of the time set for the executions. The firm of Murphy
& McHaney (white) are in the case with the understanding that a fee
can be raised. Both are Democrats and have only stood square on the
Negro. Mr. Murphy has been a former Attorney General of the State.
We need about $10,000. Can your society assist; any substantial
amount will help. Please be confidential, give the matter no publicity
for the present until the work is well under way and we get the time
for the executions stayed.[45]

Walter White replied in early December that the NAACP itself
was "in the process of arranging for defense" and promised to
supply details later. The NAACP, however, reacted suspiciously
to the involvement of Jones and Price in the legal defense efforts,
apparently because the Association feared the exposure of its
role in the defense. Further, ironically, it was dubious of the
abilities of the black lawyers. James Weldon Johnson told Robert Church that the NAACP had received Thomas Price's letter
and had "judged it is best for Mr. Price to know that the Association has already employed Colonel Murphy, but we do not
wish to say this in black and white because, as you fully understand, the Association wishes to keep its hand hidden in this
matter until we get results. We feel certain that if the people of
Arkansas knew that we were raising funds to set aside the verdicts already rendered by the courts of Arkansas, there would
be aroused opinion on the part of the public, if not on the part
of the courts, which would be prejudicial to the cases of the men
on trial."[46]
Johnson suggested that Church ask Price to visit Memphis
and discuss the defense. "We do not want Mr. Price to 'gum up'
the case," he said. "We do not know how good a lawyer he is."
Church could see, Johnson continued, "that there is a possibility
of [some] colored lawyers going [off] on a tangent to raise
money and, of course, to figure in the cases, thereby messing up
the whole matter." "We want to avoid that just now. We do not
want any publicity in this matter until we are out of the woods,"

Johnson concluded. "If we save these men, we will flood the country with publicity on what we have done, but publicity now will not help us and will only hurt them."[47]

The NAACP also arranged for U. S. Bratton to check on the roles Scipio Jones and Thomas Price were playing in the defense efforts. Bratton informed the Association that he had "had a talk with Attorneys Jones and Price, and I found from their conversation that they are not aware that the National Association has advanced any money or contracted for [legal representation]." Price and Jones, Bratton reported, had a harmonious relationship with Colonel Murphy, who they believed was being retained by Bratton and themselves. Bratton warned that the NAACP might be denied the credit for its defense of the condemned men because of the secrecy of its proceedings. "The most difficult problem will be to shape the activities so the N.A.A.C.P. can claim credit for the results," he concluded, since "as it is now the local people will naturally feel they are entitled to all credit."[48]

In early January 1920 the Arkansas blacks decided to establish a formal organization to raise defense funds. When Monroe Work, of the Tuskegee Institute, had been in Little Rock to investigate the Phillips County trouble in January, he had suggested to the black leaders that a formal organization should be established to raise defense funds and that such funds should be handled by a reputable treasurer.[49] They heeded Work's advice, and the result was the founding of the Citizens Defense Fund Commission (CDFC). As J. H. McConico, the secretary of the CDFC, said later, a principal reason for its organization was the possibility that people "would be imposed upon by unscrupulous parties unless some authorized organization took charge of the collecting and disbursing of funds."[50] Chairman of the CDFC was Dr. J. G. Thornton, McConico was secretary, and Dr. H. W. Suggs, treasurer. The CDFC agreed to pay Scipio Jones and Colonel Murphy twelve thousand dollars for their legal services, and within a few months the organization had raised half that amount and disbursed over four thousand dollars.[51] During the next two years of the legal battle in Arkansas, the CDFC would raise and spend more money than the NAACP in defense of the Phillips County blacks.[52]

The NAACP first learned of the Citizens Defense Fund Commission's existence in late January of 1920, and since the latter

Probably the black church house at Hoop Spur, three miles north of Elaine, where the "riot" began on September 30, 1919. Whites said blacks attacked them; blacks said whites fired into the church. *From Governor Brough's scrapbook of the 1919 riot. Courtesy of the Arkansas History Commission*

TEN KILLED IN ARKANSAS RACE BATTLES

ARKANSAS RIOTERS SHOOT AT GOVERNOR

One of Four Negroes Kills an Alderman—Posse Slays the Entire Band.

U. S. TROOPS IN CONTROL

Two Soldiers Wounded, One Dies—White at Little Rock Arrested in Dragnet.

MACHINE GUNS ARE FIRED ON NEGROES

Black Badly Wounded and White Soldier Hurt in New Arkansas Riot.

ORGANIZED PLOT SHOWN

Cache of Big Calibre Rifles Is Found in Office of One of the Agitators.

Special Despatch to THE SUN.

ELAINE, Ark., Oct. 3.—Fifteen negroes were captured to-day by troops of the Third Infantry after they had refused to surrender. It was necessary to fire machine guns at them. One negro was badly wounded. A white soldier was shot by one of the blacks. There have been no additional deaths to-day in the

The New York Sun, October 2–4, 1919. *Courtesy of the Library of Congress*

The body in the foreground is that of a black killed by white posse. *From Governor Brough's scrapbook. Courtesy of the Arkansas History Commission*

Arkansas Governor Charles H. Brough with officer, probably Colonel Isaac C. Jenks, in command of federal troops dispatched from Camp Pike in Phillips County to restore order. *From Governor Brough's scrapbook. Courtesy of the Arkansas History Commission*

Probably the car damaged after W. A. Adkins, Deputy Sheriff Charles Pratt, and Kidd Collins, trustee of the Phillips County jail, drove to Hoop Spur on the night of September 30. *From Governor Brough's scrapbook. Courtesy of the Arkansas History Commission*

(*Right*) Governor Brough at the
riot scene. (*Below*) White posse
hunting blacks who had taken
refuge in the canebrakes
around Elaine. *From Governor
Brough's scrapbook. Courtesy of the
Arkansas History Commission*

Blacks rounded up by federal troops. *From Governor Brough's scrapbook. Courtesy of the Arkansas History Commission*

Members of posse. *From Governor Brough's scrapbook. Courtesy of the Arkansas History Commission*

O. S. BRATTON.

SON INNOCENT, SAYS FATHER OF BRATTON

Went to Elaine as Attorney for Negroes, He Says in Statement.

That his son, O. S. Bratton, was at Elaine on legal business and had nothing whatever to do with the riot, was a statement made by U. S. Bratton Sr. yesterday afternoon. Mr. Bratton said he telephoned to Governor Brough at Elaine and explained the situation to him.

The statement by Mr. Bratton follows:

"A negro from Phillips county called at our office about two weeks ago and told us that a number of share croppers wanted us to represent them in the matter of making a settlement with their landowner. My son, Guy

O. S. Bratton, son of Little Rock attorney U. S. Bratton, arrested on charges of inciting to riot, later released. *Arkansas Gazette, October 3, 1919. Courtesy of the Library of Congress*

Federal troops from Camp Pike leading blacks, probably to the basement corral in Elaine public school. *From Governor Brough's scrapbook. Courtesy of the Arkansas History Commission*

Governor Brough addressing citizens at the Elaine Mercantile Company. *From Governor Brough's scrapbook. Courtesy of the Arkansas History Commission*

organization's secretary, J. H. McConico, was also the president of the Little Rock branch of the NAACP, he was informed of the NAACP's hitherto secret role in the case.[53] By December 1920 the NAACP was publicly announcing its role in the defense efforts, but relations between the CDFC and the NAACP were periodically strained since the CDFC felt that the NAACP failed to give it proper credit.[54]

The NAACP also remained suspicious of the black lawyers who had become involved in the defense efforts. In a letter to Work, John Shillady disparaged the role Scipio A. Jones was playing, adding that the NAACP had also learned that local Arkansas blacks were not financially supporting the defense efforts to the extent that had been expected.[55] Work disputed Shillady on both points. The black citizens of Arkansas, he said,

are quite anxious to do whatever they can and . . . a considerable amount of funds have been collected. I note what you state relative to Mr. Scipio A. Jones. I have had some knowledge of conditions and affairs in Little Rock before the Elaine trouble arose. The best information which I have supported by my own personal investigation is that Mr. Jones is an able lawyer and is the heart and center of the defense which is being made of the alleged Elaine rioters. This may not agree with your information but I feel that it is nevertheless correct. What I am trying to say is that you should not discount the influence of Mr. Jones and the part he is playing in the defense, which I am sure is just as important as what Mr. Murphy is doing. In fact, you may not know that Mr. Jones is in a position to do a number of things which Mr. Murphy cannot do.[56]

As a Dr. Sanford Reamey fled with his slaves before Union troops advancing across southern Arkansas in 1863, one of his slaves, Jemmima, had given birth to a son, who was named Scipio Africanus. With the coming of emancipation, Jemmima and her husband Horace took the name of Jones, for a previous owner, Dr. Adolphus Jones. Scipio Africanus Jones attended rural black schools in Tulip, Arkansas, and in 1881 moved to Little Rock to attend Bethel University (later Philander Smith College) and Shorter College, where he received his bachelor's degree in 1885. After teaching school for two or three years, he sought admission to the University of Arkansas's law school, but blacks were not admitted to the university, and he was required to gain his legal education by reading law under the supervision of white lawyers in Little Rock. He was admitted to the bar in 1889, and in 1915 he was elected to serve as a special judge on the municipal court. At the time of the Phillips County riot, Jones was the leading black lawyer in Little Rock, serving as counsel for several secret black societies, particularly a black fraternal order, the Mosaic Templars of America. Despite its initial suspicion, the NAACP soon learned that Work's estimate of Scipio Jones's ability was fully correct.[57]

The leadership of the NAACP appears from the outset to have understood that their defense of the Phillips County case, especially if it proved successful, would produce significant benefits for the Association, including increased contributions and public identification of the NAACP as the leading defender of black rights. Control of the Phillips County litigation was essential to this end, and the intervention of local black attorneys and leaders in the litigation could threaten NAACP control. In addition, at least some NAACP leaders appear to have shared prejudicial attitudes, commonly held at the time, toward the competence and abilities of black professionals, including lawyers. The Association, in some of its early cases, had encountered certain incompetent black lawyers whose actions had seriously damaged the cause of their clients, and other black lawyers whose goals in NAACP cases had been their own financial gain. These experiences had led Oswald Garrison Villard, one of the white founders of the NAACP, to conclude that it "is an unfortunate fact that the colored lawyers, as we have learned to our cost . . . , usually take advantage of philanthropic interest of this kind to make money for themselves."[58] Memories of earlier, unsatisfactory experience with black lawyers, therefore, was an important factor in the suspicious reaction of the NAACP in the Arkansas cases.

Despite the strained relations between the NAACP and Arkansas black leaders, Monroe Work cautioned that the "main thing is that all the agencies should work in cooperation and in harmony to get a just decision in the Elaine cases."[59] The legal defense efforts jointly financed by the NAACP and the CDFC did in fact begin to produce results by early December. The ex-Confederate and the ex-slave, Colonel Murphy and Scipio Jones, were together preparing motions for new trials to be filed in the Circuit Court of Phillips County. Colonel Murphy announced to the press that he was "not yet fully informed about the case, but from what I can gather no exceptions were made and no witnesses were summoned for the defense [at the original trials].

Able lawyers were appointed to defend the 12 men, I am informed, but the trial was held in the same county where the
uprising is alleged to have occurred and there seems to have
been a great deal of excitement and possibly prejudice. I am in
favor of giving the 12 men every possible chance before the law."
The twelve condemned blacks had been scheduled to be executed on December 27, 1919, but on January 2, 1920, Governor
Brough agreed to grant a stay of execution. "If efforts are made
to appeal the case, and if the attorneys will proceed promptly
in their efforts to secure an appeal," Brough said, "I will grant
any necessary stay of execution."[60]

U. S. Bratton found that by early 1920 his own position in
Arkansas had become untenable. After "disposing of our business here," Guy Bratton had said to his father after the freeing
of his brother, O. S. Bratton, "I would lose no sleep in forsaking
this country, even though that is the desire of that bunch of cut-
throats. For it is foolish to think we can ever do any more business down there, they have so intimidated the Negro in that
county that I doubt if he will have the nerve to come into court
again unless he is given more protection than he is at present. . . . [The Brattons are the only ones who] have had the
nerve to face the ring, and yet some of those good Christian
gentlemen, even Rev. Millar, Editor [of the] Arkansas Methodist, in newspaper articles says that the Negro is well treated."[61]

In addition to the bitterness the Brattons felt as a result
of their involvement in the Phillips County trouble, constant
threats were being made against the life of U. S. Bratton and he
found the practice of law in Arkansas impossible.[62] He therefore
left Arkansas with his family in early 1920 and established a
law practice with his son Guy Bratton in Detroit, Michigan. "I
regret leaving the state in many ways," Bratton wrote Shillady
at the NAACP in February 1920, "but really think it is best, if I
can put some other person in my shoes, as they can keep up the
fight without having to overcome the prejudice that has been so
unjustly aroused against me."[63]

The legal defense Bratton had helped to organize had, nevertheless, produced the first ray of light in a situation that had
appeared hopeless only three months earlier. Reacting in early
December to the news of the stay of execution for the condemned blacks and the preparation of the motions for new
trials, Mary White Ovington called the report from Arkansas

"quite wonderful. . . ." "It seems strange to speak of being encouraged when conditions are so terrible," she said, "but . . . it looks as though we might get really extraordinary results from these Elaine cases, and if we can get the facts not only before the country but before the world, we may hope for some improvement."[64]

4 The Hill Extradition Fight

Robert L. Hill was arrested in Kansas City, Kansas, on January 20, 1920, and was immediately taken to Topeka to await extradition to Arkansas, where he had been indicted for nightriding and murder in Phillips County. Hill was thirty years old. When he was arrested he was described as "dressed like a common plantation hand." Walter White himself had called Hill "an ignorant, illiterate country farm hand," but Hill proved to be literate, and, indeed, he had corresponded with U. S. Bratton, with Little Rock black attorney Thomas Price, with the NAACP, and with Governor Brough during the period when he was in hiding.[1]

In his correspondence Hill admitted that he had helped organize the Progressive Farmers Union, first established by a man named R. I. Lee.[2] The union, Hill said, had been incorporated with the help of a law firm in Winchester, Arkansas, and the charter of incorporation recorded in Monticello. "We did all the law required and was declared a legal body," Hill complained. "Now if the law dont protect us it is no use to have a law."[3]

The Progressive Farmers Union had sought the help of U. S. Bratton's law firm in obtaining settlements for cotton crops and statements of accounts for blacks in Phillips County, and Hill had accompanied O. S. Bratton when he visited the Ratio plantation on October 1. "Course we didn't have anything to do with the trouble," he said. "I was only rendering legal service, I was helping out the Bratton law firm . . . on the case. Mr. Bratton

55

was expected down Wednesday morning, October first and the people met Tuesday night somewhere about Hoop Spur in Phillips County and the trouble started. Course we didn't know anything of it we was at the station [at Ratio], talking with the people; and a crowd of armed men come up and arrested Mr. [O. S.] Bratton and I fled for my life."[4]

Hill had taken a correspondence course in detective training from a St. Louis firm, and at the conclusion of the course he received a badge with the letters "U. S." on it. He subsequently considered himself a detective and referred to himself as a "U.S. Detective."[5] He told the NAACP that after the Phillips County authorities had "found out I was detective helping the law firm they charged me for inciting trouble. It was a fact that the people could not get statements of their accounts and their cotton was being shipped and the custom in that section was the landlord would take the cotton and seed and ship them away and didn't ask them . . . and the people had decided to put their money together and get legal help and some how up about Elaine, Arkansas, the white people had ordered the Negroes to stop meeting and from that trouble came up." "I can't tell just the whole truth of the matter about the white people ordering them to not meet [any more] but if the Government will take up the matter they could put some one in there and find out," Hill continued. "I heard about it but the truth is that the people was trying to get a settlement through a process of law. Now, I was detective on the case but I can't say how the shooting started but it shows that the Negroes were harmless, they went back in the wood according to Newspaper that says the soldiers had to go into the [canebrakes] and get them."[6]

Hill explained to the Bratton law firm, "Course the Union was in about 25 or 30 counties, and it seems that it would be awful foolish for me to go to Phillips County only to plan killing whites of that county and there was local Unions in about 25 or 30 Counties." "I am sorry that the trouble came up. I did what I though[t] was right in the matter. I advised the people to get the help of some honest white lawyers. We didn't intend to go on farther in the matter than lawyers advise them, as the people was paying me to get them good lawyers. I thought I was right and I believe that I ought to have protection. . . . I never has had a mind to harm no one. I love my white friends well as I did the colored. So far as the union that they claim was planning an uprising, I dont know anything about it."[7]

Hill then pleaded to Bratton, "[could you] help me out, they are trying to accuse me of inciting that trouble but Dear Sir I didn't even dream of such a thing. . . . Now I know you have good influence in the Government and you can get in touch with the leaders of the state and help me out."[8] He likewise asked the NAACP to please "get up at once for my help because if they get me, they will kill me, just like they are doing, sentencing all leaders of the Union to death they say that blacks was planning to kill whites."[9] Hill admonished Thomas Price to be "sure to not mention my name and do away with this letter as soon as you have read same."[10] Price instead forwarded the letter to Walter White of the NAACP. "I am writing to the party mentioned at the address given asking him to come directly to the office in New York City where we would do what we could for him," White wrote Price. "I will appreciate it if you will also write to him urging [him] to do so."[11] Instead of making his way to New York City, however, Hill appears to have fled initially to Boley, Oklahoma, an all-black community.[12] And in early December, he reportedly wrote Governor Brough, offering to surrender if he were guaranteed a fair trial and if the reward offered for his capture were to go to the support of his family.[13] Hill then fled to South Dakota, returning to Kansas City on January 20, where he was caught.[14]

The strategy of the Arkansas authorities was to ensure Robert Hill's return to Arkansas by pressing his extradition on the state charges of murder and nightriding and, at the same time, on federal charges. The federal indictment against Hill had been issued in the fall term of the U.S. district court in Helena; in addition to impersonating a federal officer, Hill was charged, with V. E. Powell, with conspiracy to impersonate a federal officer. (Powell had been indicted in the wake of the Phillips County riot and was in custody in Arkansas.) Even if the governor of Kansas, Henry J. Allen, refused to extradite Hill on the state charges, therefore, he could still be arrested by federal officials in Kansas and returned to Arkansas to stand trial on the federal charges. And once Hill was back within the jurisdiction of Arkansas, he could be tried on the state charges as well. Fred Robertson, the U.S. Attorney in Kansas City, and other Kansas officials issued statements that implied Hill would be returned to Arkansas to face the federal charges against him even if Governor Allen refused extradition on the state charges.[15]

Charles W. Pratt, the deputy sheriff wounded near Hoop Spur at the outset of the Phillips County trouble, had been dispatched to Kansas to return Hill to Arkansas. His reception in Topeka was not entirely friendly and threats of violence were reportedly made against him.[16] Pratt, concluding that Hill's extradition was not to be a routine affair, telegraphed to Governor Brough on January 25 that he had "information that the negroes are going to make an extremely hard fight on the Hill extradition." "Do you want to furnish counsel for the state of Arkansas?" he asked the governor. "This will be a hard legal battle."[17] Governor Brough decided to send Attorney General John D. Arbuckle to Topeka to fight for Hill's extradition.

Fortunately for Hill, there was an active branch of the NAACP in Topeka, and members of the branch promptly came to his aid. James H. Guy, A. M. Thomas, and Elisha Scott, all lawyers and members of the Topeka branch of the NAACP, contacted the governor's office. Extradition papers requesting the return of Hill to Arkansas had yet to be filed, but Guy, Scott, and Thomas were promised that a hearing would be held before the governor preceding a decision on the question of extradition.[18] The Topeka lawyers, having been informed that Hill had been indicted in Arkansas on federal charges of impersonating a federal officer and conspiracy to do so, immediately sent telegrams to the U.S. senators from Kansas, Arthur Capper and Charles Curtis, urging them to contact the Department of Justice. If Hill were returned to Arkansas, they warned, "he would be lynched." Senator Curtis replied that the Justice Department had assured him Hill had the right to a hearing in federal court before facing extradition to Arkansas on the federal charges and that the department had wired the U.S. Attorney in Kansas ordering him to see that Hill was given his full rights under federal law.[19]

"If the Arkansas courts ever get their hands on [Hill]," James Weldon Johnson had said, "we are afraid he would not have a chance for his life."[20] The national office of the NAACP, like its Topeka branch, swiftly mobilized in Hill's defense when Associated Press dispatches announcing his capture came through on January 22. James Weldon Johnson asked Senator Capper to join in the NAACP's protest against Hill's extradition on the ground that he could not receive a fair trial in Arkansas. Capper, a member of the NAACP board of directors, telegraphed Governor Allen.[21]

The NAACP also asked Senator Capper to recommend a Kansas lawyer to defend Hill in the extradition proceedings. Capper suggested Hugh T. Fisher, the county prosecutor of Shawnee County, where Topeka is located. "Senator Capper and the Association very much hope that you will feel disposed to take this case in the public interest," John Shillady wrote Fisher, "as it involves the question of securing the legal rights of a Negro whom every bit of evidence we can get hold of indicates is not guilty of the crime that will be charged against him if he is extradited to Arkansas where it is certain he cannot get a fair trial." In contrast to its secret involvement in the defense of the blacks convicted in the wake of the Phillips County riot, Shillady told Fisher, the Association was "willing and prepared to let it be known that it is behind the efforts to prevent Hill's extradition [to] Arkansas."[22]

Hugh Fisher was a Republican, and at the time of the Hill extradition fight, he was about to begin a campaign for election as a state senator. He apparently perceived that his identification with Hill's cause would be to his advantage in the coming election and readily offered his services to the NAACP and in defense of Hill. Consequently the NAACP obtained the services of an extremely able and astute attorney largely without cost; Fisher refused to accept payment for his defense of Hill, requesting only reimbursement for his relatively minor incidental expenses.[23]

Hugh Fisher assumed the leadership of Hill's defense in association with the black Topeka lawyers—James Guy, Elisha Scott and A. M. Thomas—who had initially come to Hill's aid. Confronting Fisher and his colleagues was the fact that Hill was facing not only extradition proceedings but also the complicating factor of a federal indictment. Hugh Fisher quickly decided that the most crucial factor was time—time in which Hill's lawyers could muster evidence demonstrating that he could not receive a fair trial in Arkansas if he were extradited, and time in which to prepare a defense against removal to Arkansas on the federal charges. Fisher decided that the best strategy for the defense was to ensure that the extradition proceedings before Governor Allen were held first. He believed defense counsel could obtain from the governor a delay in those proceedings of sufficient duration to allow him to marshal an effective defense not only against extradition but also against the federal charges.

Because the warrant for Hill's arrest on the Arkansas charges had initially been delayed, however, Guy, Scott, and Thomas had filed a petition for a writ of habeas corpus in the Shawnee County District Court, charging that Hill was being held illegally by Kansas authorities. From the standpoint of Fisher's strategy, the initiation of the habeas corpus proceeding was a mistake, since if Hill were freed as a result of that proceeding, he would be promptly arrested on the federal charges and might be returned to Arkansas by federal officials. And if this were to occur, there would be no extradition proceeding before Governor Allen and no opportunity for the dilatory tactics Fisher hoped to pursue. Fisher was undoubtedly relieved when Judge James McClure of the Shawnee County District Court dismissed the petition, ruling that the Kansas courts could not question the validity of the indictment of Hill on the Arkansas charges. Whether or not Hill should be extradited, Judge McClure said, was "up to the good judgment of our governor."[24]

Fisher had taken action to ensure that Hill would be held in state custody pending extradition proceedings before Governor Allen; he accomplished this by persuading the governor to issue a warrant holding Hill in the custody of the State of Kansas until extradition proceedings were completed. "The Governor's warrant prevents the Federal authorities from taking Hill into custody until the requisition is heard by the Governor," Fisher reported to the NAACP. "I am satisfied that Governor Allen will give us a reasonable opportunity to secure evidence and I believe that he will deny the extradition," he continued. "The Federal authorities will then arrest Hill and we will secure an order from the Federal Court and have an opportunity to fight removal in the United States District Court in Kansas City. The time gained by the Governor holding him will not only enable us to secure evidence to present in the Federal Court but will give us a chance to make a showing [in the extradition proceedings before] the Governor."[25]

The federal Constitution provides that a fugitive from justice in one state who is apprehended in another state "shall on Demand of the executive Authority of the State from which he fled, be delivered up, to be removed to the State having Jurisdiction of the Crime," but the U.S. Supreme Court had held in 1861 that a governor could not be compelled to deliver a fugitive to the authorities of a state from which he had fled. Whether Hill would be returned to Arkansas was up to Governor Allen, and

Hugh Fisher proved to be correct in his belief that Hill's counsel could obtain a postponement of the extradition proceedings of sufficient duration to allow them to marshal evidence that Hill could not receive a fair trial in Arkansas. Although Attorney General Arbuckle of Arkansas had assured Governor Allen that Hill would receive a fair trial and would not be lynched in Arkansas, the governor agreed on January 27, upon motion by Hugh Fisher and the black attorneys defending Hill, to postpone further hearings on Hill's extradition. "If Hill is unable to overcome evidence produced at today's hearing, Kansas negroes will not want the writ [of extradition] set aside," Allen said. "Kansas cannot be recognized as a mecca for negroes fleeing from Justice," the governor continued. "In order that he may have every opportunity to present his case, I have continued the matter. . . ."[26]

Returning to Arkansas on January 28, Attorney General Arbuckle reported that the extradition hearing had been attended by large numbers of blacks and that the Topeka newspapers were printing stories charging that the convicted Phillips County blacks were not guilty. Feelings in Topeka were "bitter against Arkansas as a result of the Elaine trouble," Arbuckle said, but he added that every courtesy had been extended to him and he was convinced that Governor Allen would ultimately order Hill's extradition.[27]

E. M. Allen of the Helena Business Men's League; J. L. Solomon, president of the Helena Board of Trade; F. F. Kitchens, sheriff of Phillips County; H. D. Moore, Phillips County judge; and J. C. Knight, the mayor of Helena, signed a telegram to Governor Allen on January 29, stating that the "citizens of Helena and of Phillips County, Arkansas, urge your prompt compliance with the request of Governor Brough that Robert L. Hill will be returned to Arkansas." "We feel that he should stand trial as the active head of the organization responsible for the trouble and suffering endured by our people, white and colored, last fall," the telegram continued. "We will guarantee him a fair and impartial trial and will agree to a change of venue if desired. All we want is to see justice done, and feel that the right of a trial of the case on the actual evidence should not be denied us. There has never been a lynching in Phillips County and never will be as long as criminals receive proper and just punishment at the hands of the courts."[28]

A more serious blow to the NAACP's fight against extradition occurred on February 2, when three black leaders—Bishop J. M. Conner of the A.M.E. church; J. M. Cox, president of the Philander Smith College; and J. A. Booker, president of the Arkansas Baptist College—joined the white members of the executive committee of the Arkansas Commission on Race Relations in requesting that Governor Allen return Hill to Arkansas. "We, the . . . members of the Executive Committee of the Commission on Race Relations in Arkansas, hereby request that you honor the requisition of Gov. Charles H. Brough for Robert L. Hill, charged with accessory to murder and nightriding in Phillips County, Arkansas, in connection with the Elaine affair," the message to Governor Allen read. "The citizens of Phillips County and the Governor have assured us that Hill will be guaranteed a fair trial and the right to change of venue. We believe the return of Hill is in the interest of justice to the negro and will materially strengthen this biracial commission in the work of promoting inter-racial justice."[29]

The relations between the NAACP and Arkansas black leaders, already strained by mutual suspicions, deteriorated further as a result of this statement. The three Arkansas black leaders were strongly denounced in the NAACP *Crisis*, which portrayed their actions as a betrayal of the black cause. The *Chicago Defender* denounced the three as "rattlesnakes" and "animals." "The names of Conner, [Cox] and Booker henceforth will be as a stench in the nostrils of self-respecting men and women," the *Defender* said, "and they should be shunned as a pestilence and hated as traitors of a type that would have made Benedict Arnold blush with shame."[30]

Arkansas's Governor Brough, on the other hand, praised Conner, Cox, and Booker for signing the request for Hill's return, remarking that their actions proved that they were for law and order, while the white press in Arkansas also joined in defending the actions of the black leaders.[31] Joseph Booker publicly expressed his appreciation for the manner "in which the whole white press came to the defense of the three colored commissioners in the matter of having R. L. Hill returned to the state for a fair trial." He asked, "Would it not be far better to magnify these things that count so much for peace and prosperity and minimize those special cases of disturbance like the Elaine riot, etc., than to furnish itching ears to outsiders, who are keeping up a seething pot of hatred and misrepresentation for the sake of making money from us who are anxious to buy their newspaper rot? . . . Let me once again appeal to my people to spurn the yellow journalism which we are feeding and fattening, and turn to our home papers, schools, [and] business enterprises here in the state for what we want."[32]

In a letter to the *Arkansas Gazette*, J. T. Chambliss, a black educator from Fordyce, expressed his view of what a "great trial it must have been to Bishop Conner, Prof. Cox and Prof. Booker to ask for the return of a member of their own race for trial for his life, but no man of good intentions can afford to criticize or condemn them for rising to the high level they did." Chambliss resented "the inflammatory articles" appearing in the black press of the North and noted that while "all these inflammatory articles are coming to us it is well to remember that none of the Elaine rioters have yet been executed. Their cases are pending on appeal and their lives are in the hands of fine, honest, sober, Christian men, as good as any man north of the Mason and Dixon line. An ex-Confederate soldier, reputed to be the ablest criminal lawyer this state ever produced, is pleading their cause with force and moving eloquence. If they are finally held to be guilty as charged it is safe to say that the evidence was sufficient and their guilt proven beyond all reasonable doubt."[33]

For the NAACP and the attorneys defending Hill in Kansas, however, the actions of Cox, Booker, and Conner appeared to be a serious, perhaps fatal, blow to their efforts. "If our Governor gets a signed statement from these men it is going to make it very hard indeed to overcome," Fisher wrote Walter White. "I was satisfied that we would be successful before the Governor until I saw this statement."[34] Fisher telegraphed Shillady, warning that if the reports of their actions were "true, [it] cripples us."[35] Fisher asked the NAACP to try to counteract the Arkansas black leaders' statement. In response Shillady wrote on February 6 to all NAACP branches, "upon the receipt of this letter, the National Office urges you to write to Hon. Henry J. Allen, Governor, Topeka, Kans., urging him not to grant extradition papers for the return of Robert L. Hill to Arkansas for trial." The branches should emphasize their conviction that Hill could not receive a fair trial in Arkansas.[36]

The NAACP also began a dialogue with Cox, Conner, and Booker on the wisdom of their endorsement of extradition. William H. Pickens, the associate field secretary of the NAACP, wrote to J. M. Cox soon after the controversial statement became public.

Of course it would be irregular for you not to support any perfectly legitimate procedure of the [Commission on Race Relations], but this occurred to me; if I were a member of this committee I would at least inquire that before I gave my consent, signature or any effort to get a Negro who is not now in the hands of Arkansas, those who are in the hands of Arkansas, must first be given justice. This committee may pledge itself to justice for Hill, but such pledge can hardly be based on anything trustworthy unless they first demonstrate their capacity of good will toward the men under sentence to die for defending their own lives and the other multitude of men who are serving prison terms for the same cause. You know and I know that many of these men are as innocent as you and I are. If we had been in Phillips County in the path of that mob, we would be in prison or on our way to the electric chair.

The colored men of Arkansas who want to support the laws could reasonably ask that justice be shown to those who are now in the hands of the State but the colored men can not assist in getting any others into the hands of the State. This would require great courage, but I think it perfectly sound. As a matter of fact, you and I know that under present conditions there is small chance for Hill in an Arkansas Court. Perhaps there would be some little chance for him in the Northern part of Arkansas. But you are on the scene. You must know what you are doing. Could you kindly write me, confidentially, if necessary, just what your position is, so that we may understand? The National Association would like to co-operate with the best colored men everywhere. And these are no times for colored people to work at any cross purposes.[37]

Joseph Cox responded to Pickens' letter: "Yes, I signed the petition to Governor Allen for the return of Robert L. Hill, signed it of my own accord and knowing at the time that I would be criticized by many Negroes who live in Arkansas and by many who do not live in Arkansas." None of the black members of the Arkansas Commission on Race Relations believed that the Phillips County defendants had organized for the purpose of killing whites and taking their property, and these views had been freely expressed, Cox said. "On the day we sent the telegram to Governor Allen, we discussed the subject fully two hours and signed the petition only after we had assurance from Governor Brough, Attorney General Arbuckle and other prominent white citizens that a change of venue would be granted and that a fair and just trial would be given." Governor Brough, Cox added, "is one of the fairest executives in this country. The leading Negroes of Arkansas believe in him and he believes in the Negroes of Arkansas."[38] The Arkansas black leaders on the Commission on Race Relations "made the beginning in the way of securing a new trial for the men condemned to the electric chair," Cox wrote, and they intended to continue their efforts. The return of Hill would lead to a trial at which facts favorable to the condemned blacks would be established. The black members of the commission had interviewed the condemned blacks in prison, and Cox assured Pickens that they would "insist that the white members of the commission go and interview the men that are in the penitentiary. If they see what we saw and hear what we heard, in case the supreme court fails to grant a new trial, we will be able to lay facts before the governor that will weigh mightily in our plea for pardons, and my word for it, the white members will support us to a man."[39]

There are places in Arkansas in which the Negro can get a fair trial—just as fair as he can get in New York City or in Baltimore. As I see it, in all matters we must stand for justice, work that it may not miscarry, but do nothing to help Negroes evade it. [Although most northern blacks seemed to believe that] Phillips County is all Arkansas and Elaine is the capitol of the state, the three Negroes who signed the petition [asking for Hill's extradition] held conferences with some of Little Rock's leading Negroes, and with just two exceptions, all approved our course, [and] Attorney T. J. Price, who knows as much about Mr. Hill's order as any other man in the state and who is Mr. Hill's representative, thinks it best for him to return. Attorney S. A. Jones, who is making the appeal to the supreme court for a new trial for the condemned men, believes Hill should return. We all believe he will be acquitted. We all further believe that Hill's trial will do more than anything else to show the innocence of the other men. . . .

[Cox hoped Pickens] may see that at least our motive is right, that you may know that we believe in the good people of Arkansas, and finally that I might make a plea for the sanity of the five hundred thousand Negroes of the state; for if we believe, as some other Negroes believe, that Arkansas is a regular hell and that nowhere in the state can the Negro get justice in the courts, we would be the biggest fools possible to remain here.[40]

The Arkansas black leaders were obviously convinced that the salvation of the riot defendants could be achieved only through cooperation with and accommodation to the white political leadership that controlled the state and the ultimate fate of the defendants. With its goals of equality of the races and full enforcement of the Fourteenth and Fifteenth Amendments, the

NAACP's leadership could not, understandably, accept cooperation with and deference to a white political system geared to
maintaining blacks as second-class citizens. At the heart of the
conflict between the NAACP and the Arkansas black leaders was
a dilemma that would affect not just the Phillips County case
but the effective defense of the rights of blacks throughout the
South.

Although the intervention of "outside" groups like the NAACP
was frequently essential to the prevention or correction of injustices to southern blacks, their involvement was all too often
perceived in the South as the meddling of outsiders in southern
affairs and hence stubbornly resisted. Attempts to correct injustices and protect the rights of blacks through cultivation of
white leaders and avoidance of overt attacks on southern administration of the law, on the other hand, while reducing the
possibility of the kind of resistance engendered by the intervention of outside groups, often proved ineffective in the end. The
selection of the proper strategy to be employed in the defense
of the rights of blacks in the South therefore posed questions of
considerable delicacy, and the conflict between the Arkansas
black leaders and the NAACP in large part concerned just such
strategic considerations.[41]

By the end of February, the NAACP had obviously decided
that a final break with Arkansas black leaders should be avoided
in the interest of the defense of the Phillips County blacks. William Pickens wrote J. A. Booker that despite their differences
"we wish to do everything possible to co-operate with your efforts there."[42] He told James Cox, "I feel sure that you and President Booker and Bishop Conner are doing and will do the best
that is in you to [protect] the interest of our people in Arkansas
and elsewhere." Pickens pointed out, however, that the situations of the NAACP and the Arkansas black leaders

are somewhat different and that we can perhaps do something from
our end that might not be the wisest thing from your end. However,
there are some decided advantages in your situation. In that you have
intimate and direct touch with the situation and in that you stand face
to face with the white people and the authorities who chiefly control
the situation. It is nothing but common sense that the rest of us should
concede [a] large measure of rightful discretion for a man who stands
where you stand. At the same time we want to cooperate with you and
do the best we can to help. By no means do the colored people in one
part of the country want to assume a spirit of antagonism to those in

another part, of the country. And I, for my part, want to invite the free, full and frank understanding always with others who are striving to do the same thing that I am striving to do. If you discover any way that I can render assistance, do not hesitate for a moment to let me know.[43]

J. A. Booker responded that he and the other Arkansas black spokesmen were "glad to know that you people will do everything you can to co-operate with us here, in spirit. . . . It is quite true that our situations are different; yet here in Arkansas and in the South, a few of us think we can work out some part of these problems without leaving the South, or without provoking bloodshed at every issue." Booker continued:

we are trying to secure the lives and freedom of the men who are convicted to die in the electric chair. It is not now a matter with us as to how they came to their present condition; we know in reason that they are there by false trials; that the testimony convicting them was both forced and false; that if they had their dues they would either have short terms for misdemeanors, or would be dead or alive along with their fellow rioters. But it has now become a condition confronting us and not a theory. We must play checkers fast, if we would save their lives. What would you do under the circumstances, especially when Hill [who is] a material witness, is not indicted for the high crime which he has caused the others to meet? Like you, 'there will come a time when we can speak more plainly.' I propose to work hard and be patient till that time comes.[44]

While the conflict between the NAACP and the Arkansas black leaders ended without a break in relations between them and with mutual assurances of cooperation, there was a lingering suspicion and bitterness between the two camps. Reacting to subsequent comments by Bishop Conner regarding the Phillips County affair, U. S. Bratton declared that "Judas was [a] saint beside that fellow. . . . Hell is not hot enough for him."[45] In the spring of 1920, Bishop Conner was transferred by the general conference of the A.M.E. church to the district of Michigan and Canada. The Arkansas press reported that Conner's transfer was in retaliation for his signing the request for Hill's extradition and the "fact that he refused to condone lawlessness by negroes."[46] The press in Arkansas subsequently reported also that the lives of the black members of the Commission on Race Relations had been threatened because of their endorsement of Hill's extradition and that the commission was discussing methods by which they could be protected. The commission pointed to evidence that the Industrial Workers of the World were "trying to inflame Arkansas negroes against negroes who are co-operating with the whites in an effort to secure better understanding between the races"; it appointed committees to "expose the viciousness of the I.W.W. propaganda" and to inform the black community that I.W.W. "principles can bring nothing but disaster."[47]

The NAACP continued intense efforts to block the extradition during the postponement of the proceedings ordered by Governor Allen. Its efforts were directed primarily at getting access to Governor Allen to inform him of the Association's version of the causes of the Phillips County trouble and the unfairness of the trials that followed it. The NAACP had by this time secured information from the blacks condemned to death in Arkansas that the Helena Committee of Seven had resorted to torture to secure confessions from some of them.[48] This information, together with evidence that the Progressive Farmers Union had pursued peaceful purposes, Hugh Fisher told the NAACP, would aid substantially in the fight against Hill's extradition.

"If we get the information desired," Fisher wrote Walter White, "we are almost sure to defeat the requisition before the Governor and I believe [we will be] in such shape to fight in the Federal Court as well [and] possibly prevent Hill's removal and in any event, can put up such a fight, the publicity from which will result in good for Hill and the ideas of your Association."[49] "We are going to have a very hard fight before the Governor and a much harder one in the Federal Court," Fisher nonetheless warned John Shillady. "We are doing everything in our power from this end of the line and so far have been successful in holding Hill in Kansas, but we must have evidence under oath or we will fail."[50]

Since U. S. Bratton was the NAACP's best source of information on the events in Phillips County, the Association asked him to try to see Governor Allen in Topeka and tell him his story. Bratton agreed to do so, although he told Shillady he well knew "what this will do as to bringing down upon my head the condemnation of the southern thieves but I can not afford to remain silent when such an outrage is being permitted."[51] In mid-February, Bratton arrived in Topeka; Hugh Fisher kept his presence secret while a meeting was arranged with the governor. Bratton and he, Fisher reported to the NAACP, had "quite a long confidential conference with Governor Allen and his executive clerk." Allen was going on by train to Kansas City after the conference, so "I put Mr. Bratton on the same train that Governor Allen took, going to Kansas City, and the Governor said he would talk with him further on the train. I also asked Mr. Bratton to see Federal Judge Pollock in Kansas City and tell him his story. I am satisfied from the conference with the Governor that he will not release Hill, provided we can satisfy him that Hill did not advise the colored men to arm."[52] Bratton told the NAACP that he had the impression that Governor Allen was opposed to extradition.[53] "I want again to say that the officers and executives of this Association are delighted with the energy with which you are handling this case," John Shillady wrote Hugh Fisher. "No better work has ever been done for us. You certainly miss no points in following up this matter."[54]

James Weldon Johnson, the NAACP secretary, also saw the governor in mid-February; this interview was an additional source of encouragement to the NAACP. "I found the Governor very sympathetic and much interested in the case," Johnson reported. "He stated to me that he [was] clear on the matter of peonage conditions in Arkansas, and that he was also fully informed about the riot and its results and the manner in which the first trial was conducted." The only points Governor Allen wished to have cleared up, Johnson said, "were the personal history of Hill and the exact nature and purpose of the organization which he formed." At the initial hearing on Hill's extradition, Attorney General Arbuckle had read from purported Progressive Farmers Union literature, Allen told Johnson, and the passages he read seemed to call "on the blacks to arm themselves and rise up against the whites." Johnson added, "I told the Governor I did not believe such to be the purpose of the [Progressive Farmers Union], and I did not believe that any such passages formed a part of their literature. However, he wants more information on this point."[55] Fisher agreed with Johnson's assessment of the governor's position, reporting to Shillady "if we can present evidence to show that Hill's organization and work was for [a] legitimate purpose . . . Governor Allen will not hesitate to refuse to deliver him."[56]

Governor Brough, hearing reports that Governor Allen had not ordered extradition because he believed Arkansas was interfering with the right of blacks to organize unions, labeled the reports "absolutely incorrect"; they were "unfounded and bristle with prejudice."

Phillips County authorities were very careful in their prosecution of those implicated in the riot and, as a matter of fact, more than 200 of these negroes were released. . . . Negro lodges and organizations of every conceivable character exist in this state and are not interfered with by the authorities. The authorities of Arkansas, both local and state, will take steps at any time to suppress any organizations arming its members to take possession of land belonging to bona fide citizens, who are guilty of sending out incendiary propaganda, or plan murder of both whites and blacks who have the courage to combat this very dangerous type of Bolshevism. . . . Arkansas' attitude toward [the defendants] will be absolutely fair and impartial. If Hill is returned (and I do not see how Governor Allen can refuse to honor the requisition) he will be given an absolutely fair trial and will be assured competent counsel and change of venue, if necessary. All we are interested in is to have light thrown on the real motive and active participants in the uprising that threatened the lives and property of thousands of our citizens.[57]

The extradition hearing was not resumed until March 22, 1920, almost two months after the initial session. On the eve of March 22, a mass meeting of Topeka blacks adopted resolutions opposing Hill's extradition to be presented to Governor Allen. The resumed proceedings were held in the courtroom of the Kansas Court of Industrial Relations packed by Topeka blacks, according to press reports, and "standing room was at a premium." "Excepting Gov. Henry J. Allen, four state and federal officers and Hugh Fisher there were no white persons in the room. Outside, looking through the windows leading from the hallway into the courtroom was a sea of white faces, state house officials witnessing the strange sight."[58]

Attorney General Arbuckle again represented the State of Arkansas. He brought as witnesses Phillips County sheriff Kitchens, deputy sheriff Pratt, and a special railroad detective. He presented the confessions and evidence from the trials of the convicted blacks, seeking to demonstrate both that the Progressive Farmers Union and Hill were responsible for the trouble and that the trials had been fair.[59] A Topeka newspaper reported that Arbuckle "called negroes 'niggahs' when he referred to them. There was an audible murmur of anger heard when the lawyer from the south called the members of the black race by the name they resent."[60]

Robert Hill was represented by Hugh Fisher and the black

Topeka lawyers Elisha Scott, James Guy, and A. M. Thomas. They argued that Hill could not possibly receive a fair trial in Arkansas and backed up their argument with affidavits and depositions. Fisher reported later that Arbuckle became "so stirred up that he helped us make our own case on the point of feeling. Our tilts were not rough, but each time it seemed to exasperate him and he made a considerable number of mistakes and labored under excitement." Arbuckle "became so aroused over Mr. Guy's argument," Fisher said, "that he wasted half of his time on frivolous prejudices. On the [whole], I think he came off a bad second best in the scrap with the lawyers on the other side."[61]

Hill testified that the Phillips County trouble was caused by white resistance to the attempts of blacks to get statements of accounts on their cotton crops.[62] He testified that "on the morning after the killing at Elaine he was eight miles from the scene, ignorant of what had happened, with O. S. Bratton . . . helping him to sign up about 30 contracts with negroes to start legal proceedings to get an accounting on their cotton." He learned about the shootings only after "a white man informed him he was being sought. . . . A white family assisted him to escape [from Arkansas] and gave him money."[63] Attorney General Arbuckle did not cross-examine Hill. In his summation, he declared that "the situation is perfectly plain; there is plenty of evidence to show that crimes have been committed [and that] the defendant Hill has been indicted regularly."[64]

The extradition hearing had begun at two o'clock in the afternoon of March 22 and it continued into the early morning hours of the following day. In the afternoon of March 23, Governor Allen announced that he would not return Hill to Arkansas.[65] The NAACP, elated, wrote the governor that it desired "to express to you its deep appreciation of the decision rendered by you in denying extradition to Arkansas of Robert L. Hill and the care you have taken to see that the rights of this Negro were properly safeguarded, in so far as your responsibility for passing upon extradition proceedings was concerned. We are certain that your decision will meet with the approval of all fair-minded citizens, and that it is beyond question that the previous trials of Negroes accused of similar offenses to that of Hill proved that Hill could by no means secure a fair trial under present conditions in the State of Arkansas."[66]

"The colored people of Topeka are exceedingly pleased over

the out-come of the Hill matter as we are ourselves," Fisher wrote to the NAACP. "I think the Attorney General of Arkansas has a little more respect for the attitude of Northern white lawyers in the trial of a case of this sort, after his experience here."[67] He told the *Topeka State Journal* it was the "first time in my career as an attorney in which I was involved in a murder case that I didn't go to the scene of the crime. Frankly, I was afraid to go because of the riot spirit which I learned through correspondence exists down there [in Phillips County]. People would write to us and give us information that would help Hill and insist that their names be kept secret for fear of trouble."[68]

The reaction in Arkansas was as expected. Governor Brough "felt outrage" at Governor Allen's action; in passing on an extradition case, he said, "a governor is not called on to decide the guilt or innocence of the man indicted, but merely to decide whether he had been legally indicted. If Governor Allen attempted to decide Hill's innocence or guilt, he could not have found him innocent, in view of the absolute proof which was presented by Attorney General John D. Arbuckle at the hearing."[69] Brough charged that Governor Allen's action had been politically motivated: "The action of Arkansas throughout in dealing with participants in the Elaine insurrection, which cost scores of lives and jeopardized thousands of dollars' worth of property," he said, "is in striking contrast to the unwarranted refusal of Governor Allen of Kansas to honor a requisition for the return of Robert L. Hill, universally recognized as having been one of the leading spirits in the whole damnable conspiracy to murder white citizens and take possession of their property. Politics is not so apparent in Arkansas as in Kansas, in dealing with the race question, and our executive and judicial authorities are able to give clear, cogent reasons for their actions, without being biased because of political advantage."[70]

Brough again attacked the northern press and "other radical negro-phile publications" for slandering Arkansas, and he particularly disputed charges that some of the members of the Helena Committee of Seven were direct beneficiaries of the peonage system in eastern Arkansas. "The seven gentlemen whom I designated, so far from encouraging any oppression of the negroes, took very determined and resolute steps to prevent lynching . . . ," Brough asserted. "The attitude of outstanding negro leaders like Bishop Conner, President Booker, Doctor Cox and others, reflects the sentiment among the best negroes in the South and they deserve a debt of gratitude at the hands of all right thinking people. The South has always been the negroes' best friend and despite unreasonable and unintelligent criticism our people will continue to give the law-abiding, peaceable negro an absolutely square deal," Brough concluded. "The state of Arkansas is in a much more fortunate position today in the maintenance of her firm attitude that the guilty shall be punished by orderly, legal process, than is the state of Kansas, where political prejudice, through action of her governor, has set aside the comity between states, the majesty of the law and trampled justice under foot."[71]

An *Arkansas Gazette* editorial protested that twelve blacks had been sentenced to death and many others imprisoned yet Robert Hill, the alleged mastermind of the riot, remained free. Right and justice, the *Gazette* declared, demanded that Hill "be delivered to the Arkansas authorities to be tried for the grave offenses for which he has been indicted. Governor Allen has arbitrarily thwarted the courts of this state through perversion of the power reposed in his hands."[72]

Attorney General Arbuckle defended his handling of the extradition proceedings and denounced Allen's refusal to extradite Hill as a violation of the law of comity between states and of the governor's clear moral duty. The transcripts of the trials of the convicted blacks demonstrated that Hill had advised the blacks to arm themselves. Affidavits of newspaper reporters and U.S. army officers had supported his contention that many of the blacks taken into custody after the riot had voluntarily admitted their participation in an armed insurrection. Counsel for Hill, Arbuckle pointed out, had presented versions of the riot published by the northern black press and "read the affidavits of the men now under sentence of death, in which they stated that former statements made by them connecting Hill with the affair were made under duress and were false." Hill and his wife also testified, Arbuckle charged, in a prejudicial atmosphere, amid "loud groans and expressions of horror [that] came from the other negroes in the room."[73] Governor Allen had succumbed to political pressure, Arbuckle concluded, claiming

Kansas is Democratic except for the negro vote. On the morning of the hearing many prominent negroes from various cities and towns of Kansas came to the hearing, and telegrams were received from others. . . .

The influence of the negro political leaders, together with that of some of the most prominent white politicians, was more pressure, apparently, than Governor Allen could stand. His backbone gave way, and he refused to honor the requisition in the face of a proper showing of the demands of the law of what I believe he really felt should be done when acting free from political pressure. . . .

The testimony against Hill is not as strong, so far as developed, as might be, but warranted the return of the indictment and the return of Hill for trial. [Governor Allen's action] will not only have a tendency to excite improper feelings between the whites and the negroes, a thing which is least desired by both whites and leading colored citizens of the South as well, but it will have a strong tendency to mar the splendid relations between the states of Kansas and Arkansas, two neighbors, and may result in serious detriment in the enforcement of the law in both states.[74]

Shillady wrote to Fisher that "Arbuckle alleged that politics outweighed justice in Governor Allen's decision. He tries to magnify what he did and to minimize all the testimony that you were able to present. Our admiration for the ability with which this case has been conducted by you and your associates is heightened by the development of events."[75] "If Mr. Arbuckle heard the comments here as to his ability to handle his side of the case," Fisher replied to Shillady, "he would consider it necessary to get into the newspaper to save his reputation."[76]

The angry reactions of Attorney General Arbuckle, Governor Brough, and the *Arkansas Gazette* nevertheless paled in comparison to the vitriolic denunciations in Allen's mail from private Arkansas citizens. An apparently typical example of Allen's mail from Arkansas was a postcard sent from Helena and addressed to "The Kansas Nigger Lover." "You Kansas Nigger Lover," the card said, "it is too bad you were not at Elaine on October 1st 1919 and had your nasty 'white liver' shot out by some of your beloved brotheren." Governor Allen wrote privately that the "flood of anonymous and filthy letters which come, added to the intemperate statements of people who sign their names and the unreliable interview given out by the attorney general upon his return to Arkansas, all convince me that my judgment was correct in the presumption that the atmosphere there is so inflamed with passion as the natural result of the riot that the Hill case would not have received the proper consideration in an atmosphere of judicial calmness which should surround every man on trial for his life."[77]

The vice-president of the United States, Thomas R. Marshall, addressed the convention of the Good Roads Association at Hot Springs in mid-April. Noting that Governor Brough had been elected president of the Good Roads Association, Marshall remarked that good roads "are needed, for in the future if the governor of Arkansas wants a prisoner and they won't give him up, Governor Brough can get into an automobile and go and get him, and if I were governor of Arkansas I would set aside a section of the state as an asylum for the criminals of Kansas." The three thousand delegates "arose and cheered him for several minutes."[78] In response to the vice-president's remarks, Fisher urged the NAACP to enlist the support of leading Republicans. "You doubtless saw the statement in the press that Vice President Marshall made, to the effect that the Governor of Arkansas should create a district in his State as an asylum for criminals of Kansas to retaliate [against] Governor Allen's action," Fisher wrote John Shillady. "If Democratic politicians are taking a hand in this fight, it is time Republicans were doing likewise."[79]

Authorities in Arkansas were gleeful when Governor Allen was embarrassed by the lynching of a black man from a telephone pole at Mulberry, Kansas, in late April. The victim of the lynching had been charged with an attack on a young white girl. "It would seem that the record of the officers and people of Phillips County in preventing mob violence is much more credible than that of the people of some portions of Kansas," Governor Brough commented. "I should not be surprised to learn that Governor Allen now regrets that he did not allow the orderly process of the law to take its course [in the Hill case]." In a telegram to Governor Allen following the Kansas lynching, Brough demanded that Hill be extradited. "Phillips County has never had a lynching in its history," Brough's telegram said, "and it seems to me in all fairness that you could afford to honor my requisition for the return of Robert L. Hill to a county where a fair trial is absolutely guaranteed and where there is no danger of lynching."[80]

Governor Allen broke his silence on the Hill case in responding to Brough's telegram. "I did not refuse the extradition of Hill through any fear that he might be lynched, but through fear of that equally unfortunate thing, that he might be tried by racial passion and bitterness," Allen informed Brough. "The immoderate messages I have received from Arkansas before the hearing and the tirades since the hearing, convince me that the temper of that community made it impossible for anyone to guarantee a fair trial." "I deeply regret," Allen added, "that you should have misinterpreted my action to reflect any discourtesy to yourself or to your state."[81] The *Arkansas Gazette* deplored the fact that private citizens had sent abusive messages to Allen. "The impression prevailed in Arkansas that Allen's action was based entirely on his desire to please the Republicans and the negro vote," the *Gazette* said. "The message senders have given Allen a real defense."[82]

Both counsel for Hill and the NAACP still faced the possibility that the U.S. district court in Kansas might order Hill's removal to Arkansas to stand trial on the federal charges of impersonating a federal officer and conspiracy to do so. As soon as extradition had been denied, Hill had been promptly arrested by Deputy U.S. Marshal R. Neil Rahn on the basis of the pending federal charges.[83] Indeed, it was only due to the swift actions of Hugh Fisher and his fellow defense counsel that Hill was not removed to Arkansas on the federal charges immediately after Governor Allen refused his extradition. Hill was arraigned before a U.S. Commissioner in Topeka, who set his bond at five thousand dollars and then refused to give Fisher and his colleagues time to arrange for the bond. Fisher and his black colleagues rushed by train to Kansas City where the U.S. district court sat, arriving just in time to prevent the district court judge from signing an order removing Hill to Arkansas as requested by Arbuckle. Fisher and his colleagues persuaded the judge, John C. Pollock, to hold a hearing on April 8 to rule on the validity of the federal indictment.[84]

At that hearing, Judge Pollock rejected Fisher's motion to dismiss the indictment on the ground that it did not sufficiently charge an offense under federal law. He nevertheless allowed defense counsel to present evidence that Hill could not receive a fair trial in Arkansas and therefore should not be removed to stand trial there on the federal charges. Hill denied that he and V. E. Powell, in custody in Arkansas on the same charges, had conspired to impersonate a federal officer. He said he had a degree as a detective, awarded by a correspondence school in St. Louis. Hill's wife testified that after the Phillips County riot, white men had come to the Hill home in Winchester and threatened to kill her husband. Hugh Fisher himself testified that he would be afraid to defend Hill in Arkansas because of possible lynch mobs, and Elisha Scott, one of Hill's black attorneys, testified that Attorney General Arbuckle had told him, in regard to U. S. Bratton's representation of blacks in Arkansas, that state authorities "won't allow any white man to disturb our good working niggers."[85]

Judge Pollock decided to issue a "conditional" order requiring Hill to be returned to Arkansas to face the federal charges. Hill was to be removed to the jurisdiction of the U.S. District Court for the Eastern District of Arkansas for trial on the federal charges, but if he were acquitted, Pollock ruled, "Hill shall not be turned over to any state authority, but shall be returned to Kansas for asylum."[86] Fisher told the NAACP that this "in one sense, [was] a very great victory, for if they can acquit Hill on the Federal charge [in Arkansas], he must be returned to Kansas by the Federal authorities. This is also a vindication of Governor Allen's judgment on the State charge. I only hope that the conditional order will so incense the Governor of Arkansas, and those interested, that they will turn it down, in which event, Judge Pollock will not hesitate to hold [Hill] here."[87] Still, Fisher believed the judge plainly wrong in his refusal to dismiss the indictment altogether. He recomended to the NAACP that counsel be retained to appeal Judge Pollock's decision to the U.S. Court of Appeals. Judge Pollock strenuously objected to the idea of an appeal, threatening to order Hill's return to Arkansas without conditions if such an appeal were undertaken. "Judge Pollock gave us to understand that if we appealed the case to the Circuit Court [of Appeals], that he might conclude to give a general order of removal," Fisher informed the NAACP. "In that event, Hill would go down for trial on the Federal charge and if acquitted, they could take him on the State charge. Judge Pollock feels that he can fully protect Hill and thinks he should stand trial on the Federal charge and agreed he would order his return [to Kansas] even in the event he was convicted on the Federal charge" on the condition that no appeal be undertaken. Pollock said Fisher could draft the removal order requiring Hill's return from Arkansas even if he were convicted of the federal charges, "and if Federal executive authorities would not agree to it, he would not return him at all."[88]

"We were in the position of possibly waiving Hill's opportunity to avoid facing the State charge upon which we have no doubt [he would be convicted] through testimony they would be able to procure in their desire to get Hill," Fisher continued. Alternatively, they could agree to Judge Pollock's order and forego an appeal. "I regret very much indeed that we cannot go into the Circuit Court [of Appeals] as I am satisfied Judge Pollock is wrong on his duty to rule on the indictment."[89] The NAACP reassured Fisher that it was "more than satisfied with your handling of the Hill case."[90]

Judge Pollock's order authorizing Hill's return to Arkansas for trial on the condition that, even if he were convicted, he must be returned to Kansas was challenged by U.S. Attorney June P. Wooten of Little Rock. He referred the matter to the attorney general of the United States, A. Mitchell Palmer, who ruled, in turn, that Pollock lacked the power to issue such a conditional order.[91] Hugh Fisher urged John Shillady and the NAACP to "begin to use some pressure at Washington. If they intend to make this a political issue, I suggest that you arrange to have [Kansas U.S.] Senators Capper and Curtis confer with [Republican party national chairman] Mr. Will Hays and others and bring the necessary political influence to off-set that of the Southern Democrats."[92]

Fisher's strategy shifted to contesting the indictment of V. E. Powell. Scipio Jones was defending Powell, who was in custody in Arkansas, against the federal charges and Fisher sent Jones a demurrer to the indictment on the charge of conspiracy, urging Jones to file the demurrer in the U.S. District Court for the Eastern District of Arkansas. His strategy was to obtain either an acquittal of Powell or a dismissal of the charges, thus making it extremely difficult for the federal authorities in Arkansas to continue to press the same charges against Hill.

In late April presiding judge Jacob Trieber sustained the demurrer filed by Scipio Jones on behalf of Powell. Fisher was confident that Judge Pollock in Kansas City would dismiss the count against Hill. How could there be a conspiracy if the charge had been dismissed against Powell? He told the NAACP he had "another card to play. I am urging [Scipio] Jones to have Powell tried on the second count of the indictment which is the impersonation of the Federal officer. If Powell is cleared on that, it will further complicate the Government in Hill's case and in the end, will result in Hill's freedom."[93] Scipio Jones followed Fisher's advice, and Powell was tried in the U.S. district court in Arkansas for impersonating a federal officer. Judge Trieber directed the jury to return a verdict of acquittal. The government, he said, had failed to prove its case.[94]

Robert Hill, increasingly distressed by his months of imprisonment in Kansas, in mid-June wrote to Arkansas attorney general Arbuckle to express the hope that Arkansas authorities would allow him to be released. He was "sick and tired of staying in jail," Hill told Arbuckle and pointed out that "if you will stop and think a minute you will realize that we must all die some day and must all go before the same God."[95] In the mistaken belief that Governor Allen of Kansas possessed authority to effect his release on the federal charges, Hill also appealed to him. He was being persecuted only because he had attempted to help the Phillips County blacks to obtain fair settlements with the white plantation owners, Hill told Allen, and it seemed "like it [is] almost imposible for me to gain my liberty after proving to the public my innocent. Now even if I be convicted to penitentiary it would simply prove to me and thousand of my race, a race that has been handicaped through out the south over three hundred years that the law is not the thing for us to call on." "Now my dear sir," Hill appealed to Governor Allen, "will you act quickly for my release. . . . Well do I know that this great country as a hole near are controlled by your people at least your race of people and we has no one else to call upon that can do us eny good but you people especily in a dreadful hour as now confronts me and since I am in the bounds of your grace I beg your help."[96]

When Powell was acquitted in mid-June, Fisher was convinced that he could secure Hill's release on bail, since it was exceedingly unlikely that the government could successfully prosecute Hill on the same charge.[97] Hill was released on a bond of two thousand dollars in mid-July, pending a further hearing before Judge Pollock on October 11. Fisher arranged for Hill to go into hiding. "No one knows where he is," Fisher assured the NAACP, "except a few who can be trusted."[98]

Hill's release on bond in July 1920 effectively ended the legal battle to prevent his return to Arkansas, since the final stage of the fight consisted of political negotiations in Washington. In May U.S. Attorney General Palmer, approached on behalf of the NAACP by Philip G. Peabody, a wealthy member of the Association from Boston,[99] told Peabody that if he could prove his assertion that U. S. Bratton had been forced to leave Arkansas because of threats on his life, he would order the charges against Hill to be dismissed.[100] U. S. Bratton confirmed by telegram that there had been open "threats that if I dared go into certain portions of [the] state to represent clients [that I] would be killed." Rather than "take life in my hands and be murdered or quit practicing law and for protection of my family necessary to leave state."[101]

Hugh Fisher, A. M. Thomas, and James Guy also dictated affidavits stating that the evidence at the Hill extradition hearing had revealed that Bratton's son, O. S. Bratton, had been almost lynched in Helena and his father had been forced to leave Little Rock.[102] Armed with these affidavits and Bratton's statement, Walter White laid out the case before Assistant Attorney General William C. Herron in the Department of Justice. White said that Arkansas had not presented a convincing case for extradition on the charges of murder and nightriding; the federal charges filed against Hill in Arkansas constituted a mere subterfuge by which Arkansas hoped to obtain custody. If U. S. Bratton, a white man, had been driven from Arkansas by threats of violence, Hill, as a black man, was certain to receive an even more violent reception if he were returned to the state.[103]

White reported to the NAACP that Herron appeared to be "a fair-minded man." He conceded that the government's case against Hill was very flimsy and wired the federal authorities in Topeka to hold up all action in the federal courts pending an investigation. He ordered the U.S. Attorney in Little Rock to forward to Washington all the evidence he possessed about Hill's alleged impersonation of a federal officer. Unless the evidence "was of the very strongest character," Herron informed White, the federal charges against Hill would be dismissed, particularly in light of the threats against Bratton. "I believe," White reported to the NAACP, "that will be the disposition of the case."[104]

White's prediction proved accurate. In early October U.S. Attorney Wooten asked Federal District Judge Trieber in Arkansas to dismiss the charges against Hill.[105] And when Hill appeared before Federal District Judge Pollock on October 11 in Kansas City, the U.S. Attorney stated that on orders from Attorney General Palmer he was requesting Hill's release from custody. Judge Pollock did order Hill's release, an action, Hugh Fisher told the

NAACP, that "closes the incident, I presume, unless Hill should be so foolish to leave the jurisdiction of Kansas. I am sure they can't get any other evidence in Arkansas that will change our Governor's attitude and I suppose they have given it up in Arkansas. The fact that Governor Allen gave us sufficient time to prepare the case before the presentation to him enabled us to make the showing that we did in the Federal court. . . ."[106]

Except for reimbursement of his incidental expenses, Fisher had won Hill's freedom for the NAACP without charging any fee, although he did advise the NAACP that, in connection with his campaign for the state senate, "I may call upon you . . . to get in touch with the colored citizens of Topeka. At present I know that this is not necessary as the colored people are very loyal and appreciative of what I have done."[107] "I hope you will be elected State Senator," Shillady replied, "and if you put up as good a fight for everything else as you have for Hill you are going to be a corker."[108]

James H. Guy, one of the black Topeka lawyers who had aided Fisher's defense of Hill, summed up the legal battle: "this has been a hard and tedious fight for a man's freedom, [but] the outcome has been doubly worth the effort. The disclosure of conditions in the state of Arkansas as they exist between the whites and blacks in the cotton districts, shows nothing less than down right peonage, pure and simple, and should cause every American to rise in stout opposition to such a system."[109]

The failure of Arkansas authorities to obtain custody of Hill, embittered the white leadership of Arkansas, especially that of Phillips County. The chief spokesman for the Helena Committee of Seven, E. M. Allen, pointed out in correspondence with Governor Allen that many of the large property owners in Phillips County were of northern origin. "The Northern born people here feel your insults very deeply," E. M. Allen told the governor, "we are the ones you are reflecting upon, not the Southerners, and we feel that you should be put into possession of the real facts, regardless of the humiliating position we are in."[110] Hill had visited Phillips County on numerous occasions during the summer of 1919 to organize the Progressive Farmers Union, Allen informed the governor, and he had urged the blacks to arm themselves for the day of reckoning. Hill "was pointed out to me at Elaine the morning after one of his meetings by a negro farmer who said: 'Captain there's a little nigger who is talking a lot of foolishness to the folks around here and if somebody don't stop him he is going to bring on a lot of trouble.'" Although Hill had been at Ratio with O. S. Bratton when the shooting at Hoop Spur occurred, Allen said, after Bratton's arrest Hill had fled to his mother's house at Ratio and made his way through the woods to Ed Hicks's house north of Elaine. Hearing that white men had been killed, Hill had replied, so Allen said, "'that's the stuff, that's the way to do it.'" "Hill had the ability of rousing the spark of savagery lying dormant in every negro's heart," Allen continued. "Education cannot eliminate it, and civilization thus far has failed to do it." Even Massachusetts-born and Harvard-educated W. E. B. Du Bois, said Allen, revealed this spark of savagery by "consistently advocat[ing] riot, murder and bloodshed in his paper 'The Crisis'."[111]

In his correspondence with Governor Allen, E. M. Allen vigorously denied that blacks in Phillips County were being exploited through peonage. The Helena Business Men's League, he assured the governor, "would take immediate action against any landlord, white or black, who attempted to hold a tenant or sharecropper for debt." "The only thing the white people demand here is white control, and while I am Northern born I realize the absolute necessity for that," Allen noted. "If a negro is self-respecting, industrious and law abiding he will be given every opportunity to succeed in this County." The leaders of Phillips County, Allen concluded, "are splendid citizens, Governor, and are always working for the progress, improvement and the good name of our section of the State. They are by no means perfect, but the average is high."[112] Allen assured the Kansas governor that Hill would receive a fair trial in Arkansas.

As a free man once again, Hill expressed his gratitude to the NAACP and volunteered his services to the Association. He had found a job in a packing plant in Topeka but had been injured in an accident. "Now since you are the saving of my life I have decided to give the bal[ance] of my life to the association soon as I am able," he said. "I really believe that I can do good now if you can provide away for me to get a lifing out of what I does. I will take the work up now I believe I owe this tribute to this organization. . . . I am the Hill that you kept from going back to Arkansas."[113] James Weldon Johnson suggested that Hill could help the NAACP best by joining the Topeka branch of the Association.[114]

In its successful defense in Kansas, the NAACP had had several crucial advantages. There existed in Topeka not only an active branch of the NAACP but also a politically involved black community upon which the Association could rely; the Association also had important influence with both senators from Kansas, Senator Capper being a member of the NAACP's board of directors. Through him, the Association had gained Hugh Fisher's services in directing the legal battle with dedication and skill. The NAACP was able also to maximize the advantage of its access to national political leaders, especially in the Department of Justice, in that way being able to obtain the dismissal of the federal charges against Hill.

Many of the resources the Association had possessed in its defense of Hill in Kansas were not available to it in Arkansas. There the NAACP's relations with the Arkansas black community were strained at best, and its successful defense of Hill had made the Association, if possible, even more unpopular than before with the white political leadership that substantially controlled the fate of the Phillips County blacks. The organization also encountered serious problems in its relations with the Arkansas attorneys it had retained to represent the convicted blacks. The NAACP still faced a difficult and at times complex legal battle over the fate of these seventy-nine men, a battle that would not end for another five years.

5 Victory and Defeat: The Phillips County Cases in the State Courts

On December 18, 1919, Scipio Jones and Colonel G. W. Murphy filed motions for new trials on behalf of the twelve black men convicted and sentenced to death in the trials that had followed the Phillips County riot. In the motions filed in the Circuit Court of Phillips County in Helena, Jones and Murphy stated that the twelve condemned blacks were entitled to new trials because adverse publicity and racial hostility in the community, as well as the atmosphere surrounding the original trials, had precluded the possibility of fair trials. The condemned blacks had been denied, at their original trials, adequate time to consult with their attorneys and adequate notice of the charges against them; consequently "they were convicted and sentenced to death without due process of law."[1] Further, equal protection of the laws had been denied, because of the systematic exclusion of blacks in the county from service on both grand juries and petit (trial) juries. No black "has been appointed a jury commissioner, or selected to serve as a juror, either grand or petit, for more than thirty years," the motion for new trials said, although the black population of Phillips County exceeded the white population by "at least five to one." The result of this discrimination, Jones and Murphy argued, was "that the defendants have thus been by said discriminatory practices and by said trial, deprived of their rights under the Constitution of the United States, and especially the 14th Amendment thereto,

84

and were, in and by said trial and proceedings, and still are, denied the equal protection of the law."[2]

Jones and Murphy presented to the circuit court affidavits testifying that the Helena Committee of Seven had employed torture to secure confessions and testimony against the defendants in the original trials. O. S. Bratton was apparently the first source of information about the use of torture and his information was confirmed later by the condemned blacks after their transfer to the penitentiary in Little Rock.[3] In early December 1919, U. S. Bratton reported to the NAACP that the attorneys defending the condemned blacks were "in a position to prove beyond any question that the prisoners were placed in chairs wherein electricity was applied and they were shocked severely. In addition . . . the prisoners were further mistreated by applying some preparation, possibly harts horn,[4] to their nose, almost strangling them to death. This process was continued along with brutal whipping until they talked to the liking of the brutes that had them in charge."[5] "I think these motions [for new trials] will be revelations to the world in that they will show the true [dimensions] of the outrages that have been perpetrated on these people."[6]

Colonel Murphy and Scipio Jones filed affidavits in which Alf Banks, Jr., and Will Wordlow, two of those under sentence of death, detailed the treatment they had received before their trials in Helena. "I was frequently whipped with great severity, and was also put into an electric chair and shocked, and strangling drugs would be put to my nose to make me tell things against others, that they had killed or shot at some white people and to force me to testify against them," Alf Banks said in his affidavit. "I had not seen anything of the kind, and so told them, at first; but they kept on, and tortured me so that I finally told them falsely that what they wanted me to say was true and that I would testify to it." He had been blindfolded when being tortured, Banks said, and at one point his interrogators had pretended to be about to hang him to frighten him into cooperating. He was forced to testify falsely at the trials of the other blacks, Banks said, and as "they were taking me to the court room they told me if I changed my testimony or did not testify as I had said, when they took me back, they would skin me alive." They "used negroes they had in or about the jail to do most of the whipping, but some white men would be present,"

Banks concluded. "I would never have testified falsely as I did if I had not been made to do it."[7]

Will Wordlow related a similar story of whippings and other forms of torture in his affidavit. "I do not know of any negro who killed or advised or encouraged the killing" of any whites during the riot, Wordlow said, "and [I] would not have voluntarily testified that I did. As I was taken to the court room, I was given to understand that if I did not testify as they had directed, I would be killed."[8]

Colonel Murphy and Scipio Jones argued the motions for new trials before Judge J. M. Jackson of the Phillips County Circuit Court, but on December 20, Judge Jackson denied the motions. He allowed sixty days for Jones and Murphy to appeal his decision to the Arkansas Supreme Court.[9] Governor Brough announced on December 22 that he would stay the executions of the condemned blacks to allow time for such an appeal, and the appeals in the cases were docketed in the supreme court on January 9, 1920.[10]

There were two sets of cases, each involving six of the condemned blacks, appealed to the Arkansas Supreme Court. The first set (*Ed Ware et al.*) concerned the convictions of Ed Ware; Will Wordlow; Albert Giles; Joe Fox; Alf Banks Jr.; and John Martin, while the second set of cases (*Frank Moore et al.*) involved the convictions of Frank Moore; the brothers Frank and Ed Hicks; J. E. Knox; Ed Coleman; and Paul Hall. Both sets of cases were argued before the Arkansas Supreme Court on March 22, 1920, with each side allowed an hour and a half to present its case. The State of Arkansas was represented by Robert C. Knox; all of the Phillips County blacks, by Colonel Murphy.[11]

Colonel Murphy raised a new issue in his argument. Arkansas law, he said, required that a jury "shall, in all cases of murder, on conviction of the accused, find by their verdict whether he be guilty of murder in the first or second degree." Despite this statutory requirement, Murphy argued, the juries in the *Ed Ware* cases had not specified in their verdicts what degree of murder they were finding the defendants guilty of. And in Frank Hicks's case, Murphy noted, the jury had made a similar error, but Judge J. M. Jackson had corrected it by writing into the jury's verdict words to the effect that they had found Hicks guilty of murder in the first degree. Both failures by the juries were additional grounds for reversal of the convictions.[12]

The Arkansas Supreme Court announced its decision on March 29, just short of a week after Governor Allen of Kansas had refused to extradite Robert Hill. In the cases of Ware, Banks, Martin, Giles, Fox, and Wordlow, the court said, the questions were essentially the same and, therefore, the cases could be decided together: "The only issue raised by the appeal in each of the above cases is, could the court lawfully proceed to judgment and sentence on the verdict?" The statutes of Arkansas were clear in requiring juries in murder cases to specify the degree of murder of which defendants were being convicted, and the "court has uniformly held that a verdict of conviction in a case of murder, which does not find the degree of murder, is so fatally defective, that no judgment can be entered upon it."[13] This rule of Arkansas law was so firmly established in the jurisprudence of the state that the court had reversed murder convictions on its basis even when counsel for defendants had not even raised the issue on appeal. Yet in the case of Ed Ware and the others, the court said, the juries had returned verdicts saying only that "We, the jury, find the defendants . . . guilty as charged in the indictment," without specifying the degree of murder which formed the basis of the verdicts.

The statute expressly requires the jury to ascertain the degree in all cases of murder. Its terms are imperative. The court has uniformly construed it to be mandatory, and as before stated it has become a fixed part of our criminal jurisprudence. It is the duty of courts to enforce legislative provisions when the Legislature acts within constitutional limits, and a departure by the courts from imperative rules established by the Legislature for the protection of all in order to meet the exigencies of particular cases is an evil not to be thought of, let alone be acted upon.

It is well settled in this State, however, that when a verdict is so defective that no judgment can be entered upon it, a verdict is no bar to a new trial and conviction of the defendant for murder in the first degree upon a remand of the case. It therefore follows that the judgment must be reversed and the cause remanded for a new trial.[14]

The convictions of Ed Ware and the five others were therefore reversed by the supreme court, although all could be subjected to new trials for first-degree murder.

Frank Moore et al. received less favorable treatment at the hands of the supreme court; their convictions were affirmed. The court noted that the first argument for the reversal of the convictions in the cases of Frank Moore and the five others was based on the fact that no blacks served on the grand juries that indicted, nor the trial juries that convicted, all of the defendants, and "that no colored man had served on any jury in Phillips County—where the trials occurred—for many years." This objection, the supreme court held, should have been raised, if it was to be raised, at the outset of the trials; under Arkansas procedure, it could not be raised belatedly in motions for new trials. "This assignment of error," the court held, "is answered by saying that the question was first raised in the motion for a new trial, and it, therefore, comes too late to be now considered."[15]

The court acknowledged that an additional argument for reversal in the cases was that the verdicts were contrary to the law and the evidence and

that the trials occurred under such circumstances as that appellants have been convicted without due process of law. The facts upon which these contentions are chiefly made were not developed at the trial, but are brought into the record by affidavits filed in support of the motions for new trials.". . . It is now insisted that because of the incidents developed at the trial and those recited in the motion for new trials, and the excitement and feeling growing out of them, no fair trial was had, or could have been had, and that the trial did not, therefore, constitute due process of law. It is admitted, however, that eminent counsel was appointed to defend appellants, and no attempt is made to show that a fair and impartial trial was not had, except as an inference from the facts stated above, the insistence being that a fair trial was impossible under the circumstances.[16]

The court rejected the argument that a prejudicial atmosphere and the coercion of testimony by torture, as alleged in the motions for new trials, had contravened due process standards. It was unable, the court said, "to say that this must necessarily have been the case. The trials were according to law, the jury was correctly charged as to the law of the case, and the testimony is legally sufficient to support the verdicts returned. We cannot, therefore, in the face of this affirmative showing, assume that the trial was an empty ceremony, conducted for the purpose only of appearing to comply with the requirements of the law, when they were not in fact being complied with."[17]

The court rejected the argument that even if Frank Hicks had allegedly fired the shots that killed Clinton Lee, the evidence was insufficient to convict Frank Moore, Ed Hicks, J. E. Knox, Ed Coleman, and Paul Hall with the shooting of Lee. The court held that "the testimony of the numerous witnesses who were examined and cross-examined at the trial supports the finding that these appellants were present when Frank Hicks killed Clinton Lee, and that they aided, abetted and assisted him in doing so, and if this is true they are as guilty as Hicks himself." "According to these witnesses," the court continued, "these appellants were all armed, and before leaving the place from which they started the purpose of going to Elaine to fight the white men found there was announced, and we think this testimony warranted the jury in finding that Hicks' act in firing the fatal shot was done pursuant to a conspiracy previously formed, which contemplated violence, and the possible killing of white men."[18]

Finally, the court considered whether Judge Jackson's amendment of the verdict of the jury in order to specify that the verdict found Frank Hicks guilty of murder in the first degree, constituted a reversible error. The court pointed out that Judge Jackson had written on the margin of the transcript of the record, explaining his amendment of the jury's verdict. "The interlineation made in this verdict was made before I signed the bill of exceptions," Judge Jackson had written, "and correctly shows the verdict as it was returned by the jury." Such interlineations, the supreme court held, "may be a proper part of the record, and will be so treated by us unless it appears such interlineations were not properly acknowledged." Since, with Judge Jackson's interlineation, the jury's verdict in Frank Hicks's case did specify the degree of murder of which he was convicted, the court upheld that verdict.[19]

"We have given these cases the careful consideration which their importance required," the supreme court concluded, "but our consideration is necessarily limited to those matters which are properly brought before us for review, and as no error has been made to appear in [any of the cases] the judgments must be affirmed. It is so ordered."[20] Frank Moore, Ed and Frank Hicks, J. E. Knox, Ed Coleman, and Paul Hall therefore remained under sentence of death, and with the Arkansas Supreme Court's decision affirming their convictions, the state judicial remedies for challenging their death sentences appeared to have been exhausted.

At the outset of the defense, U. S. Bratton and Colonel Murphy had agreed upon the basic strategy to pursue. Motions for new trials in the Phillips County Circuit Court would be filed, they had agreed, and if the motions were denied, appeals to the Arkansas Supreme Court would be taken. And, assuming the Arkansas Supreme Court affirmed any or all of the convictions, further appeals would be filed in the United States Supreme Court. If the U.S. Supreme Court denied review, Murphy and Bratton further agreed, a last-ditch effort to save the condemned defendants would be made by filing a petition for a writ of habeas corpus in the U.S. district court on the ground that the condemned blacks had been denied due process of law in violation of the Due Process Clause of the Fourteenth Amendment of the Constitution. The filing of a petition for a federal writ of habeas corpus, however, could not occur until all state remedies were exhausted, and at the time, an appeal to the U.S. Supreme Court was considered to be a part of the exhaustion of state remedies requirement.[21]

In the *Moore* cases, where the convictions had been affirmed by the Arkansas Supreme Court, therefore, a petition for a writ of certiorari was filed on May 24, 1920, in the U.S. Supreme Court seeking a review of the cases by that Court. As Colonel Murphy's law partner, E. L. McHaney, explained to the NAACP, although defense counsel "are not very hopeful of any favorable result on this petition in the Supreme Court of the United States, yet we thought it wise, if not absolutely necessary, to take this course with these cases, in order to exhaust all direct remedies which are, or may be, afforded by law, before applying in the District Court of the United States here in Little Rock for writs of habeas corpus." "If we fail to get any relief in the Supreme Court of the United States," McHaney added, "it has been our purpose all along to take this course with these cases."[22] The NAACP agreed to this strategy of appealing to the U.S. Supreme Court. Although "the cost will be five or six times as great," Walter White said, "we would rather for this to be done, for in that way we can bring to light some of the trouble which exists in the South at the present time and which has existed for the past fifty years."[23]

Under the decision of the Arkansas Supreme Court, on the other hand, the *Ed Ware* blacks had to be retried by the state, and the six men whose convictions had been reversed were transferred back to Helena by train on April 2.[24] Scipio Jones appeared on behalf of the defendants in the Phillips County Cir-

cuit Court on April 26 to seek a delay in the retrials, but Judge
Jackson set the trial date for May 3.[25]

The continuing sensitivity of Phillips County officials regarding their handling of the riot was evident when Ben Freeman,
the white editor and publisher of the *Green Forest News*, published an editorial commending Kansas Governor Allen's action
in denying the extradition of Robert Hill. "Governor Allen of
Kansas did right this week in refusing to honor a requisition of
the negro, Robert L. Hill, charged with leadership in the uprising of the negroes at Elaine, Phillips County, last fall in which
several people lost their lives," Freeman wrote. "We know the
conditions in that section pretty well and we know the judge
that tried the other negroes: Therefore, we do not hesitate to
say that we do not believe Hill could get a fair and impartial
trial there. However, in making this comment, we are not passing upon Hill's guilt or innocence."[26]

As the preparations for the retrial of the Ware blacks were
underway, county prosecutor John E. Miller filed a complaint,
charging Freeman with contempt of court because of his editorial comments, and Judge Jackson issued an order commanding
Freeman to appear within five days to answer the contempt
charge.[27] When Freeman failed to appear, Judge Jackson issued
a warrant for his arrest, but it was reported that Freeman had
fled to Kansas.[28]

As the retrial of the Phillips County blacks began, the press
reported that it was "clear that [defense] counsel intended to
fight for every inch of the ground."[29] Colonel Murphy and Scipio
Jones filed a motion to transfer the cases to the U.S. district
court on the ground that there had been no blacks summoned
to serve on either the grand or trial juries and the defendants
could not receive the equal protection of the laws in the state
court. When Judge Jackson denied this motion, Murphy and
Jones petitioned for a change of venue on the ground a fair trial
could not be obtained for the defendants in the county, particularly because of the local publicity given to the Committee of
Seven's report that the riot had resulted from a planned insurrection against the white community.[30]

Apparently because of fear of retaliation, Murphy and Jones
could get only four local blacks to testify in support of the motion for a change of venue and to verify that a fair trial could
not be had in the county. Commenting later, U. S. Bratton de-

clared, "I tell you it is discouraging when those who are disposed to fight the battles of those down trodden people can not
rely on members of their own race. Col. Murphy could not even
get supporting affidavits for a change of venue, notwithstanding
the thousands of the race who had the intelligence to know just
what was necessary to secure a change and all of whom knew
that they would be stating the truth when they swore to the
affidavit. It looks like that God will simply have to take them up
bodily and lift them out of that country, for they do not seem to
have the faculty for helping themselves."[31]

After a hearing lasting an hour and a half, Judge Jackson denied the motion for a change of venue.[32] Playing their final card,
Murphy and Jones filed motions to quash the indictments because no blacks had been selected to serve on the original grand
jury and to quash the panel of potential jurors summoned by
the sheriff for the trial juries, because no blacks had been included. Both the grand and trial juries, Jones and Murphy argued, had been selected by racially discriminatory methods
that violated the Equal Protection Clause of the Fourteenth
Amendment. Judge Jackson denied these motions also, and the
trials finally began.[33]

Colonel Murphy fell gravely ill in the middle of the new trial
and was taken to a Helena hospital in critical condition on May
5. Scipio Jones therefore took on the major burden of the defense alone. For a black attorney, it was an extremely hostile
environment. Jones made a drugstore in the black section of
Helena his headquarters and each evening would select a house
of a black family at random and ask to be put up for the night.
"He slept and left early the next morning. No two nights were
spent in the same house. No one knew where Scipio Jones
put up."[34]

On May 3 John Martin became the first defendant to be retried. He testified that his testimony at the first trial was the
result of torture, but on May 4 he was convicted by the jury of
first-degree murder. William Wordlow, who was tried next, also
testified that he had been tortured, but on May 5, he, too, was
convicted. Albert Giles, Joe Fox, Alf Banks, and Ed Ware were
all convicted of murder during the following week. On May 11
Judge Jackson overruled motions for new trials and sentenced
all six to death in the electric chair.[35] "Tranquility now reigns
where on October 1, 1919, the rising sun found armed forces

confronting each other in the cane and underbrush in the vicinity of Hoop Spur and the smoke of battle ascended toward a cloudless sky," the *Arkansas Gazette* reported at the end of the retrials. "The plantations are alive with busy workers and there are no longer secret meetings of armed negroes at midnight. Peace has come again to Phillips County."[36]

Judge Jackson set July 23, 1920, as the execution date for Ed Ware, John Martin, Albert Giles, Joe Fox, William Wordlow, and Alf Banks, and once again under sentence of death, the men were transferred to the state penitentiary at Little Rock on May 15; Frank Moore, Ed and Frank Hicks, J. E. Knox, Ed Coleman, and Paul Hall, whose cases were on petition for a writ of certiorari in the U.S. Supreme Court, were already there on death row.[37] Ed Ware and the others protested that they had not received fair trials. "We and our attorneys feel that the officials did not deal fairly with us," Ed Ware said on behalf of the group. "There was no direct evidence that I fired a shot or that I even had a gun on me during the trouble," Ware continued. "We believe that they never could convict us if prejudice was left outside. We also think that the Lord will never let us die, for we are innocent." "All we can do," Ware added, "is read the scriptures, pray to the Lord and sing, and time passes on."[38]

Colonel Murphy and Scipio Jones filed notice that they would again appeal the *Ware* cases to the Arkansas Supreme Court, indicating that the primary basis of the appeal would be racial discrimination in the selection of the juries for the retrials in violation of the Equal Protection Clause of the Fourteenth Amendment. Governor Brough told the press that he was extremely doubtful that there was any federal constitutional question raised by the cases. The trials had been conducted throughout, he said, "with absolute justice" and "the state had dealt patiently with the negroes."[39] Still Brough granted a stay of execution to allow time for an appeal to the Arkansas Supreme Court.[40]

As the fight over Robert Hill's extradition was reaching its conclusion in the fall of 1920, the situation of the condemned blacks once again became a focus of attention. On October 11, the same day Hill was ordered released from custody in Kansas, the U.S. Supreme Court denied the petition for a writ of certiorari in the *Moore et al.* cases.[41] Also on that day, Colonel Murphy died in Little Rock at the age of seventy-nine. The leading counsel for the defense had been taken away. "I think," Scipio Jones said, "that he died on the very hour [that the Supreme Court denied review]."[42]

Colonel Murphy was praised in editorials in the Little Rock newspapers. The *Arkansas Gazette* said that he had been "a man of great heart. He was aggressive and fearless, but he was also tender and sympathetic. He enjoyed the love and affection of many friends and his name was everywhere held in the highest respect."[43] The *Arkansas Democrat* declared that with the death of Murphy "the finest figure of the Old South has passed. . . . Always fearless in his life, devoted to the right as he saw it, [nothing more typical] of Colonel Murphy's later years could be mentioned than his fight in behalf of the negro rioters of Elaine. . . . Murphy was still waging the fight for the negroes when death called." Colonel Murphy believed undue haste had been permitted in the handling of the Phillips County cases, and in spite of the strong feelings against the rioters, he fought for their lives with a resourcefulness and a vigor unexcelled during a long life of service."[44]

"We regret very much to have to advise you of the death of Col. Murphy on account of his intimate association with the Helena cases, growing out of the Elaine trouble," Murphy's law firm wrote the NAACP on October 18. "But such is the fact. In his loss, we have not only suffered, but these defendants have lost the aid and counsel of the ablest criminal lawyer this state has ever known. The other members of his firm will proceed with the cases to the best of their ability along the lines he had in mind and had outlined, and will do the very best we can do to carry out his objects and purposes, and also carry out the agreements of the firm with you and the Association."[45]

The death of Colonel Murphy forced the NAACP to choose another lawyer to act as principal defense counsel, but the choice was not easy. Colonel Murphy's law partner, E. L. Mc-Haney, was the logical successor, but McHaney had earlier aroused some hostility at the offices of the NAACP, because of his aggressive requests for money. In the spring of 1920, McHaney, accompanied by Scipio Jones, had gone to New York City to consult with the NAACP on the defense of the Arkansas blacks. Following this meeting, McHaney wrote the NAACP that the Phillips County cases had taken up "practically all of Col. Murphy's time, to the exclusion of nearly all other business." He predicted that the cases would probably take "two to three years before finally being wound up." "Speaking for my firm," McHaney continued, "I will say that I feel that a fee of $25,000.00 will be a very moderate compensation for the service which we will be compelled to render if we go through with all these cases to the end. As a lawyer, you know that when we fix a fee for a client, we should take into consideration a great many things. One of the great things that we ought to take into consideration in this case is the feeling that has been, and will continue to be, engendered against us for our connection with these cases. This feeling is particularly pronounced in these cases on account of their having grown out of racial troubles, in which several well and favorably known white men lost their lives, and would go against any one who sought to protect [the blacks allegedly responsible], even through the agencies and instrumentalities provided by the law."[46] His law firm, McHaney assured the NAACP, had "not taken this matter into consideration here, but do feel that we ought to be reasonably compensated for the time and attention to be given [the Phillips County cases]." He did not believe that the black community in Arkansas could raise a "fund sufficient to pay us and to pay [Scipio] Jones and the cost necessary to be incurred," but rather the "honest, God fearing, Liberty loving white people of the United States ought to come to [the assistance of the Phillips County blacks]." "We hope that you will not feel that we are, in writing you this letter, soliciting employment, or a fee for the promotion of our own selfish interest," McHaney concluded. "We are not. We have been able up to this time to keep the wolf from the door, and keep ourselves reasonably busy in the legitimate practice of the law through professional methods."[47]

McHaney's request for money had apparently irritated Colonel Murphy. "The Col. is a sincere fighter but his partner McHaney has absolutely no interest other than get the money," Bratton wrote John Shillady. "Had it not been for the Col.'s disposition to take such cases as he desires I never would have been able to [have] induced the doing of anything. McHaney was grumbling all along as to the cases and fee. He was scared to death for fear of the local feeling, and besides said the bunch at Helena were his special friends." As for Colonel Murphy, Bratton said, "when he takes a case the money part of it is the smallest consideration."[48]

The NAACP board of directors agreed to pay the firm of Murphy, McHaney & Dunaway "$5,000 in addition to what has al-

ready been paid, to be divided between Messrs. Murphy, Mc-
Haney and Jones, as they saw fit, which sum should include all
expenses incurred." In return for the $5,000, Murphy, McHaney
& Dunaway should agree to appeal the cases to the U. S. Supreme Court. After some negotiations, the law firm agreed to
the $5,000 fee.[49]

When Walter White consulted with Bratton in Detroit after
Murphy's death, Bratton strongly recommended that McHaney
not be allowed to continue in the cases; he advised the NAACP
to retain another law firm.[50] "The sad news of the death of Col.
Geo. W. Murphy of Little Rock, Ark., has just reached me," Bratton had written. "I am at a loss to know what can be done in
the matter of the Helena negroes. I know of no attorney in Arkansas who I think would dare to go into [the] cases and do his
duty as an attorney should."[51]

In late October, White wrote to ask J. H. McConico, the president of the Little Rock branch of the NAACP, for his advice.
"Since the death of Colonel Murphy, we have been in something
of a quandary regarding proceedings in the Arkansas Defense
Cases," White informed McConico. "Mr. Bratton . . . strongly rec-
ommends that we secure other counsel to succeed Colonel Murphy retaining Scipio A. Jones as Attorney of Record. Mr. Bratton
urges this as he does not seem to have much confidence in either
the integrity or ability of Mr. McHaney to press the cases to a
successful conclusion. However, we are definitely obligated to
the firm of Murphy, McHaney & Dunaway and to Scipio A. Jones
to pay a sum of $5,000 to carry the cases up to but not including
the United States Supreme Court. Of course, if we retain additional counsel, it will mean a sum additional to this one."[52]

McConico replied in early November that he was in "accord
with Mr. Bratton as to the 'Sincerity and integrity' of McHaney
and Dunaway." McHaney and Dunaway "are both young and
ambitious and I am sure will engage in no activity that would
impair their popularity with their people socially or otherwise."
McConico suggested other attorneys whom the NAACP might
retain to replace Colonel Murphy.[53] Despite such misgivings, the
NAACP decided to continue with the firm of Murphy, McHaney
& Dunaway. This decision was undoubtedly made because,
given the financial arrangements that the Association had already entered into with the firm, the retention of additional
lawyers would impose a burden upon the Association's limited
resources. But because of its suspicions of the motives and in-

tegrity of McHaney, the Association increasingly relied upon
Scipio Jones as the chief counsel in the Phillips County cases,
the firm of Murphy, McHaney & Dunaway coming to play a secondary role.

The Association was confronted with a grave crisis as a consequence of the U.S. Supreme Court's denial of certiorari in the
Moore cases. Since that decision appeared to have blocked the
final avenue of appeal on behalf of Frank Moore, Ed and Frank
Hicks, J. E. Knox, Ed Coleman, and Paul Hall, it became the
duty of Governor Brough to fix a final date for their execution
or, alternatively, to commute their sentences. Pressure was
brought to bear on the governor, on the one hand, to commute
the sentences and, on the other hand, to let the death penalties
stand.

In the basement of the Episcopal church in Helena on October
19, 1920, a meeting of 380 members of the Richard L. Kitchens
Post of the American Legion adopted a resolution urging Governor Brough not to commute the death sentences of any of the
twelve. Any action of that kind, the resolution said "would do
more harm in the community and breed lawlessness, as well as
disregard for constituted authority, as at the time of this race
riot the members of the [American Legion] Post were called
upon to go to Hoop Spur and Elaine to protect life and property,
and in compliance with this request, there were two American
Legion members killed and one seriously injured, besides other
non-members who also perished, and when the guilty negroes
were apprehended, a solemn promise was given by the leading
citizens of the community, that if these guilty parties were not
lynched, and let the law take its course, that justice would be
done and the majesty of the law upheld."[54]

The legionnaires pointed out that appeals of all of the cases
had been undertaken and "attorneys of their own selection were
permitted to handle their cases," and "we most earnestly protest
against the commutation of any of the sentences of these twelve
negroes convicted of murder in the Elaine riot in October 1919,
their having received a fair trial and [having been] proven
guilty, and the leniency of the court was shown in the balance
of the cases tried, these being the ring leaders and guilty murderers, and that law and order will be vindicated and a solemn
promise kept." The legionnaires appointed a committee, composed of Herbert Thompson; T. H. Faulkner, Jr.; J. B. Lambert,
and L. J. Wilkes, Jr., with authorization to meet with Governor

Brough and "to take such steps as they may deem necessary to carry out the wishes of this resolution and leaving nothing undone to have these sentences carried out."[55]

In a message to the national headquarters of the American Legion, the NAACP protested this action of the Helena American Legion post: "The National Association for the Advancement of Colored People inquires if it is the intention of the American Legion to permit its branches not only to exclude colored veterans of the world war, but to urge publicly the execution of colored men whose cases are before the courts."[56]

Seventy-four members of the Helena Rotary Club, "representing twenty-five of the leading industrial and commercial enterprises of this City," met on November 10 and adopted a resolution expressing support of the American Legion statement. Similar action was taken by sixty members of the Helena Lions Club, "representing sixty of the leading industrial and commercial enterprises of this City."[57] And on November 14 five of the original members of the Committee of Seven in Helena—E. M. Allen, Sebastian Straub, T. W. Keesee, H. D. Moore and E. C. Horner—signed a joint letter to Governor Brough.[58] We "earnestly urge you," they wrote, "to let the law take its course untrammeled by Executive Clemency."

With all the provocation our people refrained from mob violence. The reason they did this was that this Committee gave our citizens their solemn promise that the law would be carried out. This Community can be made a model one so far as resorting to mob violence is concerned, but should the Governor commute any sentence of these Elaine rioters, this would be difficult, if not impossible. We respectfully urge you to support law and order as we supported it. There were 150 Negroes legally guilty of murder in the first degree—actually present and assisting in the wilful and deliberate murder of white citizens—and this Committee assisted in seeing that only leaders were brought to trial. Leniency has already been shown. We think the law itself is on trial. All our citizens are of the opinion that the law should take its course.[59]

Governor Brough apparently went to Phillips County to learn the facts for himself, and at one point he seriously considered commuting the sentences of Ed Coleman, Paul Hall, and J. E. Knox. Brough asked the legionnaires to submit to him their version of the facts on these three convicted men. The legionnaires reported that, in their opinion, J. E. Knox had been vicepresident of the Elaine lodge of the Progressive Farmers Union, had aided in selecting whites to be assassinated and had been among the leaders of the group of blacks that killed Clinton Lee. "We, therefore, feel that Knox conspired deliberately from time to time, both in and out of the lodge meetings, to murder white people," the legionnaires reported to Brough, "and pursuant to his fixed purpose to engage in murder, he assisted in organizing these negroes and stood by and approved the killing of young Lee."[60] Ed Coleman, the legionnaires said, had participated in the selection of the whites to be executed in the uprising and had given his rifle to Frank Hicks, who had proceeded to shoot and kill Clinton Lee. While "the evidence in the court records does not disclose it, it is well known among the negroes that [Coleman] handed his high-powered rifle to Hicks immediately prior to the time that Hicks fired the shot that killed young Lee," the legionnaires reported. Paul Hall, the legionnaires also said, had helped select whites to be killed during the insurrection, and he had "stood by and aided, abetted and encouraged Frank Hicks to shoot and kill young Clinton Lee."[61]

The legionnaires told Brough they wished to "enter our solemn protest against the commutation of the sentences of [any] of these persons." They were convinced that only those blacks who were leaders in the insurrection and who had actually committed murder or conspired to do so had been tried for murder, and indeed there were "probably 25 to 50 other negroes who were technically guilty of the same offense [but who] were not prosecuted with a view of giving them the extreme penalty because of the fact that it was thought that probably they were, to a certain extent, influenced and misled by the leaders who were prosecuted." They felt, the legionnaires told Governor Brough, "that we would be untrue to the memory of the members of our post who lost their lives combating this effort on the part of armed murderers to murder white citizens of our community, not even sparing women and children, if we did not enter our solemn protest against the commutation of sentences of those whom we believe were the ringleaders and the main instigators of these crimes."[62]

Governor Brough met with delegations from Elaine and Helena for several hours on November 15, then released an announcement to the press that he had decided to refuse clemency. All six of the blacks in the *Moore* cases were guilty of first-degree murder; he should not commute their sentences. The people of Phillips County had exercised commendable restraint in dealing with the riot, a restraint caused by "the definite promise to the people of Phillips County [by the Committee of Seven] that the law would be enforced and that there would be no outside influence permitted to interfere with its due and solemn enforcement."[63] Brough acknowledged that "he was not unaware that the facts connected with the Elaine insurrection have been misrepresented by certain sections of the northern press," and he was also aware that his official action in this matter would probably be subjected to similar criticism. This fact, Brough said, should "not deter me from seeing to it that the law is carried out as adjudged by the courts, for it is my belief that the cause of law enforcement and maintenance of law and order can only be served by a strict compliance with the law." The governor had been impressed by the fact that "every business, civic and other organization in the community which refrained from mob violence, has taken a strong stand for carrying out the decree of the court to the letter."[64]

Although the Arkansas black leaders had assured the NAACP that they would be in a favorable position to secure either clemency or pardons for the condemned blacks and that the white members of the Commission on Race Relations would support them in this, it was obvious from Governor Brough's statement that he had yielded to the pressure from Phillips County officials. Scipio Jones's press release in response to the governor's statement pointed out that defense counsel did not propose to "try our cases in the newspapers."

We do not understand why the great pressure should be brought to bear upon the Governor at this particular time regarding the six cases already passed upon by the Supreme Court of Arkansas, nor do we understand why the Governor should issue a statement in connection with them at this particular time, unless it might be possible that it was desired to give notoriety to this matter at this time, with the hope that it might possibly influence the decision of the [Arkansas] Supreme Court in the other six [Ware] cases. [All groups agree] that the death penalty was promised, solemnly and religiously, if the mob would stay its hand. This is not news to us. We had understood from the very beginning that somebody had to be executed because the mob [had] been promised blood, [and] like Shylock of old, it is still insisting on blood.". . . when it becomes known how the evidence was obtained, which formed the basis of the convictions in all these cases we predict a change of sentiment, even in Phillips County.[65]

The Arkansas white press generally supported Governor Brough's statement and ignored Jones's remarks, although the

Arkansas Democrat urged the state not to be unduly hasty in executing the six blacks in the *Moore* cases.[66] And assuming that the six were eventually executed, the *Democrat* editorialized, "as these men pay the price of their folly, let us not be too proud of the imperfect functions of human justice under which black dupes must die while their 'mastermind' [Robert Hill], the mulatto they trusted, roams the broad earth under the protecting aegis of the great commonwealth of Kansas."[67] The *Arkansas Gazette*, on the other hand, warmly endorsed Governor Brough's position, though it would no doubt "bring from certain newspapers and periodicals in sections of the country beyond the confines of the South another flood of vilification and misrepresentation. The absolute refusal of the North, East and West to credit the statements of leading men of Helena and Phillips County as well as the statements of the governor of Arkansas, the press of Arkansas and prominent Arkansans who investigated or had intimate knowledge of the Elaine insurrection, is unusual and somewhat remarkable." Misrepresentation by the northern black press was to be expected, the *Gazette* said, "but the misrepresentation by more decent publications came as a surprise."[68]

"In refusing to commute the sentences of the negroes, Governor Brough is putting down lynching," the *Gazette* continued. "Law abiding citizens of Phillips County were promised prompt and rigid enforcement of the law in the case of these murderers. The state should not falter now in carrying out that promise." There was no doubt of the guilt of the condemned blacks, the *Gazette* maintained, and in the process of securing their convictions the people of Phillips County "conducted themselves with admirable calm during the trying days just following the insurrection. They protected the innocent negroes and they protected the reputation and good name of Arkansas." Black agitators in the South would nonetheless continue to misrepresent what had happened, the *Gazette* predicted, and such "men are responsible largely for the present plight of the negroes under sentence of death. They teach the negroes to hate the whites and since the negroes listen to them rather than to those people who have proven themselves real friends of the negroes, the negroes must take what comes to them as the result of bad counsel."[69]

The mandate of the U.S. Supreme Court denying review in the *Moore* cases was not delivered to the Arkansas Supreme

Court until the end of November, further delaying the setting of a new date of execution. Brough said he would announce a new execution date "as soon as [the cases] are cleared of legal formalities, and since the United States court is the last court of appeal, denial of a review there automatically ends the legal battle for the lives of the men. . . . It will be recalled that I granted these condemned men a stay of execution of sentence when their cases were being appealed originally . . . , and I have not shown a desire to hurry these men to their deaths before full justice has been done." In his statement that he would not commute the sentences, the governor said, "I wanted to make it clear that I would not extend executive clemency in these six cases, which are nearing an ending in the courts, and I shall be prepared to take action in the remaining cases, also, just as quickly as they are cleared of legal formalities."[70]

When the denial of review by the U.S. Supreme Court reached the Arkansas Supreme Court on November 29, the *Arkansas Gazette* announced that the last hope for the six condemned blacks was gone.[71] But one week later, the Arkansas Supreme Court announced its decision in the *Ware* cases, which had been appealed to the court following the retrial and reconviction of the defendants, and for the second time, that court reversed the convictions in all of the *Ware* cases.[72] The supreme court acknowledged that counsel for the defendants at the retrial of the *Ware* cases had filed motions to transfer the cases to the U. S. district court and for a change of venue from Phillips County. Judge J. M. Jackson's ruling in the Phillips County Circuit Court refusing to transfer the cases to the federal court had been proper, the supreme court held, since there "has been no interpretation of our Constitution and laws by this court to show that in advance of a trial negroes could not enforce in the judicial tribunals of this State all the rights belonging to them in common with their fellow citizens of the white race."[73] Judge Jackson had also been correct in denying the motion for a change of venue. The court could not hold as a matter of law, the decision said, that the publication of the Committee of Seven's report on the riot "was sufficient foundation to justify the affiants in swearing that they believed that the minds of the inhabitants of the county were so prejudiced against the appellants that they could not obtain a fair and impartial trial." One member of the court, Judge Carroll D. Wood, dissented on this point and expressed the opinion that the motion for a change of venue should have been granted by the trial court.[74]

The final argument for reversal was that the defendants were "colored men, of African descent, and that the sheriff in summoning the talesmen for the completion of the jury had discriminated against them, on account of their race and color, by rejecting and refusing to summon any colored man, of whom there were many qualified to serve on the jury, solely because of their color, thereby denying to them the equal protection of the laws, and due process of law, in violation of the rights guaranteed to them under the first section of the Fourteenth Amendment to the Constitution of the United States."[75] Motions alleging racial discrimination in the selection of both the grand jury and the trial juries had been filed by counsel for the defendants, the court pointed out, and "it does not appear that the State, orally or otherwise, in any manner controverted the facts set forth in the motions." By refusing to allow the defense to submit evidence that would support its allegations of racial discrimination in the selection of the jury, the court held, the trial court had in effect held that even if the allegations of racial discrimination in the selection of jurors were true, such allegations were still legally insufficient to justify a ruling in favor of the defendants. This ruling by the trial court, the supreme court held, was not only contrary to the decisions of the U.S. Supreme Court in interpreting the Equal Protection Clause of the Fourteenth Amendment, but was also contrary to the law of Arkansas. A defendant "indicted for crime does have the right, when he is put upon his trial and called upon to face the panel from which the jury is to be selected to try him, to challenge the panel, and he is not called upon or required to make his objection before that time," the supreme court ruled. "The motions to set aside the panel of the petit jury, therefore, at the term when the appellants were put upon their trial and at the time when they were called upon to select a jury for their trials, were in apt time."[76]

Therefore, we conclude that, under the decisions of the Supreme Court of the United States . . . , the discrimination of the jury commissioners against the colored race in the selection of the petit jury, by which negroes were excluded from that jury solely on account of their color, rendered that selection illegal as to the appellants. That sort of discrimination in the selection of both grand and petit juries is in contravention of the Fourteenth Amendment to the Constitution of the United States, and the Civil Rights Act of March 1, 1875. . . . A majority of the court is of the opinion that the trial court erred in refusing to hear evidence on the motions to set aside the regular panel of the petit jury and erred in overruling such motions without hearing the evidence. The above errors must cause a reversal in all the cases.[77]

Chief Justice Edgar A. McCulloch and Judge Thomas H. Humphreys dissented from the decision reversing John Martin's conviction, because his counsel had failed to request a specific ruling on his motion to quash the panel from which his trial jury was drawn,[78] but the court was unanimous in its reversal of the convictions of the other five defendants. As a result, Ed Ware, William Wordlow, Albert Giles, Joe Fox, Alf Banks, and John Martin were entitled to yet another trial of the murder charges against them.

The NAACP accused Governor Brough of attempting to influence the supreme court to affirm the convictions in the *Ware* cases through his statements to the press on his decision to refuse executive clemency. The NAACP charged, "in direct contravention of all precedent, [Brough] issued a long statement to the newspapers . . . giving reasons why he believed the men were guilty and declaring that if the State Supreme Court refused to grant the appeals of the condemned men, he as Governor would grant no clemency." Through his actions, Brough had "made every effort to hang these Negroes, even attempting to influence the court by newspaper articles in which he cited the various Arkansas organizations which were demanding their death."[79]

If Governor Brough's intent had been that ascribed to him by the NAACP, the Arkansas Supreme Court had quite clearly refused to bow to such pressure. Yet the men in the *Moore* cases faced execution as a result of trials that had involved the same racially discriminatory jury selection processes condemned by the court in the *Ware* cases. Because the original trial counsel for the blacks in the *Moore* cases had not raised the issue of discrimination in the selection of their juries at the first trials, the Arkansas Supreme Court had held that the issue could not be raised in motions for new trials. The result was that the *Moore* blacks remained on death row, subject to execution, while the *Ware* blacks were entitled to retrials for the second time—retrials in which they could, at least theoretically, be acquitted.

Commenting on the state supreme court's decision, Scipio Jones pointed out that despite the favorable results for the *Ware* defendants, defense counsel "have been unsuccessful in all our efforts to secure a new trial for the other six condemned men, and the governor's such a busy man that he has not been able to devote sufficient time, I think, to investigation of the cases." "And, too," Jones added, "he visited the scene during the Phillips County trouble and may be prejudiced against the negroes, though he may have no intention to be so. Excitement [over] the insurrection had not subsided when the trials were held."[80]

Governor Brough apparently never set a new date for the executions. And since his term as governor of Arkansas expired in January of 1921, the responsibility for acting on the *Moore* cases fell upon the new governor, Thomas C. McRae.

A congressman from 1885 to 1903, president of the Arkansas Bar Association from 1917 to 1918, McRae was elected governor in 1920.[81] Any expectation that Governor McRae might act more favorably than Brough in the *Moore* cases had been dampened by his statements on pardons and commutations of sentences during his gubernatorial campaign. In June 1920 McRae had declared he realized "that a candidate for governor only causes a smile when he declares for upholding the courts by refusing pardons, but I want to make it clear that I stand for upholding our courts and juries. My observation is that few criminals are unjustly sentenced, and that many of them escape their just deserts."[82] Instead of commuting the sentences in the *Moore* cases, the new governor set the date for the execution of Frank Moore, Ed and Frank Hicks, J. E. Knox, Ed Coleman, and Paul Hall for June 10, 1921.[83]

The men in the *Ware* case now faced trials for murder for the third time, the NAACP again requesting a change of venue. The Association entertained the hope that more favorable results could be obtained for the *Ware* group in a less prejudiced forum than the Phillips County Circuit Court. The situation of the *Moore* defendants, however, was now more desperate than ever, and counsel for the NAACP would soon have to play the final card in the strategy to save their lives—a petition for a writ of habeas corpus in the U. S. district court.

⑥ The Genesis of *Moore* v. *Dempsey*

By the beginning of 1921 the NAACP had spent more than eight thousand dollars on the defense of the Phillips County blacks. The locally organized Citizens Defense Fund Commission (CDFC) in Arkansas had spent over ten thousand dollars. When the NAACP published its contribution to the defense efforts in the *Crisis* in February 1921 without mentioning the defense contribution of the CDFC, the old suspicions and resentments between the Association and the Arkansas black leaders resurfaced.[1] As secretary of the CDFC, J. H. McConico wrote to the NAACP asking that the omission of the CDFC's contributions in the *Crisis* be corrected.[2] McConico filed a report on the CDFC's activities, asserting that the Commission had been primarily responsible for the defense from the outset.

Since January of 1920, the report said, "the Citizens' Defense Fund Commission has had supervision of the legal fight—paying Attorneys, Court Costs and Attendant Expenses. The Commission got in touch with the NAACP and requested that the two organizations work in Union and keep each other informed as to each step taken. The Commission *has* done this and has mailed Statements of Disbursements to Headquarters of the NAACP. While collecting and putting into these Cases more than $10,000.00, no member of the Commission has received one cent and has steadfastly refused to accept the services of any one who desired to profit in any manner. In view of this service, as well as the fact that the Commission has disbursed more money upon the Cases in question than any other organization, we felt that any published Statement as to cost which omitted this fact [was incomplete]—especially when data were available."[3]

Responding on behalf of the NAACP, Walter White wrote to Scipio Jones that the Association had retained Colonel Murphy in November of 1919, well before the CDFC had been organized. McConico had acknowledged soon after the CDFC was organized that the CDFC "was aware of the fact the NAACP had taken up the defense of the Elaine rioters and wished to aid financially and morally." Contrary to the implication in the CDFC report, White said, the NAACP had received only one previous report from the CDFC, in April of 1920: "The Association has always been willing to give full credit to the Citizens' Defense Fund Commission and has no desire whatever to minimize the splendid services which have been rendered to the cause by the Commission." But the NAACP did object to the discrepancies in the CDFC's report, as well as to recent statements by Bishop J. M. Conner, in which he asserted that he had retained and paid for the lawyers in the Phillips County cases and that the NAACP had paid nothing.[4]

The NAACP acted to defuse the conflict by publishing an account of the Commission's contributions to the defense in the April 1921 issue of the *Crisis*. It praised the CDFC's efforts but at the same time, was careful to point out that the Association had been active in the defense effort well before the CDFC was organized. "On November 21, 1919, the NAACP entered into an agreement with the late Colonel George M. Murphy to defend all of the colored defendants in the Arkansas cases, and paid on November 30 the first $1,000 on the attorneys' fees. In January following, the Citizens [Defense Fund] Commission was organized and began to collect funds to aid in the defense of these cases, and with remarkable success as the statement . . . will show."[5]

While the CDFC correctly claimed to have contributed more to the defense than had the NAACP up to early 1921, the CDFC's contributions to the defense rapidly diminished thereafter. Indeed, as early as the spring of 1920, the CDFC informed the NAACP that it had "about spent [its] force so far as collecting funds; we only have about One Thousand Dollars on hand. This amount we will use toward getting some relief for the men serving prison sentences on condition that the NAACP will look after the twelve murder cases from this point."[6] And by the winter of 1922, Walter White was commenting that for a time the CDFC "aided to a large extent in raising funds for the defense but finally its means were exhausted and according to information, it is not now in existence."[7] The conflict between the NAACP and the CDFC unfortunately diverted the attention and energy of both organizations from the immediate problems confronting the defense. These included preparations for the defense of the six men in the *Ware* cases who faced a third series of murder trials, and the more serious situation of the six men in the *Moore* cases, whose execution had been set for June 10, 1921.

The *Ware* cases were again scheduled for trial before Judge J. M. Jackson in the Phillips County Circuit Court in the spring of 1921, but in early May, Jones and McHaney filed motions for changes of venue. In support of the motions, several Phillips County blacks signed affidavits in which they testified that the defendants could not get a fair trial in the county.[8] Judge Jackson delayed his ruling on the motions for almost two months, but on June 21 he granted the changes of venue; the retrials of the *Ware* defendants were ordered to be held in October at Marianna in Lee County.[9]

The situation of the NAACP and the defense counsel in the *Moore* cases grew increasingly desperate as the execution date approached. Like Governor Brough before him, Governor McRae was subjected to conflicting pressures on the issue of clemency. On May 13 petitions requesting a stay of execution signed by more than one hundred black citizens of Arkansas were presented to the governor by a committee of prominent blacks headed by Bishop J. M. Conner. They urged the governor to delay the executions until after the October retrials of the *Ware* cases.[10] In early June, McHaney and Jones conferred with the governor and urged him either to grant clemency or at least to postpone the executions.[11] Jones and McHaney filed petitions with the governor detailing the torture to which the condemned men and the witnesses testifying against them had been subjected.[12]

As the day of the scheduled executions drew even nearer, telegrams from around the country supporting clemency poured in to the governor's office.[13] On June 7 a delegation of black ministers representing forty churches in the Negro ministerial alliance in Pine Bluff called on McRae to plead for mercy. Indeed, delegations of persons supporting clemency for the condemned men called upon Governor McRae throughout the day of June 7, among them the mother, father, sister, and wife of Frank Moore.[14] Faculty members and the Jubilee Chorus from the Arkansas Baptist College visited "the Walls"—the contemporary term for the state penitentiary—to conduct "an old-fashioned prayer and song service with the six Elaine negroes sentenced to be electrocuted." The *Arkansas Democrat* reported that "plans for the executions were being carried out at the penitentiary. The death chamber was cleaned and the apparatus tested. . . . Coffins had been ordered."[15]

One of the most interesting individuals who intervened on behalf of the *Moore* defendants at this time was Colonel Robert T. Kerlin, professor in the English department at the Virginia Military Institute. Kerlin wrote to the NAACP in early May that the execution of the six men would be "an outrageous crime." He proposed to write an open letter to the governor of Arkansas denouncing the proposed executions, since as "a southern white man I may draw new and wider attention to the case . . . and public opinion may accomplish something."[16] Walter White encouraged Kerlin to proceed. A draft of his letter was completed by mid-May and forwarded to White for his comments. "I wish to be able to stand by this letter as I shall be obliged to do," Kerlin told White. "If I have made any mistake it will be made the most of, to the discredit of the cause."[17] With the exception of one or two minor points in the letter, White replied to Kerlin, he could "think of no possible way of bettering it. It is a powerful and splendidly worded statement. . . . I cannot but express our very hearty appreciation for the splendid service which you are thus rendering not only to these unfortunate men alone, but to the state of Arkansas and to America."[18]

On May 25 Kerlin dispatched his letter to Governor McRae, urging the governor to heed

the still small voice . . . that bids you stand for the eternal right . . . , a vindicator of human dignity, [not] the voice of the tempter of all men to . . . [submit] to the ill-guided multitude. . . . [The churches of Arkansas could help to prevent the commission of] a crime like that of Calvary . . . in a land where the Bible is an open and revered book, and the people are of the stock that has led the world in civilization. . . . [Never] in the history of our Republic has a more tremendous responsibility before God and the civilized world devolved upon the shoulders of the chief executive of any state than has devolved upon [McRae's] *in re* the Negroes of Phillips County condemned for murder and to death in the electric chair and so sentenced by the courts of your state.[19]

The convicted men had not received fair trials and torture had been used against them to force them to confess and against other blacks to compel them to testify against those condemned to death. The so-called Phillips County insurrection, Kerlin contended, had occurred because of the exploitation of blacks through the peonage system in the county; given the large number of blacks killed in the trouble, it was fair to ask whether the riot had been "a riot of the blacks or of the whites." Despite these circumstances, Kerlin said to Governor McRae, in "the case of six of those condemned men the sentence of death has been sanctioned by you and you have appointed the day of execution. It is a deed to be contemplated with horror. In the execution of those men a race is suffering crucifixion. I entreat you to take the matter into your private chamber and give it an hour's earnest consideration, as before the Eternal Judge."[20]

Colonel Robert T. Kerlin was a Missouri native with a Yale Ph.D., who was a Methodist minister and served as a chaplain in the Missouri Volunteers in the Spanish-American War. He taught English at Virginia Military Institute for eleven years. Active in Socialist party and labor union affairs, he was also the author of *The Voice of the Negro*, among other books.

Robert Kerlin's letter created a sensation in Arkansas. E. M. Allen declared that Kerlin's letter "appears to be the work of those hysterical theorists who are responsible for the affairs said to be prevalent in some of our larger colleges." Kerlin "openly slanders and discredits the citizens and courts of Phillips County and the Supreme Court of the United States." Allen asserted, "The condemned negroes were defended by the ablest and most honorable members of the Phillips County bar. Judge John I. Moore, former acting governor of the state; Major Greenfield Quarles, a graduate of V.M.I., a friend of the negro race all of his life and long known among the negroes as a man of deep sympathy and understanding. Every effort was made by these attorneys and the courts to produce evidence to lighten the cases against their clients, but the admissions made by the condemned men themselves precluded the possibility of letting them take the stand in their own behalf."[21] Allen denied that a system of peonage existed in Phillips County. Everyone who had investigated the riot, he argued, was "met time and again with the statement on the part of renters and share croppers that they never had a moment's difficulty with the landlords. Statements of accounts and settlements are always made by landlords according to the custom prevailing since the Civil War. . . . The ones sentenced to death are the deliberate murderers who planned and carried out the details of the insurrection, who confessed to murder and who wanted to continue killing but who were unable to hold their men together after the soldiers arrived."[22]

Taking note of such attacks, Robert Kerlin wrote to Walter White that the "Huns of Arkansas are evidently getting ready to come after my scalp. They are denouncing my letter as a mass of falsehoods and are writing to the Superintendent of [the Virginia Military Institute] to denounce me." The Superintendent, Kerlin said, "disapproves of my letter—being afraid of loss of patronage," and he requested that White send him materials that could be used in his defense before the VMI Board of Visitors.[23] White complied with the request, pointing out that the NAACP "must come to the rescue of this man who has done so much and at so great a sacrifice in this cause."[24] The NAACP's help was not enough, however and Robert Kerlin was later dismissed from his position at VMI.[25] The Virginia Military Institute Board of Visitors, incensed at his appeal to the governer of Arkansas, in August 1921, demanded his immediate resignation. Kerlin brought suit for $50,000 damages and hired two black attorneys to handle his case; as the *Baltimore Sun* said on May 7, 1923, it was the first time apparently in Virginia's history that "negroes have represented a white man." The suit was dismissed by the courts and Kerlin took a teaching job at the State Normal School in West Chester, Pennsylvania. He died in 1950 at 83 years of age.

The fact that a southern white had condemned the execution of the blacks prompted Judge Jackson to write Governor McRae. "So far as the letter of Robert T. Kerlin is concerned," Judge Jackson told the governor,

let me call your attention to the fact that in almost every criminal case in which the public eye has been centered, there arise maudlin sentimentalists who take some statement published in a newspaper and from that protest to high heaven against the punishment of the criminal. There is no basis of fact for the statements in the Kerlin letter. The statement that the Progressive Farmers' and Householders Union was a peaceful union founded for legitimate purposes is wholly untrue. The statement that the insurrectionists shot only in self-defense is false. The statement that the negroes were indiscriminately hunted, harried and shot down is a wicked lie. The principal facts were proven by the boys of the American Legion, who, as members of the sheriff's posse, put down the riot, [and] the identity of the defendants was established by testimony of the negroes themselves. Careful investigation was made during the trials of alleged whipping of the negroes to obtain testimony and from all that human testimony can show . . . this was not done. . . . In my judgment, the sentences imposed by law should be carried out. . . . The defendants had a fair trial, and I doubt if anywhere a racial clash has been handled with the same degree of absence of mob violence, leniency and respect for law as that which was shown in the Elaine insurrection. So far as I know this is the first time the people have been tempered enough to try to handle such cases in the courts; for I assure you there was an an armed insurrection with the deliberate purpose to kill and plunder.

The reason that our people respected the law was that they were assured that the judgments of the courts would be carried out. So you can readily see that interference with the judgments of the courts in these cases would destroy the only incentive for observance of the law. If the promises made to our people, promises by our Christian leaders, are not carried out, then no more promises will be made. . . . The responsibility must rest on you in this matter. I gladly take my share, and urge you in the name of law and order, the protection of our women and children, and the peace of our community not to interfere with the judgment of the court.[26]

At a public meeting in Helena on June 7, a resolution was passed calling upon the governor to allow the executions to proceed. On June 8 a delegation from Helena called upon Governor McRae to communicate these views in person. Included were H. E. McRae, the governor's nephew, and John I. Moore, who strongly opposed commutation, despite E. M. Allen's assertion of the effectiveness of his representation at the trial of the *Moore* blacks.[27] Kerlin's letter, as well as the presentations of Jones, McHaney, and other opponents of the execution of the condemned men, had apparently raised serious doubts in Governor McRae's mind about his course of action, and he asked John Miller, prosecutor in the Phillips County cases, to file a report of his view of the facts.

Miller duly filed, in early June, a report fully supporting the version of the trouble endorsed by the Helena Committee of Seven and other officials in Phillips County. "A reading of the records in these cases is sufficient answer to the letter of Mr. Kerlin," Miller reported to the governor. "The letter shows on its face that he is unadvised of the facts surrounding this awful event, and I am inclined to believe the writing of that letter was prompted by some outside influence, rather than the pleading of the 'still small voice.'" Miller was not inclined to follow Kerlin "as the unappointed Moses to lead us out of the wilderness of error in which he says we are at this time." If Kerlin had impartially investigated the Phillips County affair, "and had asked men of unquestionable integrity and honor for the facts then that letter never would have been written, if he is the man he would have us believe him to be, and on this question I must reserve my opinion."[28]

Scipio Jones and E. L. McHaney had submitted to Governor McRae affidavits sworn to by Walter Ward, John Jefferson, and George Green; all three blacks said they had been tortured to compel them to testify against the *Moore* defendants. McRae submitted these affidavits to John Miller for his consideration, and Miller reported back that

a casual reading of them will suffice to show the reader that they were written by some subtle hand with one end in view of creating public sentiment. These are not the only affidavits that have been procured, and doubtless, if you will take the time to investigate you will find that the parties who are making this fight for these negroes can supply you with other affidavits written by the same party and sworn to by other prisoners. This is but natural and is to be expected. It is not the first time that prosecuting witnesses have changed their testimony under the careful leadership of some interested party.

As you know, I am not a resident of Phillips County and at the time this insurrection occurred I had only held one court in that county. I was practically unknown and did not know scarcely any one in the county. I am under no obligations to any one, either politically or otherwise, and I went about my investigation of this matter with only one desire and that was to arrive at the actual facts and the actual cause of this trouble. When I arrived at Helena, I found something like 300 negroes in jail, being held for investigation. The investigation was under way and was being conducted by some of the very best and most honorable citizens of the county. They were not vindictive and used no cruel methods in their investigation. . . . [I]t was not my desire, nor the desire of the good people of Phillips County to convict men and women who had been led into the matters by others and who had taken no great or active part in the insurrection, [and] therefore they were turned loose and asked to return to the farms, which they did, and they are now living on the farms and happy and free from the sinister influences that had so nearly resulted in their undoing. The investigation showed conclusively that the entire county around Elaine had been organized by Robert L. Hill, and the men who are condemned to die, for the purpose of acting in concert to gain their fancied rights. There had been no wrong committed, but the average plantation negro had been led to believe that he was being wronged by the white man. Those men who had innocently participated were released, but the ones who had assisted in the killings were tried and convicted.[29]

Had the shooting at Hoop Spur not begun the insurrection prematurely, Miller declared, "it is my honest opinion that there would not have been a white man, woman or child left in that part of the country to tell the story of their death and the devastation of the country."[30]

Continuing his report, Miller noted that the lodge of the Progressive Farmers Union had met at the Hoop Spur church, posting armed sentries around the church, and it was these sentries who had fired upon the automobile that carried Adkins, Pratt, and the black trusty and had killed Adkins and wounded Pratt. Couriers had been immediately dispatched to union members in other sections of the county with the message to prepare to fight the whites, and by daylight, Miller said, "something like 100 men had assembled at Frank Moore's house armed and ready to fight in accordance with the teachings of the lodge and their leaders." Under the leadership of Moore, Frank Hicks, and others, these men proceeded in the direction of Elaine. In order to arrest the armed blacks, the members of the American Legion post at Helena were deputized, "and in their efforts to arrest the men who had thus rebelled, some of them were killed and several of the negroes were killed, but my investigation failed to show that a single negro was killed unnecessarily."[31]

His investigation demonstrated, Miller continued, that the members of the Progressive Farmers Union were told by their leaders to arm themselves with high-powered rifles and to be prepared to fight the whites at the appointed time.

The testimony that the witnesses gave at the trial of these men is true. It cannot be otherwise, notwithstanding the affidavits [produced by Jones and McHaney] to the contrary. The witnesses detailed every little circumstance, every conversation, and their testimony exactly agreed with the physical facts and the physical conditions and the things that the officers saw and know existed. The witnesses could not have told of these things if they had not known, and no man could have framed up the testimony for them to have given in the manner in which it was

SUBJECTS OF PROF. KERLIN'S APPEAL

The twelve blacks sentenced to death in the riot cases. *The Chicago Defender,* February 4, 1922. *Courtesy of the Library of Congress*

Phillips County courthouse, where the first trial proceedings were held. *Courtesy of the Arkansas History Commission*

ARKANSAS RIOTING PLANNED BY NEGRO

Investigation Reveals Plot for Uprising Against White People.

UNION OF ARMED BLACKS

Organizer Worked on Superstition of Race—Leader of Band of 20 Is Sought.

HELENA, Ark., Oct. 6.—A statement was made to-day on the recent riots by E. M. Allen of the committee of seven, authorized by local officers and Gov. Brough to investigate the trouble, charging that the affair was an organized negro uprising, fostered by a negro who preyed on "the ignorance and superstition of a race of children for monetary gains."

Mr. Allen, who was one of the leading men marked for death, after hearing confessions, examining circulars and other evidence procured by State and military officers in connection with the work of the committee, issued the following statement to explain what the committee had found to be the situation leading to the killing of five white men

The New York Sun, October 7, 1919. *Courtesy of the Library of Congress*

Arkansas Governor Charles H. Brough. *Courtesy of the Library of Congress*

John F. Miller, prosecutor in the Helena trials, former congressman and later U.S. District Court judge. *Courtesy of the Library of Congress*

J. S. Utley, Arkansas attorney general, a prosecutor in the riot cases, who presented the State of Arkansas's case to the U.S. Supreme Court in 1923. *Courtesy of the Arkansas History Commission*

John D. Arbuckle, Arkansas attorney general. *Courtesy of the Library of Congress*

ALLEGED LEADER IN UPRISING AT ELAINE HAS BEEN CAPTURED

DOESN'T WANT HILL RETURNED

Boston, Jan. 23.—The National Equal Rights League telegraphed Gov. Henry J. Allen of Kansas yesterday, urging him not to extradite to Arkansas Robert L. Hill, president of the "Progressive Farmers and Household Union," the negro organization which is said to have been responsible for the negro uprising near Elaine, Ark., three months ago.

The league's telegram characterizes the negroes' union as "one of reputable colored farmers to secure court protection of their pay for their cotton against fraud by planters and not to kill off whites."

Hill, who is held at Topeka, Kan.,

Topeka, Kan., Jan. 21.—Robert L. Hill, negro, under arrest here, admits his identity and declares he will resist extradition. He asserts he is innocent of the charge of murder.

Hill was arrested by Topeka officers, who traced him through a letter he had written to his wife, asking her to meet him in Topeka.

Robert L. Hill, president of the "Progressive Farmers' and Household Union," the negro organization which is said to have been responsible for the negro uprising near Elaine, Ark., three months ago, which resulted in deaths of six white men and many negroes, is

Robert L. Hill, head of the Progressive Farmers Union, arrested in Kansas City, Kansas. *Arkansas Democrat*, January 21, 1920 and January 23, 1920. *Courtesy of the Library of Congress*

Henry J. Allen, governor of Kansas, who in 1920 refused to extradict the black union representative Robert L. Hill to Arkansas to stand trial for inciting the riot. *Courtesy of the Library of Congress*

E. H. Dempsey, keeper of the Arkansas State Penitentiary, where the twelve convicted men awaited execution from 1919–1924. He is the Dempsey of *Moore v. Dempsey*, on which the Supreme Court acted in 1923. *Arkansas Gazette. Courtesy of the Library of Congress*

Renew Hope in Case of Elaine Men

Little Rock, Ark., Sept. 2.—It has been announced that efforts would be made to obtain from the Supreme Court of the United States a writ of certiorari in behalf of six Arkansas farmers condemned to die on September 23 for their connection with the Arkansas riots of 1919. It is then contemplated applying to a federal court for a writ of habeas corpus.

It was for appealing to the governor of Arkansas in behalf of these men that Prof. Robert T. Kerlin was handed a resolution of dismissal by the board of visitors of the Virginia Military Institute, Lexington, Va.

Six others are to be tried at Marianna, Ark., in October.

General counsel for the condemned men said to a Defender reporter: "We have great confidence of victory in the final outcome if given proper assistance."

The cases have been lingering in the courts for over two years and, due to the unusual amount of prejudice that has attended them, citizens of both races have interested themselves in the fight for justice.

The Chicago Defender, September 3, 1921. *Courtesy of the Library of Congress*

KERLIN CASE PROVES SOUTH IS BACKWARD

Southern "Uplifters" Demonstrate Their Brand of "Racial Justice" by Demanding Professor's Dismissal at Military Institute

Belgian Congo Is Too Hot for Whites Now; Disease Kills Them

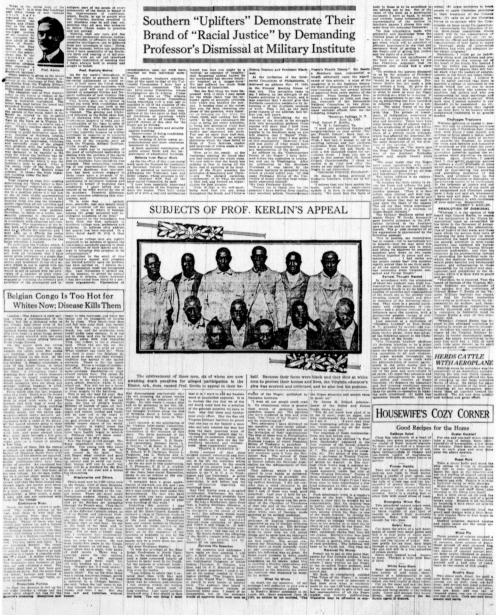

SUBJECTS OF PROF. KERLIN'S APPEAL

HERDS CATTLE WITH AEROPLANE

HOUSEWIFE'S COZY CORNER

Good Recipes for the Home

(*Above and above right*) Robert T. Kerlin, Virginia Military Institute professor, who lost his faculty post after he protested death sentences of the twelve convicted Arkansas blacks. *The Chicago Defender*, February 4, 1922 (above) and September 3, 1921 (right). *Courtesy of the Library of Congress*

SOUTH SEES DANGER IN COL. KERLIN

Southerners Show Weakness on Race Issue by Expelling Professor

Richmond, Va., Sept. 2.—When Prof. Robert T. Kerlin of the Virginia Military Institute was dismissed from that institution the lie about white Southerners being the friends of the Race was exposed and a true friend was subjected to a nauseating and shameful treatment of that same prejudice which he had fought against.

Col. Kerlin

Col. Kerlin was dismissed, according to a resolution adopted by the board of visitors of the institution where he was pro-fessor of English, because of his interposition in behalf of the six men condemned to die in connection with the Arkansas riots at Elaine some months ago. The directors maintained that his recent work, with its bearing on inter-racial relations, had tended to show that the professor was out of sympathy with the strongest aims, purposes and disposition of the institution. Reference was made to the fact that the public which supports the school viewed with no little disdain Col. Kerlin's desire to force the sham out of Southern race relations.

Board Met in Secret

The inquiry into the activities of the deposed member of the faculty was conducted with the utmost secrecy in the Hotel Richmond. Two days and nights the deliberations continued. Rumors had spread in various circles that the question of the dismissal of Mr. Kerlin was being discussed. Since his espousal of the cause of the Race a growing coldness toward him and his work by both teachers and students at the institute had been in evidence.

Whereas in former years members of the faculty had met and counseled with the professor of English, his recent revelation of the sinister and malign tendencies of South race prejudice and his effort to show in its true light the worth of the people who are being persecuted had resulted in a sort of social and professional ostracism. For some months he had lived a sort of martyr to the cause which he had taken up with no thought of gain save that which came from seeing justice done. Some of his closest friends are said to have strongly objected to the public stand which he took. He showed the same courage in supporting his views that he had shown years ago as a soldier in defense of the stricken Cubans.

Born in 1866, he had been instructor in English at the Virginia Military Institute since 1910. He had attended many schools, holding the degree of M. A. from Central College, Missouri, credit for work at Johns Hopkins University, the University of Chicago, Harvard, and a Ph. D. degree from Yale in 1906.

ELAINE RIOTERS BEING RAILROADED, IS CHARGE

Former Bar Association Head Assails Arkansas for Sentences.

Washington, Jan. 9.—(By I. N. S.)—Appearing before the United States supreme court to plead for negroes condemned to die in connection with the Arkansas riots of 1919, Moorfield Storey, former president of American Bar Association, today charged the Arkansas courts, newspapers, leading citizens, Rotary club, American Legion and other organizations of Helena, Ark., with attempting to "railroad the negroes to death."

Arkansas Democrat, January 9, 1923. *Courtesy of the Library of Congress*

Judge Jacob Trieber of Arkansas U.S. District Court, who, as a former Phillips County resident, disqualified himself from presiding at the habeas corpus hearing. *Courtesy of the Library of Congress*

Judge John E. Martineau, of the Pulaski Chancery Court, whose intervention delayed and, therefore, in the end, prevented the executions. *Courtesy of the Arkansas History Commission*

given. The witnesses appeared before the Grand Jury and then, in the presence of the Grand Jury, a body of representative citizens, gave this testimony and it is true.

[L]et me tell you that [Phillips] County has suffered more than most counties would endure. They knew they were right and they passed such outbursts as that of Mr. Kerlin by, trusting in the officers of the law, and now to commute the sentences of these men, or to longer postpone their execution, would, in my opinion, be the gravest insult that can be given to a body of law-abiding people. I warn that if such a course is taken it will not be safe; that some time in the future, although I hope not, there may be other trouble of this kind, and if there is, I shudder to think of what may be the outcome if the law is not vindicated this time. . . . [A]s an officer who has honestly tried to discharge his duty as required by the law, I make this appeal to you. I also appeal to you on behalf of the citizens of Phillips County who have suffered long and patiently from the insults of such men as Kerlin, who have tried to mould public sentiment without stating the facts as they existed. I have remained silent in the face of what has been said about these cases, hoping some one would make an investigation with an end in view of ascertaining the facts and with a motive prompted by that desire, and not by money, and when such an investigation is made it will be determined that what I have said is true. I, therefore, hope that you may allow the law to be carried out and justice be done in these cases.[32]

Governor McRae now took the position that if a fair trial had indeed been denied the condemned blacks, that issue should be raised in the courts, but he would not himself interfere with the executions on that ground.[33] Jones and McHaney had, of course, planned all along to file a petition for a writ of habeas corpus in the U.S. district court in Little Rock as a last resort. Judge Trieber, of the court, was temporarily sitting on the U.S. Court of Appeals in St. Paul, Minnesota, and was not scheduled to return to Arkansas until after the scheduled execution date. His absence from the bench (apparently no substitute was available) thus blocked what had been planned as the last card in the defense strategy, and, as McHaney said, unless Governor McRae "grants [a] postponement, we have no tribunal, during the recess of the federal court, to which we may make any further appeal."[34] It appeared that there was nothing further that Jones and McHaney could legally do to save the six condemned men.

But in desperation they filed petitions for writs of habeas corpus in the Pulaski County Chancery Court in Little Rock, where Chancellor John E. Martineau had presided since 1907. It was only two days before the scheduled executions. Their petitions asserted that the condemned men had been illegally convicted with testimony secured through torture, that they had been denied a fair trial because of the mob atmosphere in Helena at the time of their trials, and that they had been tried by juries illegally selected in a racially discriminatory manner. These were the same petitions they were blocked from filing in the U.S. district court.[35] Chancellor Martineau ordered the warden of the state penitentiary, E. H. Dempsey, to appear with the men at a hearing on June 10 to show cause why they should be executed; he issued an injunction prohibiting the carrying out of the executions until the habeas corpus hearing could be held. Chancellor Martineau had temporarily saved the lives of the six men.[36]

Arkansas Attorney General J. S. Utley promptly challenged Chancellor Martineau's authority either to issue the writs of habeas corpus or to issue the injunction prohibiting the executions. On June 9 he filed a petition for a writ of prohibition in the Arkansas Supreme Court asking that court to order Martineau to dismiss the petitions for writs of habeas corpus and to vacate the injunction.[37] The supreme court considered the attorney general's petition on June 10. Chief Justice McCulloch took the position that the court should immediately issue the writ of prohibition ordering the dismissal of the habeas corpus petitions as well as the injunction by the chancery court. Such an action would have cleared the way for the executions to have been carried out on schedule. Jones and McHaney requested, however, that the supreme court postpone issuance of the writ of prohibition pending a hearing. A majority of the court agreed to their request. The execution of the *Moore* blacks was accordingly postponed until after the hearing on the petition for a writ of prohibition.[38]

The *Arkansas Democrat* of Little Rock was the first dissenting voice among the ranks of the state's white press on the handling of the Phillips County riot. "Thinking people everywhere in this State must be glad that sanity has won in the cases of the six Elaine negroes who were to have been electrocuted," the *Democrat* said in an editorial. "At the time the date of these executions was fixed for June 10, the Arkansas Democrat deplored it as an unfortunate action, because of the uncertain status of the other six [*Ware*] cases which are awaiting new trials." The cases of all twelve of the men convicted and sentenced to death must be considered together, since all "were convicted of the same offense, upon the same evidence, and if one is guilty, any or all may be guilty; if one is innocent any or all of the others may be innocent."[39]

Suppose then, that the new trials of the six who were sent back result in acquittal, or in conviction of a lesser offense than first degree murder. Does any man deny that in simple justice the six who did not get new trials should then get them, or should receive commutations to make their punishment commensurate with that dealt out to their fellows? [Suppose] we should find that the State, because of unseemly haste to enforce a previous sentence, had taken away their lives. There is a remedy, say the Spanish, for everything except death. With what force that terrible fact would then bear upon our hearts and consciences.

[There had been some consideration] in State official circles, of proceeding with the executions on Friday, in defiance of the order of the Pulaski chancery court. . . . What terrible advertising that would have given our beloved State before the world! Beside such an act of official anarchy all the other instances of unfavorable advertising which we have bemoaned in recent months would have been dwarfed into insignificance. Here, the world would have said, and said rightly, was a state so thirsty for the blood of a half-dozen wretched negroes that her own officials were not willing to let the law take its course, but must go ahead with execution, taking their own chance with the courts later. What a counsel of madness![40]

The argument that carrying through with the executions was necessary to prevent the lynching of the six blacks who were to be returned to Helena for new trials could not be sufficient justification for lawless action on the part of state officials. "Let us be calm, unrushed, unswayed by blind, unreasoning passion," the *Democrat* concluded. "If these negroes must die; if there is to be no clemency or no postponement of their execution, at least let everything be done properly and in order, and in a semblance of respect for the common decencies!"[41]

The *Arkansas Democrat* published the petitions for writs of habeas corpus filed in the chancery court on behalf of the condemned men, including the allegations that much of the testimony at their trials had been the product of torture. This was the most extensive publicity the contentions of the NAACP and the defense counsel had yet received in the white press of Arkansas. The *Arkansas Gazette*, for its part, roundly condemned the *Democrat's* editorial, declaring it would "doubtless be greedily seized on by those individuals in the North and East who have in this matter so flagrantly misrepresented Arkansas and done this state so great [an] injustice." The *Moore* defendants, the *Gazette* argued, had been convicted of killing Lee; the *Ware* men, of killing Adkins and Tappan. "It is clear that even if the six negroes who are accused of the murder of Adkins and Tappan should finally be found not guilty, their acquittal would not mean that the six who were sentenced to die [on June 10] were not guilty of the murder of Lee," the *Gazette* said. "In fact one of the six negroes now in the death cells at the penitentiary admitted firing the shot that killed Lee."[42]

While the press was debating the merits of the postponement of the executions, arguments were held before the Arkansas Supreme Court on June 12 on the question of the writ of prohibition. The courtroom was reported to have been crowded with both whites and blacks.[43] Arguing for the state, Assistant Attorney General Elbert Godwin denounced the petitions for writs of habeas corpus that had been filed in the chancery court as involving one of the "bitterest attacks ever made on a court of any community," and argued that, under Arkansas law, chancery courts had no jurisdiction whatever in criminal cases. McHaney argued on behalf of the condemned men that the state's evidence in the original trials had been secured through torture, in violation of due process. Chief Justice McCulloch stopped him in mid-argument. Such contentions, he said, were irrelevant to the issue of the chancery court's jurisdiction to issue the writs and the injunction. McHaney contended that, under the U.S. Constitution and the federal Habeas Corpus Act of 1867, state courts could issue writs of habeas corpus in cases in which due process of law had been denied.[44]

The Arkansas Supreme Court, announcing its decision on June 20, held that the writ of prohibition should be issued because the chancery court did not have jurisdiction in criminal cases. Writing for a unanimous court, Chief Justice McCulloch pointed out that the "doctrine has been announced by this court that courts of equity in this State are not clothed with jurisdiction to review proceedings in criminal cases or to interfere with such proceedings, either by injunction or under the writ of habeas corpus."[45] To McHaney's argument citing the Habeas Corpus Act of 1867, McCulloch replied that the act "does not apply to any courts except to the Supreme Court and the circuit and district courts of the United States, and it defines the practice in those courts and the powers of the courts under the remedy afforded by the writ of habeas corpus. The statute does not purport to apply to the courts of the States, and Congress had no authority, had it attempted to do so, to prescribe the process of the State courts and the practice to be followed in matters within their jurisdictions. What the result would be of an application to a Federal court under the statute referred to and upon the facts stated in the petition we need not inquire."[46]

Further discussion would seem to be useless. It was not contended in the argument here that there is any other charge in the motion upon which relief could be granted, except the one to the effect that the trial court was dominated by a mob, which suspended the functions of the court and prevented a fair trial. There are no other facts in the petition which would warrant a review of the judgment of the circuit court of Phillips County. The allegations with regard to newly discovered evidence and the retraction by the State's witnesses, which is, in effect, an allegation of the discovery of new evidence, affords no ground for a review of the judgments of conviction, for there is no provision in the laws of this State for the granting of a new trial after the lapse of the term [of the court at which a conviction was obtained] on the ground of newly discovered evidence. . . . It follows that the chancery court is without jurisdiction to proceed, and the writ of prohibition will therefore be granted, and the writ of habeas corpus as well as the injunction order issued by the court will be quashed.[47]

Walter White immediately telegraphed to Scipio Jones asking what further steps could be taken to save the men from execution.[48] White also notified NAACP president Moorfield Storey of the supreme court decision. Due to "pressure brought to bear from Phillips County, the Arkansas Supreme Court . . . issued a writ of prohibition dissolving the injunction of the Chancery Court," White said. "I cannot say at this time what the results will be or what action our lawyers have taken or will take. We can only hope for the best."[49]

Jones had told White that there was no immediate danger of the executions' taking place, since Governor McRae had not set a new date, and that defense counsel intended to file a petition for a writ of error in the U.S. Supreme Court, seeking its review of the Arkansas Supreme Court's decision. Such an action would further delay the executions.[50] Governor McRae had the power to set a new execution date fifteen days after the Arkansas Supreme Court's decision, but before that time, Jones and Mc-

Haney appealed the decision to the U.S. Supreme Court. The executions were once again indefinitely postponed.[51]

Phillips County and the Arkansas State Penitentiary Board had recently become embroiled in a tragicomic dispute over the cost of room and board for the condemned men in the penitentiary. A 1921 law required counties in which defendants were sentenced to death to pay one dollar per day for the support of such prisoners on death row. By June 1, 1921, Phillips County owed the state penitentiary $1440 for the housing and maintenance of the twelve men. C. E. Toole, clerk of the State Penitentiary Board, had written to Phillips County Judge William Larkin that, unless the board's "claims aggregating $1440 for the safekeeping of 12 prisoners from your county from February 1, 1921, to May 31, 1921, is allowed and paid by your [county] court before the next board meeting, which is July 6, [the board] will instruct the attorney general of Arkansas to file suit for the collection of this amount. The Penitentiary Board is in no way responsible for the fact that the court order [sentencing the twelve blacks to death] of Phillips County has not been executed, and the penitentiary management feels that your county should honor at once this claim for the keeping of these men."[52] Toole told the judge that unless Phillips County did pay its bill, the prisoners in the *Ware* cases, who were scheduled for retrials, would be sent back to the Phillips County jail. Judge Larkin refused, on behalf of the county, to pay the penitentiary bill; he maintained that Phillips County was not responsible for the long delay in carrying out the executions of the twelve men.[53] Attorney General Utley, supporting the position of the State Penitentiary Board, threatened to sue Phillips County unless it paid its bill.[54]

In the midst of this dispute, Judge Jackson, of the county circuit court, granted the change of venue for the retrial of the *Ware* cases, and Phillips County authorities sought to transfer the prisoners from the penitentiary to the Lee County jail at Marianna. It would cost Phillips County twenty-five cents a day less to house the prisoners in the Lee County jail than it cost at the penitentiary. State penitentiary warden Dempsey refused to release the prisoners to the custody of Phillips County Sheriff J. D. Mays, until each of the prisoners had a guard from the State Penitentiary Board to ensure adequate protection during transfer to Lee County.[55] Governor McRae met with the State Penitentiary Board and Sheriff Mays on June 25, and a mutually agreeable plan to protect the prisoners in transit was negotiated.[56] "Because of the fact that sentiment in eastern Arkansas has become greatly inflamed as a result of the long delays in the execution of the Elaine rioters," the press reported, "elaborate precautions against mob violence were taken by the officers" in transferring the prisoners to Lee County. "There was a well-founded rumor," it was reported, "that officers had learned of a plot to lynch the negroes somewhere on the way to Marianna." Sheriff Mays hid the prisoners in Little Rock for six hours after taking them from the penitentiary and then arranged for a special train to take the men to Marianna without incident.[57]

Phillips County officials persisted in their refusal to pay the bill for the upkeep of the condemned men in the state penitentiary, however, and so the state attorney general sued the county in the circuit court. The Circuit Court of Phillips County ruled in favor of the State Penitentiary Board. Phillips County promptly appealed the judgment to the Arkansas Supreme Court, but on January 29, 1923, the supreme court upheld the circuit court's decision and ordered Phillips County to pay the eight thousand dollars it then owed for housing. (In March 1923 the state legislature passed a special act relieving Phillips County of its obligation to pay this judgment.)[58]

McHaney had in the meantime secured important new evidence to use in the defense. Writing the NAACP in August 1921, he told the Association that defense counsel "now have two white witnesses who were in the trouble at Helena and Elaine from beginning to end and who are going to testify for us." Using these witnesses, McHaney said, "we expect to show that the white men started the trouble by going to the meeting house [at Hoop Spur] and breaking up the meeting of [the Progressive Farmers Union], and that the white folks fired the first shot. We will be able to prove by these witnesses that the colored men in jail were whipped and tortured most unmercifully to compel them to give evidence against the others, especially the men who had been tried and convicted."[59]

Three of the blacks awaiting retrial in Marianna, McHaney noted, were charged with killing Lieutenant James Tappan, but one of the white witnesses "will testify that he was standing right by Tappan when he was shot and that he was killed by a member of his own posse, and that there was not a colored man nearer than a half mile of him." One of the white witnesses, McHaney also reported, would also testify that he, himself, "did a great deal of whipping of the prisoners."[60] The white witnesses to whom McHaney referred were T. K. Jones and H. F. Smiddy. At the time of the riot they had been employed as special agents of the Missouri-Pacific Railroad, working in the Memphis division. Jones was the supervisor of Smiddy and of W. D. Adkins, who had been killed in the shooting at Hoop Spur. In September 1921 Jones and Smiddy, at the request of E. L. McHaney, swore in affidavits their observations during the riot and after it.[61]

T. K. Jones said that on the evening of September 30, 1919, Phillips County Chief Deputy Sheriff Dick Dazell had asked the special railroad agents to accompany Deputy Sheriff Charles Pratt from Helena to Elaine, where he was to arrest a man. Adkins agreed to accompany Pratt. Jones and Smiddy went to bed in the Cleiborne Hotel in Helena. At approximately two o'clock in the morning, Jones said, Dazell telephoned the hotel to inform Jones and Smiddy that Pratt and Adkins had encountered trouble at Hoop Spur. Jones, Smiddy, Dazell, and six other men left immediately by car, arriving at Hoop Spur at 3:30 or 4 A.M. They found Adkins lying dead just north of the black church at Hoop Spur. The interior of the church itself was in disarray.[62] The group proceeded to Elaine, where Dazell telephoned Sheriff F. F. Kitchens. During the afternoon of October 1, Jones said he "heard some planters talking and from their conversation I understood that a number of white men had gone to the Hoop Spur church house the night before for the purpose of breaking up the meeting of the negroes there and that the white people had shot into the church and started [the] shooting." One of the planters "said to the other that, 'My negroes don't belong to that blankety blank union.' The other said, 'How in the hell do you know they don't?' He answered and said, 'I told my negroes about two weeks ago that if they joined that blankety blank union I would kill every one of them.'"[63] Jones said he had performed guard duty during the riot and had seen no blacks firing shots, and, indeed, had not seen "a single negro with a gun or weapon of any kind during the whole day I was in the country." Jones added, "From the information I gathered while I was down there, the whole trouble started because the white folks objected to the negroes having this union; that the negroes were organizing to employ counsel to represent them in getting settlements from their white landlords, and the white folks objected to this procedure."[64]

During the Committee of Seven's interrogation in Helena of the blacks taken into custody, Jones saw

a great many negroes whipped on the third floor of the county jail to compel them to give evidence against themselves and others about the trouble. . . . I know that the negroes were frequently whipped and otherwise tortured after they were taken before the Committee and brought back. They would take the negroes before this Committee and bring them back to the whipping room of the jail, and apply the lash until the negroes were willing to testify and would testify to anything that was wanted of them to save themselves from further torture. They were not only whipped but formaldehyde was put to their noses and [they] were stripped naked and put into an electric chair which they had in the room to further frighten and torture them. I not only personally saw a great many negroes whipped with a leather strap that would cut blood at every lick, but I whipped probably two dozen of them myself. . . . I do remember I helped to whip Frank Moore and J. E. Knox.[65]

"In this manner the testimony that was used in the trials of these cases and the others was acquired," Jones continued. "So far as I know no negro made a voluntary statement that implicated any other negro in anything criminal, and I believe I would have known it if it had been done. The negroes would be told that such and such a statement they had made was a blankety blank lie; that they knew such and such was true, and after being whipped the negroes would say, 'Boss, yes, sir, that is so; I will say anything you want me to say,'—or something to that effect." "Those that did the whipping of the negroes in the Phillips County jail other than myself and Mr. Smiddy," Jones said, "were Mr. Dick Dazell, Louis Anselman, Charles Gist, and some others whose name I do not now recall."[66]

Jones said he was present in Helena during the trials of the Phillips County blacks, and the "only evidence against [the blacks] to connect them with any criminal offense was the evidence that we had extorted in the manner above set out." During the trials, he continued, "[l]arge crowds thronged the court house and grounds, all of whom were unfriendly to the defendants, and desired their condemnation to death. The feeling against them was so bitter and so strong and so universal that it was absolutely unanimous and no man could have sat upon a jury in any of these cases and have voted for acquittal and remained in Helena afterwards." A mob had in fact formed to lynch the blacks after they had been brought to the Helena jail, "but the presence of United States soldiers and advice of some level-headed [people] prevented the purpose of the mob. They were told that if the mob would not lynch the negroes that they would be tried and convicted." He had made the affidavit relating these facts "freely and voluntarily to the end that justice may be done," Jones concluded, "and I stand ready at any time to testify in any court orally as to the facts and statements herein made."[67]

H. F. Smiddy related essentially the same story as Jones in his affidavit. Smiddy, however, also said he had examined the black church at Hoop Spur, "and on the inside we found a condition that showed that the last people who had been in the church had left there hurriedly. Benches were turned over, window lights broken out on all sides of the church, glass scattered all over the floor, women's and men's hats and coats scattered around over the floor and every evidence of a stampede in the church house." Progressive Farmers Union literature, Smiddy said, was found in the church. He examined the outside of the church and "found where the church had been shot into from the north side." The church was subsequently burned, Smiddy testified, adding "I was told that it was burned down to destroy the evidence that it had been fired into by those that went there to break up the meeting."[68]

Smiddy joined a posse of fifty to sixty men, he said, and as "we marched down the thicket to the southwest I saw about five or six negroes come out unarmed, holding up their hands, and some running and trying to get away. They were shot down and killed by members of the posse. I didn't see a single negro during all the man hunt that was armed, and I didn't see a single negro fire a shot." Smiddy claimed he had been with Lieutenant James Tappan when he was killed, and although he did not know who had killed the lieutenant, he felt "perfectly sure that he was accidentally killed by a member of our own posse [which was firing] on the other side of the thicket from us." During the riot, Smiddy further stated, large groups of men from Mississippi arrived in the county "and began the indiscriminate hunting down, shooting and killing of negroes. They shot and killed men, women, and children without regard to whether they were guilty or innocent or had any connection with the killing of anybody, or whether members of the union or not. I do not know how many negroes were killed in all, but I do know that there were between two hundred and three hundred negroes killed that I saw with my own eyes."[69]

He had personally escorted black prisoners back and forth from the Helena jail to be interrogated by the Committee of Seven, Smiddy swore, and if the blacks' stories were not satisfactory to the committee, they would be whipped with a seven-pound strap.

I have personally applied the lash to a great number of these negroes. . . . [The] lash was applied on the old sores made at the first whipping, and usually the second whipping would get the negro to say what was wanted if he had refused in the first instance. While the negroes were being whipped they were stretched out on their stomachs on the concrete floor, with four negroes [jail trusties] holding them down, one holding each hand and one holding each leg. In this manner evidence was extorted from the negroes which was used against them in their trials, and so far as my observation went, and I was present throughout all of it, the only evidence on behalf of the State that the State had was acquired in this manner.[70]

The affidavits of Jones and Smiddy thus corroborated the affidavits defense counsel had secured from a few Phillips County blacks, who swore that torture had been used to secure testimony against the condemned men. This new evidence came at a crucial time for the defense, since the U.S. Supreme Court on August 4, 1921, had refused to review the decision of the Arkansas Supreme Court ordering the Pulaski County Chancery Court to dismiss the writs of habeas corpus and the injunction with regard to the *Moore* prisoners. McHaney and Jones immediately sought to obtain review of that decision by filing a petition for a writ of certiorari in the U.S. Supreme Court, but the Court was in adjournment until October and, in any case, was unlikely to grant the petition for certiorari after having already refused to grant a writ of error. Governor McRae set September 23 as the new execution date, following. The lives of the condemned men were once again in peril.[71]

On September 21 Governor McRae refused to commute the sentences or to postpone the executions, and Jones and McHaney played the final card in their strategy to save the condemned men: they filed a petition for a writ of habeas corpus in the U.S. District Court for the Eastern District of Arkansas.[72] Defense counsel were invoking what Blackstone had called "the most celebrated writ in the English law." Developed by the English courts as a common law writ, and received into American law during the colonial period, the writ of habeas corpus allows a court to order those holding an individual in custody to produce that person in court and justify the legality of his detention, and empowers the court to order the individual's release from custody if his detention is found to be unlawful. Habeas corpus is, therefore, a fundamental judicial protection against the arbitrary and unlawful imprisonment of individuals. "Although in form the Great Writ [of habeas corpus] is simply a mode of procedure, its history is inextricably intertwined with the growth of fundamental rights of personal liberty," the U.S. Supreme Court has said. "For its function has been to provide a prompt and efficacious remedy for whatever society deems to be intolerable restraints. Its root principle is that in a civilized society, government must always be accountable to the judiciary for a man's imprisonment: if the imprisonment cannot be shown to conform to the fundamental requirements of law, the individual is entitled to his immediate release."[73]

Article I, section 9 of the Constitution provides that the "Privilege of the Writ of Habeas Corpus shall not be suspended, unless when in Cases of Rebellion or Invasion the public Safety may require it." Although this language appears to assume the general availability of the writ of habeas corpus, the power of the federal courts to issue the writ has historically depended upon congressional statutes conferring it upon them under certain circumstances. The first Congress provided in the Judiciary Act of 1789 that the federal courts should have the power to issue writs of habeas corpus, but the availability of the writ was limited to those persons who were confined in custody by federal authorities. And with but two exceptions, the power of the federal courts to issue writs of habeas corpus was not extended to persons held in the custody of state authorities until after the Civil War.[74]

In the wake of that conflict, Congress passed the Habeas Corpus Act of 1867, and under its provisions extended the habeas corpus jurisdiction of the federal courts to persons held in the custody of either federal or state authorities in violation of their federally protected rights. The federal courts, the act provided, "shall have power to grant writs of habeas corpus in all cases where any person may be restrained of his or her liberty in violation of the constitution, or of any treaty or law of the United States. . . ." Upon petition for a writ of habeas corpus filed on behalf of an individual allegedly being held in custody in violation of federal law, the act provided, the "court or judge shall proceed in a summary way to determine the facts of the case by hearing testimony and the arguments of the parties interested, and if it shall appear that the petitioner is deprived of his or her liberty in contravention of the constitution or laws of the United States, he or she shall forthwith be discharged and set at liberty."[75]

It was under the Habeas Corpus Act of 1867 that Jones and McHaney filed the petition for a writ of habeas corpus in the U.S. district court on behalf of the *Moore* blacks. Their petition charged that the defendants in the *Moore* cases were being unlawfully restrained "of their liberty" by the warden of the Arkansas state penitentiary, E. H. Dempsey, who "will, unless prevented from doing so by the issuance of the writ [of habeas corpus], deprive them of their lives on the 23rd day of Sept. 1921, in violation of the Constitution and laws of the United States." Jones and McHaney essentially recited the NAACP's version of the Phillips County riot claiming that blacks had been peacefully attempting to obtain settlements for their cotton and statements of their accounts when they were attacked by whites. The strong opposition of the whites in the county to the efforts of blacks to obtain settlements and statements of accounts, the petition also noted, was evidenced by the jailing of O. S. Bratton for a month and the filing of a barratry charge against him.[76] Furthermore, the evidence against the men in the *Moore* cases, the petition said, had been secured by the Committee of Seven through the use of torture. If blacks failed to give satisfactory testimony to the committee, they were whipped with "leather straps with metal in them, cutting the blood at every lick until the victim would agree to testify to anything their torturers demanded of them," while some of the blacks were placed in an electric chair "naked and the current turned on to shock and frighten them into giving damaging statements against themselves and others; also strangling drugs were put up their noses for the same purpose and by these methods and means false evidence was extorted from Negroes to be used and was used against [the *Moore* defendants]."[77]

The condemned men had been indicted by a wholly white grand jury on October 29, 1919, the petition pointed out. It charged that on the "3rd day of November 1919, [they] were taken into the court room before the judge, told of the charge, and were informed that a certain lawyer was appointed to defend them; that they were given no opportunity to employ an attorney of their own choice; that the appointed attorney did not consult with them, took no steps to prepare for their defense, asked nothing about their witnesses, though there were many who knew that [the *Moore* men] had nothing to do with the killing of [Clinton] Lee; that they were immediately placed on joint trial before an exclusively white jury and the trial closed so far as the evidence was concerned with the State's witnesses alone; that after the court's instructions, the jury retired just long enough to write a verdict of guilty of murder in the first degree, as charged, and returned with it into court—not being out exceeding two or three minutes, and they were promptly sentenced to death by electrocution for December 27th, 1919."[78]

During the trial, the petition went on, "large crowds of white people bent on [their] condemnation and death thronged the courthouse and grounds and streets of Helena." Given the widespread publicity devoted to the story that Phillips County blacks had planned an insurrection against the whites, the fact that several whites were killed during the riot, "and on account of all the race prejudice which normally exists and which was enhanced a thousand fold at the time, by bitterness beyond expression, [it] was impossible for [the condemned blacks] to get a fair and impartial trial in said court before a jury of white men." Indeed,

the feeling against [the men on trial] was such that it over-awed the Judge on the bench, the jury, the attorney appointed to defend them and everyone connected with said court; that all, Judge, jury and counsel were dominated by the mob spirit that was universally present in court and out. . . . [As a] result of the mob domination of court, counsel and jury, the court, although a court of original jurisdiction in felony cases, lost its jurisdiction by virtue of such mob domination and the result was but an empty ceremony, carried through in the apparent form of law, and that the verdict of the jury was really a mob verdict, dictated by the spirit of the mob and pronounced and returned because no other verdict would have been tolerated, and that the judgment against [the *Moore* blacks] is, therefore, a nullity.[79]

Since the evidence against them had been procured through the use of torture, their trial had been mob-dominated and the grand juries and trial juries that had indicted and convicted them had been selected in a racially discriminatory manner, the petition summed up, the condemned blacks had been "deprived of their rights and are about to be deprived of their lives in violation of Section 1, of the 14th Amendment of the Constitution of the United States and the laws of the United States enacted in pursuance thereto, in that they have been denied the equal protection of the law, and have been convicted, condemned, and are about to be deprived of their lives without due process of law; that they are now in the custody of the defendant, E. H. Dempsey, Keeper of the Arkansas State Penitentiary, to be electrocuted on the 23rd day of September, 1921; that they are now detained and held in custody by said Keeper and will be electrocuted on said date unless prevented from so doing by the issuance of a writ of Habeas Corpus." The petition concluded with a request that the U.S. district court issue a writ of habeas corpus "to the end that [the condemned men] may be discharged from said unlawful imprisonment and unlawful judgment and sentence to death."[80]

Jones and McHaney attached to the petition for a writ of habeas corpus the affidavits of Walter Ward; George Green; John Jefferson; Alf Banks, Jr.; and William Wordlow, each having testified that he had been tortured into giving false testimony at the trials.[81] The affidavits of T. K. Jones and H. F. Smiddy, the white railroad special agents whose testimony corroborated the affidavits of the blacks, were likewise attached to the petition.[82] To support the allegation of extreme prejudice against the condemned men on the part of the whites of Phillips County, Jones and McHaney also attached to the habeas corpus petition the press release of the Committee of Seven, in which the blacks were accused of plotting an armed insurrection against the whites; and a letter from the Committee of Seven and resolutions from the Helena American Legion post, Lions Club, and Rotary Club, all urging the execution of the condemned men and pointing out that Phillips County white citizens had been promised the execution of the blacks if they would refrain from lynching them.[83]

With the filing of the petition for a writ of habeas corpus in the U.S. District Court for the Eastern District of Arkansas on

September 21, 1921, Scipio Jones and E. L. McHaney were once again able to postpone the executions of men in the *Moore* cases. The habeas corpus proceedings in the federal courts stayed the carrying out of the death sentences by the State of Arkansas. Jones and McHaney had now resorted to the last possible judicial avenue by which the condemned men could be saved. Considering the law governing the issuance of writs of habeas corpus by the federal courts that prevailed at the time, the possibility of success for Jones and McHaney appeared to be extremely doubtful. More time had been bought for the condemned men, but a long and difficult legal battle in *Moore* v. *Dempsey* lay ahead for the NAACP and its counsel, and the outcome was not promising.

7 Moorfield Storey's Appeal: *Moore* v. *Dempsey* in the Supreme Court

Judge Jacob Trieber presided over the U.S. District Court for the Eastern District of Arkansas in which the habeas corpus petition in *Moore* v. *Dempsey* was filed, but, as a former resident of Phillips County, he disqualified himself from presiding at the habeas corpus hearing.[1] Consequently, U.S. District Judge J. H. Cotteral of Guthrie, Oklahoma, came to Little Rock to conduct the hearing.[2]

The response of the State of Arkansas to the petition for a writ of habeas corpus could not have been more favorable to the NAACP and the six condemned men. Arkansas Attorney General Utley merely filed a demurrer to the petition, but did not dispute its factual allegations. The petition, the demurrer said, did "not allege facts sufficient to entitle the [*Moore* group] to the relief prayed for in [the] petition."[3] Because the attorney general confined himself to a demurrer, and did not challenge the defense allegations, the federal courts, in passing upon the petition, would treat as true those factual allegations. The state, in declining to produce the numerous witnesses who had previously disputed the testimony of torture and mob domination, had given defense counsel an important advantage in the federal proceedings. Indeed, the attorney general's response to the habeas corpus petition was a vital factor in the NAACP's ulti-

mate victory in the *Moore* litigation.[4] A hearing on the petition
and the demurrer was held before Judge Cotteral on September
26. On the following day, Judge Cotteral sustained the state's
demurrer and ordered the dismissal of the petition for a writ of
habeas corpus. At the same time, he ruled that there was "probable cause for an appeal in this cause," thus authorizing defense
counsel to approach the U.S. Supreme Court. For a third time,
the NAACP would appeal the cases of the *Moore* blacks to the
highest court in the land.[5]

While these legal actions were proceeding, a serious conflict
arose between the national office of the NAACP and E. L. Mc-
Haney. McHaney, informing the NAACP that he had secured affidavits from the two special railroad agents, had asked the
NAACP for more money to employ additional counsel for the
retrial of the *Ware* cases in October and also an additional fee
for his firm. "I would like to know definitely, by wire, on receipt
of this letter," McHaney wrote the NAACP, "if we may be authorized to employ local counsel in Marianna, Ark., and promise
him that he will be paid his fee of $2500.00 and we would like
also to know whether we can be supplied with a reasonable
amount of money, say $5000.00 for expenses."[6]

The board of directors of the NAACP considered this demand,
but because McHaney's firm had agreed, after Colonel Murphy's
death, to represent the Phillips County blacks for the mutually
acceptable fee of $5000, the board refused to authorize the pay-
ment of additional money. They felt "that the contract of the
Arkansas attorneys with the Association obligated them to carry
through the cases for the sums agreed upon and that the demand for $7500 was both exorbitant and beyond the resources
of the Association." The board directed the secretary of the Association to "prepare a letter to be sent to the Arkansas counsel
pointing out that the Association had paid them well for the
defense of the condemned men and expected them to see the
case through in accordance with their agreement, as the Association intended to fulfill all its obligation."[7] On September 15
James Weldon Johnson accordingly replied to McHaney, pointing out that "the Association has no such amounts on hand and
I see no immediate prospect of its getting them. As I understand
the arrangement which was entered into between the Association and your firm," Johnson reminded McHaney, "you were to
receive in addition to $3000.00 paid Colonel Murphy and the

amounts that were paid out for costs and incidental expenses, the sum of $5000 and for this $5000 you agreed to perform all the services outlined in the agreement which we had with Colonel Murphy including all legal services except the final argument in the United States Supreme Court."[8]

On September 16, before he had received this letter, McHaney sent a telegram to the Association. He and his firm "are not getting the support we are entitled to receive in these cases here and we respectfully tender our resignation as attorneys for the defendants and ask that you secure other counsel."[9] James Weldon Johnson then told McHaney that the Association declined "to accept your resignation and shall expect you to carry the cases through to a conclusion in accordance with your agreement with us. We shall carry out all our obligations with you and assume you will do no less."[10] But McHaney and his firm at this point, in effect, ceased to be the principal counsel for the NAACP in the Phillips County cases, although the break was not complete and there was some subsequent involvement of the McHaney firm.[11] McHaney's actions produced considerable bitterness among NAACP officials; they felt the law firm had broken a clear commitment to see the cases through to the end. Walter White later denounced the "vicious conditions" the NAACP had encountered in the Phillips County cases, charging that McHaney and his firm "remained in the cases until they felt that they had gotten all of the money out of us that they could and then they dropped the cases. We had no recourse at law in Arkansas."[12] And Mary White Ovington complained that what "has provoked me has been that the colored lawyer seems to have been doing all the work, while the white lawyer has taken much of the money and left us at the crucial moment."[13]

Although Scipio Jones had initially been viewed with suspicion by the NAACP, Mary White Ovington's reference to the "colored lawyer" doing all of the work was an indication that Jones had come to be appreciated by the Association. After the "resignation" of E. L. McHaney and his firm, Jones became the principal Arkansas counsel in the cases; the NAACP was referring to him as "the Association's attorney in Arkansas" by the late fall of 1921.[14]

Jones and the NAACP were confronted with two immediate problems during that fall. An appeal of the U.S. district court's dismissal of the habeas corpus petition in *Moore* v. *Dempsey* had to be perfected in the U.S. Supreme Court and preparations had to be undertaken for the defense of the men in the *Ware* cases who faced retrial in Marianna. Scipio Jones recommended that a white law firm in Marianna be retained to represent the *Ware* group, and although the Association was reluctant to spend additional funds, Jones was finally authorized to retain the firm.[15] When the *Ware* cases were called for trial in the Lee County Circuit Court on October 10, 1921, the prosecution requested that the cases be continued until the April 1922 term of the court and this request was granted.[16] Scipio Jones reported to the NAACP that it was his opinion that the request for a continuance was "an indirect admission that the State has not sufficient evidence to justify the conviction [of the *Ware* defendants] and did not have [such evidence] at the former trials."[17]

By late October 1921 Jones had filed the transcript of the record and an appeal in *Moore* v. *Dempsey* in the U.S. Supreme Court.[18] He urged the NAACP to "secure the ablest constitutional lawyer possible" to argue the case.[19] The president of the NAACP, Moorfield Storey, was the logical choice to conduct the case in the Supreme Court, and officers of the Association immediately began to urge him to take it on. "You are our 'ablest constitutional lawyer,'" Mary White Ovington wrote to Storey, "and I know you will be tremendously interested to learn that these cases have reached our highest tribunal. Of course, we want to aid you in every possible way."[20] Walter White wrote Storey with the same request, but Storey resisted their appeals. "You suggest that I should present the case to the Supreme Court of the United States," Storey replied to White, "and for many reasons I should like to do so. I am, however, an old and very busy man, and I should be glad to have some younger man take the case. Mr. [U. S.] Bratton, who is the counsel thoroughly familiar with the matter from the beginning, and whose heart is interested in the business, could present the case to the court with a feeling and I think with a power that no one else could equal." "Why wouldn't it be well to ask him to act?"[21] The *Moore* case was unlikely to appear before the Court for at least a year, Storey continued, and "I am trying to retire from practice, and am now engaged in a case which takes a portion of every week, and seems likely to take it for some months. I do not want to undertake the argument of this case, and I wish you would consider my suggestion of Mr. Bratton. He was in at the beginning, and is, I think, from what I know of him, a competent lawyer."[22]

Walter White responded to Storey on October 26: "it is a source of keen disappointment to us that you feel that you are unable to argue the Arkansas cases in the United States Supreme Court. I wrote you . . . with a great deal of reluctance, because we realized how busy you were, that you were quite rightly conserving your strength as much as possible, and that you have rendered so great service to the cause." White noted that the executives of the NAACP would soon be meeting, at which time he would raise the question of retaining U. S. Bratton to argue the case, but, he continued, "Our great desire to have you present [the argument in the *Moore* case], was due to your interest and because of your prominence as a lawyer. While I agree that Mr. Bratton is an able lawyer yet his lack of prominence, his connection with a labor union and his lack of impressiveness will militate against him. This, of course, is written to you out of frankness and with no desire to disparage Mr. Bratton's interest and ability."[23]

The NAACP officers refused to accept Storey's position as final. In early November Johnson urged Storey to reconsider. No "name that we could mention would have such significance to colored people of the country in arguing these cases before the Supreme Court as your own, and in case of a victory in the court your name would mean a double victory for the Association," Johnson wrote. A younger lawyer could be retained to handle the details of conducting the case, and if "that detailed work were lifted from your shoulders, I wonder if you could not then appear."[24]

"I do not wish to refuse absolutely to appear for the Arkansas Negroes in the Supreme Court of the United States," Storey replied to Johnson, "but I must be satisfied before I do appear that they have a good case. I do not mean by that that they have a case that is good on the facts, but that there is some authority which will sustain their present application to the court. I have not had time to study the question," Storey continued, "and I am not likely to have, for I have a great many things on my mind, and very little time to spare. I probably have not many more years to live, and there are things that I want to accomplish while I can."[25] Storey left the door open to his participation in the *Moore* case, noting that the "Arkansas cases have always appealed to my sympathy, and that carries me a great way. If any good lawyer would prepare the cases and then submit them to me for my judgment, and I find I can speak with some conviction, I will try to do so, but I do not want to appear in court with a case that I cannot maintain."[26]

The NAACP allowed the situation to remain fluid as all concerned waited for the months to pass before the Supreme Court would reach the case. In July 1922, the Association publicly announced that Storey would argue the *Moore* case before the Court. Storey wrote James Weldon Johnson: "I note that you announce that I have promised to argue the Arkansas cases in the Supreme Court. I promised only if after reading the record I found that I had an arguable case. I have never seen the record. Can you get me a copy?"[27] The NAACP had lured Storey into agreeing to read the record at least. Having read it, Storey reported to the Association that it was his opinion the case could not be won in the Supreme Court. "I received the record in the Arkansas cases," Storey wrote Mary White Ovington on November 13, "and I am very much afraid that under the decision of the Supreme Court in the case of [Leo] Frank, whom you will remember was tried under very bad circumstances in Atlanta, we shall not be able to win the case, but I am going to try."[28]

Storey was finally committed to arguing the *Moore* case, but his prediction of the chances for success was gloomy news for the NAACP. "It is a bit discouraging to read that you fear we shall not be able to win the Arkansas cases under the decision of the Supreme Court in the case of [Leo] Frank," Walter White wrote Storey, "but we are indeed glad that you are going to try."[29] Storey was more encouraging in his response to White: "It is rather my habit when I enlist in a case to grow more and more confident that my cause is just, and that process is going on in the Arkansas cases. The Supreme Court in the Frank case made it clear that a case can be presented in which habeas corpus will issue, and I cannot help thinking that if that is so, it would be impossible to find a stronger case than the one which we have."[30]

The Supreme Court decision troubling Storey was *Frank* v. *Mangum*, handed down by the Court in 1915.[31] Leo M. Frank, charged with the murder of a thirteen-year-old girl, Mary Phagan, was brought to trial on that charge in Atlanta, Georgia, during the summer of 1913. Frank was convicted by a jury of murder in the first degree, but in a motion for a new trial and subsequent proceedings, his counsel alleged that a hostile mob had dominated Frank's trial and so influenced both judge and jury as to deny him the fair trial guaranteed by due process of law. A large crowd, hostile to Frank, thronged about the court-house at his trial, greeting the prosecutor with thunderous applause and shouting, "Hang the Jew, or we'll hang you." When the jury's verdict of guilty was announced, the roar of approval from the crowd was so loud that the trial judge for a time could not hear the responses of the jurors as they were polled. Frank's conviction was upheld by the Georgia Supreme Court on each of the three occasions on which it was appealed, and the U.S. Supreme Court refused to grant a writ of error.[32]

Frank's lawyers had then sought his release from state custody by filing a petition for a writ of habeas corpus in a U.S. district court. They charged that Frank had been denied a fair trial, as required by the Due Process Clause of the Fourteenth Amendment of the U.S. Constitution, by virtue of the mob domination of the proceedings and the fact that his trial counsel, at the urging of the trial judge, had waived Frank's right to be present in the courtroom when the jury's verdict was announced. The trial judge had urged both Frank and his counsel to absent themselves from the announcement of the verdict because he feared that there might be violence against them if the jury failed to convict Frank.[33] The U.S. district court dismissed the petition for a writ of habeas corpus, and an appeal was taken from this decision to the U.S. Supreme Court. In *Frank v. Mangum*, decided on April 19, 1915, the Supreme Court upheld the dismissal. A majority opinion, written by Justice Mahlon Pitney, gave an interpretation of the Due Process Clause of the Fourteenth Amendment, as well as of principles governing the habeas corpus jurisdiction of the federal courts with regard to persons in state custody on convictions for state crimes, that clearly cast serious doubt upon the NAACP's chances of winning *Moore v. Dempsey* some eight years later.[34]

Addressing the power of the federal courts to issue writs of habeas corpus for persons in state custody, the Supreme Court had held in *Frank* that a federal court should not normally issue a writ of habeas corpus until the state prisoner seeking the writ had exhausted the judicial remedies available to him in the courts of the state holding him in custody and had applied to the U.S. Supreme Court for a writ of error, seeking its review of the final decision of the state courts. Where "it is made to appear to a court of the United States that an applicant for habeas corpus is in the custody of a state officer in the ordinary course of a criminal prosecution, under a law of the state not in itself repugnant to the Federal Constitution," the Court said, "the writ, in the absence of very special circumstances, ought not to be issued until the state prosecution has reached its conclusion, and not even then until the Federal questions arising upon the record have been brought before this court upon writ of error."[35]

On the other hand, the Court rejected the contention that in habeas corpus proceedings involving persons in state custody the federal courts were limited to inquiring only into whether the state courts possessed valid jurisdiction over the subject matter and the person of the individual in custody. Under the Habeas Corpus Act of 1867, the Court pointed out, Congress had liberalized the traditional rules that governed the scope of judicial inquiry under habeas corpus in order to protect all persons in the United States from being held in custody in violation of the U.S. Constitution and laws. Consequently, under the act of 1867 a "prisoner in custody pursuant to the final judgment of a state court of criminal jurisdiction may have a judicial inquiry in a court of the United States into the very truth and substance of the causes of his detention, although it may become necessary to look behind and beyond the record of his conviction to a sufficient extent to test the jurisdiction of the state court to proceed to judgment against him."[36] The Court announced limitations on the writ, as well, saying, if a person "is held in custody by reason of his conviction upon a criminal charge before a court having plenary jurisdiction over the subject-matter or offense, the place where it was committed, and the person of the prisoner, it results from the nature of the writ itself that he cannot have relief on habeas corpus. Mere errors in points of law, however serious, committed by a criminal court in the exercise of its jurisdiction over a case properly subject to its cognizance, cannot be reviewed by habeas corpus. That writ cannot be employed as a substitute for the writ of error."[37]

In addition to elucidating these general criteria, the Court pointed out that a person seeking a writ of habeas corpus must claim to be held in violation of the Constitution and laws of the United States. The charge in Leo Frank's case was that Frank's conviction and sentence to death in the Georgia courts violated the Due Process Clause. Defining the due process of law guaranteed by the Fourteenth Amendment and thus applicable to state criminal proceedings, the Court held that "it is perfectly well settled that a criminal prosecution in the courts of a state, based upon a law not in itself repugnant to the Federal Constitution, and conducted according to the settled course of judicial proceedings as established by the law of the state, so long as it includes notice and a hearing, or an opportunity to be heard, before a court of competent jurisdiction, according to established modes of procedure, is 'due process' in the constitutional sense."[38] Under such a general and flexible definition of due process, relatively few constraints upon the conduct of criminal proceedings by the states were imposed, although the Court conceded that a state trial that was actually dominated by a mob would indeed violate the Due Process Clause. "We, of course, agree that if a trial is in fact dominated by a mob, so that the jury is intimidated and the trial judge yields, and so that there is an actual interference with the course of justice, there is, in that court, a departure from due process of law in the proper sense of that term," the Court said. "And if the state, supplying no corrective process, carries into execution a judgment of death or imprisonment based upon a verdict thus produced by mob domination, the state deprives the accused of his life or liberty without due process of law."[39]

But in evaluating whether a state criminal defendant has been denied due process, the Court held, a federal court in a habeas corpus proceeding must not limit its inquiry to the conduct of the trial alone but must consider any appellate review as well, since

the proceedings in the appellate tribunal are to be regarded as a part of the process of law under which he is held in custody by the state, and to be considered in determining any question of alleged deprivation of his life or liberty contrary to the 14th Amendment. . . . It follows as a logical consequence that where, as here, a criminal prosecution has proceeded through all the courts of the state, including the appellate as well as the trial court, the result of the appellate review cannot be ignored when afterwards the prisoner applies for his release on ground of a deprivation of Federal rights sufficient to oust the state of its jurisdiction to proceed to judgment and execution against him. This is not a mere matter of comity, as seems to be supposed. The rule stands upon a much higher plane, for it arises out of the very nature and ground of the inquiry into the proceedings of the state tribunals, and touches closely upon the relations between the state and the Federal governments.[40]

The Court examined the appellate review afforded Frank as well as the trial proceedings and ruled that the State of Georgia had supplied a "corrective process" in allowing for a motion for a new trial and an appeal to the state supreme court. In fact, the Court noted, Frank's case had been reviewed three times by the Georgia Supreme Court and on each occasion that court had rejected his contention that he had been denied due process because of mob domination of his trial. The Court said, "[w]e hold that such a determination of the facts as was thus made by the court of last resort of Georgia respecting the alleged interference with the trial through disorder and manifestations of hostile sentiment cannot, in this collateral inquiry, be treated as a nullity, but must be taken as setting forth the truth of the matter; certainly until some reasonable ground is shown for an inference that the court which rendered it either is wanting in jurisdiction, or at least erred in the exercise of its jurisdiction; and that the mere assertion by the prisoner that the facts of the matter are other than the state court, upon full investigation, determined them to be, will not be deemed sufficient to raise an issue respecting the correctness of that determination. . . ." As far as the mob-domination issue in Frank's case was concerned, the Court consequently held, there "was here no denial of due process of law."[41]

Turning to Frank's contention that he had been denied due process of law because he had not been present when the jury's verdict was announced, the Court pointed out that this issue had not been raised by Frank's counsel in the motion for a new trial. The Georgia Supreme Court had ruled that Georgia procedure prohibited the raising of such an issue except in a motion for a new trial, and the state court therefore refused to pass upon the point when it was raised in a subsequent appeal. The U.S. Supreme Court held that the states were free to adopt reasonable rules governing the method and manner in which legal questions might be raised in proceedings in their courts. "There is nothing in the 14th Amendment," the Court held, "to prevent a state from adopting and enforcing so reasonable a regulation of procedure."[42] The court ruled in addition that "[t]he presence of the prisoner when the verdict is rendered is not so essential a part of the hearing that a rule of practice permitting the accused to waive it, and holding him bound by the waiver, amounts to a deprivation of 'due process of law.'"[43] In Frank's case, the State of Georgia, "through its courts, has retained jurisdiction over him, has accorded to him the fullest right and opportunity to be heard according to the established modes of procedure, and now holds him in custody to pay the penalty of the crime of which he had been adjudged guilty," the Court concluded. "In our opinion, he is not shown to have been deprived of any right guaranteed to him by the 14th Amendment or any other provision of the Constitution of the United States; on the contrary, he has been convicted, and is now held in custody, under 'due process of law' within the meaning of the Constitution."[44]

Applying the principles enunciated by the Supreme Court in *Frank* v. *Mangum* to the facts in *Moore* v. *Dempsey*, it appeared first of all that the *Moore* case presented no problem from the standpoint of exhaustion of state judicial remedies. The case had been reviewed by the Arkansas Supreme Court on direct appeal from the Circuit Court of Phillips County, and aspects of the case had again been passed upon when the Arkansas Supreme Court issued a writ of prohibition ordering the quashing of the writs of habeas corpus and the injunction issued by the Pulaski County Chancery Court. Both decisions of the state supreme court had been appealed to the U.S. Supreme Court, but the Court had declined review. The Court's holding in the *Frank* case that state remedies must be exhausted and review sought from the Supreme Court before habeas corpus proceedings could be properly begun in the federal courts had been fully complied with in *Moore*.[45] The principal problem that the decision in the *Frank* case posed to the winning of the *Moore* case in the Supreme Court was the Court's ruling in *Frank* that if a state supplied a "corrective process" by which allegations of violations of federal constitutional rights could be fairly evaluated by a state appellate court, the state would be considered to have given a criminal defendant due process of law. And, the Court had additionally held, the state appellate court's resolution of the factual allegations on violation of federal constitutional rights was to be given great weight in any subsequent habeas corpus proceeding in the federal courts. There must be some reasonable ground to show that the state appellate court either lacked jurisdiction or erred in the exercise of its jurisdiction before that court's resolution of such factual allegations could be impeached in a federal habeas corpus proceeding, and "the mere assertion by the prisoner that the facts of the matter are other than the state court, upon full investigation, determined them to be" was not a sufficient ground for a federal court to override the state court's resolution of the factual issues.

Although the Court in the *Frank* case had conceded that mob domination of the proceedings would constitute a denial of a fair trial, and mob domination was one aspect of the allegation that due process had been violated in the *Moore* case, Arkansas had seemingly provided a "corrective process" by affording appellate review in the state supreme court of the convictions. The state supreme court had resolved the factual allegations of an unfair trial and the use of torture to secure evidence in the *Moore* case adversely to the convicted men. Addressing the argument that the trials had been unfair, the Arkansas Supreme Court had said that it was "unable . . . to say that this must necessarily have been the case. The trials were according to law, the jury was correctly charged as to the law of the case, and the testimony is legally sufficient to support the verdicts returned. We cannot, therefore, in the face of this affirmative showing, assume that the trial was an empty ceremony, conducted for the purpose only of appearing to comply with the requirements of the law, when they were not in fact being complied with."[46]

In order for Moorfield Storey and the NAACP to win in the Supreme Court, it would be necessary for them to successfully argue either that the Arkansas Supreme Court had erroneously resolved the factual allegations on the unfair trial and torture issues or that the appellate review afforded by Arkansas had not allowed a full and fair opportunity for the airing of the charges of violation of due process. The *Frank* decision had also shown that the issue of racial discrimination in the selection of grand and trial juries could not be validly raised in these habeas corpus proceedings. For the Court in the *Frank* case had held that the issue of Frank's absence during the announcement of the verdict in his trial having not been raised at the appropriate time under state procedure, the state courts had properly refused to pass upon the question. And, the Court had indicated, issues that the state courts refused to pass upon due to their not having been raised at the appropriate time under reasonable state procedural rules could not subsequently be raised in a habeas corpus proceeding in the federal courts. As the issue of racial discrimination in the selection of the grand and trial juries in the *Moore* case had not been raised at the appropriate time under Arkansas procedure, and the Arkansas Supreme Court for that reason had refused to pass upon that issue,[47] under the principles of the *Frank* case, it could not be raised in the subsequent habeas corpus proceedings in the federal courts.[48]

While the decision in *Frank* v. *Mangum* posed a difficult hurdle for Moorfield Storey and the NAACP, other factors provided some reason to hope for a successful outcome. First of all, the Supreme Court had not been unanimous in its decision in the *Frank* case. Justice Oliver Wendell Holmes, joined by Justice Charles Evans Hughes, had filed a powerful and persuasive dissenting opinion in the case. In that opinion, Holmes pointed out that

habeas corpus cuts through all forms and goes to the very tissue of the structure. It comes in from the outside, not in subordination to the proceedings, and although every form may have been preserved, opens the inquiry whether they have been more than an empty shell. . . . Whatever disagreement there may be as to the scope of the phrase 'due process of law,' there can be no doubt that it embraces the fundamental conception of a fair trial, with opportunity to be heard. Mob law does not become due process of law by securing the assent of a terrorized jury. We are not speaking of mere disorder, or mere irregularities in procedure, but of a case where the processes of justice are actually subverted. In such a case, the Federal court has jurisdiction to issue the writ.[49]

Holmes disputed both the majority's ruling that the resolution by the state courts of the factual issues on a claim of violation of a federal right must be given almost conclusive weight in federal habeas corpus proceedings and their holding that the availability of a state corrective process for the consideration of violations of federal rights precluded an independent determination of such rights by the federal courts in habeas corpus proceedings. "When the decision of the question of fact is so interwoven with the decision of the question of constitutional right that the one necessarily involves the other, the Federal court must examine the facts," he said. "Otherwise, the right will be a barren one. It is significant that the argument for the state does not go so far as to say that in no case would it be permissible, on application for habeas corpus, to override the findings of fact by the state courts. It would indeed be a most serious thing if this court were so to hold, for we could not but regard it as a removal of what is perhaps the most important guaranty of the Federal Constitution."[50]

If the proceedings in the state trial court and the state appellate court had occurred in the presence of an armed force prepared to shoot if the result was not to its liking, Holmes continued, "we do not suppose that this court would allow itself to be silenced by the suggestion that the record showed no flaw." Or, to put another extreme case, Holmes said, if the trial court had been intimidated by an armed force prepared to shoot if the outcome of the trial was not to its liking, and the state supreme court on appeal could find no errors in the record of the trial, "we still imagine that this court would find a sufficient one outside of the record, and that it would not be disturbed in its conclusion by anything that the supreme court of the state might have said." If a petition for a writ of habeas corpus "discloses facts that amount to a loss of jurisdiction in the trial court, jurisdiction could not be restored by any decision above," Holmes said. "And notwithstanding the principle of comity and convenience . . . that calls for a resort to the local appellate tribunal before coming to the courts of the United States for a writ of habeas corpus, when, as here, that resort has been in vain, the power to secure fundamental rights that had existed at every stage becomes a duty, and must be put forth."[51] Assuming the facts about mob domination in the habeas corpus petition on behalf of Leo Frank were true, Holmes concluded, "we are of [the] opinion that if they were before the [Georgia] supreme court, it sanctioned a situation upon which the courts of the United States should act; and if, for any reason, they were not before the supreme court, it is our duty to act upon them now, and to declare lynch law as little valid when practiced by a regularly drawn jury as when administered by one elected by a mob intent on death."[52] The power of Holmes' dissent was undoubtedly enhanced by the widespread belief that a gross miscarriage of justice had occurred. And this belief could only have been reinforced when, after his sentence had been commuted to life imprisonment by the governor of Georgia, Leo Frank was kidnapped in August 1915 from a Georgia prison and lynched.[53]

Another favorable factor for the *Moore* defendants was the turnover in the personnel of the Supreme Court between 1915, when the *Frank* case was decided, and January of 1923, when *Moore* v. *Dempsey* was argued before the Court. Only three of

TABLE 1
Composition of the U.S. Supreme Court in the
Frank and *Moore* cases

The *Frank* Court (April 19, 1915)	The *Moore* Court (Feb. 19, 1923)
Edward D. White, C.J.	William Howard Taft, C.J.
Joseph McKenna	Joseph McKenna
Oliver W. Holmes	Oliver W. Holmes
William R. Day	Willis Van Devanter
Charles E. Hughes	James C. McReynolds
Willis Van Devanter	Louis D. Brandeis
Joseph R. Lamar	George Sutherland
Mahlon Pitney	Pierce Butler
James C. McReynolds	[1]

1. Justice Pitney was replaced by Edward T. Sanford, who was sworn in on February 19, 1923, the day the *Moore* case was decided. Except for the chief justices, the justices in the table are listed in order of seniority on the Court.

the justices who had joined in the majority in the *Frank* case remained on the Court in 1923—Justices McKenna, Van Devanter, and McReynolds—while Justice Holmes, who had so strongly dissented in the *Frank* case, also remained on the Court. Justice Joseph Lamar had died in 1916 and was replaced by Justice Louis D. Brandeis. The early 1920s had witnessed a significant turnover in the membership of the Court, with William Howard Taft replacing Edward D. White as Chief Justice in 1921, and Justices George Sutherland and Pierce Butler replacing Justices John Clarke and William R. Day in 1922 and 1923. And Justice Mahlon Pitney, who had written the majority opinion in *Frank*, retired on December 31, 1922, just a little over a week before *Moore* v. *Dempsey* was argued. His replacement, Justice Edward Sanford, was not sworn in until February 19, 1923, with the result that the *Moore* case was decided by an eight-person Court. (For the personnel of the Courts that decided the *Frank* and *Moore* cases, see table 1.)

The changes in the Court, however, were not necessarily favorable to Storey and the NAACP. Under Chief Justice Taft the Court was more conservative than it had been during the tenure of Chief Justice White. The Taft Court conceived the primary values protected by the Due Process Clause of the Fourteenth Amendment to be those related to economic and property rights, and despite the frequent opposition of Justices Holmes and Brandeis, it unhesitatingly struck down socioeconomic leg-

islation that it perceived as interfering unduly with the fundamental right of property.[54] Issues of civil liberty, such as were
involved in the *Moore* case, were not by any means assured of a
friendly reception.

Moorfield Storey, although finally committed to conducting
the defense of the Phillips County blacks, remained convinced
that it would be helpful to have the participation of U. S. Bratton in the presentation of the case to the Court. He told Walter
White so, after he had read the record in the case. Scipio Jones,
who pointed out to White that public feeling against Bratton
remained intense in Arkansas, was afraid that "Mr. Bratton's
connection with these cases will be used against us should we
be forced to apply again for executive clemency."[55] White communicated Jones's views to Storey. Jones "personally would like
very much to have Mr. Bratton in the cases," White said, "[but]
he entertains serious doubts about the advisability of having
him appear as the bitterness against Mr. Bratton in Arkansas
would probably militate against us in the event we were forced
to apply again for executive clemency."[56] White wrote Jones that
he was "in somewhat of a quandary as to what needs to be done
about Mr. Bratton. . . . We want to do nothing that would en-
danger the lives of the men now in jail in Arkansas, nor to jeop-
ardize the success of the trials [of the *Ware* men at Marianna]."
White continued, "On the other hand, it will have a splendid
psychological effect if Mr. Bratton, a white man from Arkansas,
who knows conditions behind these cases thoroughly, should
open the argument in the appeal to the Supreme Court." White
asked Jones to reconsider his opposition to Bratton's participation, and Jones finally agreed that Bratton should take part in
the oral argument.[57]

Jones still objected to having Bratton's name appear on the
brief to be filed in the Supreme Court: "If Mr. Bratton's name
appears on our printed briefs, when the Attorney General [of
Arkansas] receives his copy of the brief, the newspapers of
[Little Rock] will make capital of the fact that Mr. Bratton was
counselor for the Elaine prisoners, which in my opinion, will
prejudice the mind of the public against our clients and deprive
them of any chances they may have for executive clemency."
Jones suggested that Bratton participate in the oral argument,
but that his name should not appear on the brief.[58] Storey objected to White that it "would be very awkward to have Mr.
Bratton appear to argue the case without having his name on

the brief, and I do not think I can ask him to do it. If Jones thinks it is going to injure the chances of his clients in Arkansas to have Mr. Bratton appear, I certain[ly] shall not insist upon his so doing."[59] White assured Storey that he would have Scipio Jones "write Mr. Bratton and let him know exactly what the situation is in Arkansas" and that "Mr. Bratton is a man of a very broad mind and deeply sympathetic with us in these cases and I feel sure that there will be no hard feelings of any sort."[60] Consequently, Bratton was retained to participate in the oral argument, but his name did not appear on the brief filed in the case, which was prepared by Moorfield Storey. When he accepted the NAACP's retainer, Bratton assured White that "it will indeed be a pleasure for me to render any possible service in the way of assisting in getting the real facts and conditions before the Supreme Court."[61]

Moorfield Storey's brief, filed with the Supreme Court, vigorously argued that the U.S. district court's decision dismissing the petition for a writ of habeas corpus in *Moore* v. *Dempsey* should be reversed and that the district court should be directed to adjudicate the merits of the allegation that the *Moore* defendants had been denied due process of law by the State of Arkansas. The Phillips County blacks had been seeking lawful means to escape the peonage system under which they were being forced to live and work, Storey argued, and there was no convincing evidence that they had conspired to initiate an insurrection or to kill white people. And those blacks who had been condemned to death in the wake of the Phillips County riot had been subjected to trials that had lacked adequate notice of the charges against the defendants and inadequate representation by counsel. The trials incorporated evidence procured through torture, and they were dominated by a lynch mob atmosphere.

The "corrective process" provided by Arkansas for the review of the alleged violations of federal rights at the trials, Storey contended, had been inadequate, since in passing upon the charge that the trials had therefore been unfair, the Arkansas Supreme Court had merely held that it was "unable . . . to say that this must necessarily have been the case." Storey declared, "The court in dealing with the case treats the allegations in the motion for a new trial that the witnesses were tortured to make them testify against the defendants, and all the other allegations which show that at the trial the court was surrounded by a mob determined on a verdict of guilty, as incidents, and say that they cannot say that a fair trial was 'necessarily' impossible."[62]

It is difficult to conceive the state of mind of the court which would lead it to say that the torture of witnesses to make them give false testimony does not affect the fairness of the trial, but the thing which distinguishes this case from the *Frank* case is that the Supreme Court of Arkansas did not pass on the question whether the allegations in the motion for a new trial of violence, prejudice, torture and mob pressure on the jury were true or not. The court assumed that they were true, and said it did not follow from them that the trial was *necessarily* unfair. This is in substance saying the defendants must actually prove that the trial was unfair, whereas the well-established rule of law is that where circumstances like this are proved, the trial cannot stand unless it is affirmatively proved that it was fair. . . .[63]

Unlike the situation in the *Frank* case, Storey therefore asserted, the state had not provided an adequate "corrective process" for violations of the federal right to due process through review by the state supreme court. Rather the Arkansas Supreme Court had been "content to deny a new trial and send these defendants to their death without even considering whether the allegations contained in the motion [for a new trial] were true or not." "We contend," Storey charged, "that this opinion of the court shows what the feeling in the State was, and how indifferent the court was to the rights of the defendants."[64]

Storey pointed out to the Court that under Arkansas law, the supreme court could review and reverse criminal cases tried in the state circuit courts only upon the basis of legal errors occurring during proceedings in the trial court. The state supreme court could not pass upon or review questions of fact related to a criminal conviction. And since the allegation of the denial of a fair trial was essentially a question of fact, the state supreme court "could not, without exceeding its jurisdiction, reverse the action of the circuit [court] in refusing a new trial." Because of the legal limitations on the scope of the Arkansas Supreme Court's review of criminal convictions, Storey argued, the only court that had had the power to pass upon the charge of an unfair trial was the Circuit Court of Phillips County.

The theory of the decision in *Frank* v. *Mangum* . . . is that, in a situation like that now presented, a State cannot be said to have deprived an accused person of life or liberty without due process of law if it has provided an independent tribunal for the examination of his complaint, and this tribunal, sitting in an atmosphere free from the alleged disturbing elements, has held the complaint unfounded. Arkansas, as has just been shown, has made no provision of this kind. It would be preposterous to say that the requirements of the Fourteenth Amendment are satisfied by giving one seeking a new trial because the court in which he was tried was guilty of the grossest irregularities nothing but the empty right to have the facts upon which his application is based passed upon by the very judge whose conduct is complained of, and that, too, only at a time when the adverse influences, if they ever existed at all, must still be operative with all their force.[65]

The Court had held in the *Frank* case, Storey continued, that the Due Process Clause guaranteed to defendants in state criminal trials the right to a fair trial and that mob domination of a trial would result in the denial of this due process protection. The trial in the *Moore* case, he argued, "was in every respect unfair, the time occupied and the character of the evidence show how little effort was made to really determine the merits of the case. The public demanded victims, and the public demand overawed the courts with the result that these helpless and ignorant Negroes were convicted with a view to their prompt execution." Storey continued, "The evidence on which they were convicted was manufactured, the witnesses were beaten and terrorized, and the record of the whole case shows what, if consummated, is only judicial murder."[66] The circumstances in the *Moore* case differed greatly from those in the *Frank* case since Frank's trial had lasted for weeks and he had been represented by competent and effective counsel, with whom he was in constant deliberation regarding the conduct of his case. In the *Moore* case, Storey pointed out in contrast, "we have a trial lasting about three-quarters of an hour, held very shortly after the indictment, with no opportunity given the defendants to consult counsel, with no earnest defense, with no conference between clients and counsel, no opportunity to summon witnesses, no opportunity to take the stand in their own defense, none of the several rights which men on trial for their lives are entitled to be accorded in courts of justice."[67]

We have the whole community inflamed against the defendants, prepared themselves to lynch them, only refraining from so doing because they are assured by leading citizens that the trial should accomplish the same purpose, a condition of things where no man who was on that jury and had ventured to vote for acquittal or delay could have lived in Phillips County. . . . We have false statements printed in the newspapers; we have society substantially organized to convict these people; and more than that, we have witnesses deliberately terrorized and forced on pain of death or torture to give false testimony. We have the testimony of the men who inflicted the torture; we have a mass of evidence which shows, if evidence can show anything, that the defendants never had a fair trial and in fact that they were innocent. . . . [The courts of Arkansas] had not before them all the evidence which was presented to the District Court of the United States, and the questions which we ask this court to consider were never considered by those courts. The allegations of fact were never considered by the Supreme Court of Arkansas as they were by the Supreme Court of Georgia in the *Frank* case, but the opinions apparently assume that they were true. This distinction between the cases is vital.[68]

"There can be no question that the citizens of Helena were determined that these men should be convicted, and that they manufactured the evidence for the purpose; and for the court to say that it cannot assume that the accused *necessarily* did not have a fair trial shows clearly that the Supreme Court of Arkansas was itself influenced by the same feeling that influenced the leaders of society throughout the region where these tragedies occurred," Storey declared in conclusion. "If this Court on reading this petition, these affidavits and this record is not satisfied that if there ever was a case in which *habeas corpus* should be granted this is the case, no argument of counsel will convince them, and we submit with confidence that either *habeas corpus* should be granted in this case or *habeas corpus* is not a practical remedy for such outrages as the evidence in this case discloses. This is in fact the extreme case which the minority of this court used as an illustration in the *Frank* case."[69]

Arkansas Attorney General Utley sought to answer Storey's arguments in a brief filed on behalf of the State of Arkansas. More than half of this brief was devoted to reproducing the facts already in the record,[70] but on the legal merits, the attorney general denied that there had been a denial of due process of law in the *Moore* case, arguing, therefore, that the petition for a federal writ of habeas corpus had been properly dismissed by the district court.

"It is a well established principle of law that the due process of law that is required by Section 1 of [the Fourteenth Amendment] of the Constitution of the United States, that a criminal prosecution in the Courts of a State, based upon a law not itself repugnant to the federal Constitution, and conducted according to the settled course of judicial proceedings as established by the law of the State, so long as it includes notice and a hearing, or an opportunity to be heard, before a court of competent jurisdiction," the attorney general argued, "is due process of law in the sense that term is used in our Federal Constitution."[71]

The Phillips County Circuit Court, in which the trial was held, Utley pointed out, had been properly convened and constituted, the grand jury indictments had been lawfully returned, the defendants had been arraigned, the jurors had been lawfully summoned and qualified, the evidence and the motion for a new trial properly heard. It appeared, the attorney general continued, that the appellants "were charged with violating the law of murder and that such law is not repugnant to the Federal Constitution; that the prosecution of appellants by the State of Arkansas was conducted according to the well established course of judicial proceedings as established by the laws of said State; that appellants were present in person and by counsel at all stages of said proceedings; that the trials were had in accord with competent jurisdiction, according to well established modes of procedure." Therefore, "appellants were not denied the equal protection under the law, nor are they entitled to the relief sought under Section One of [the Fourteenth Amendment] of the Constitution of the United States."[72] Quoting extensively from the majority opinion in the *Frank* case, which he noted was "almost exactly in point with the case at bar,"[73] Utley contended that the federal writ of habeas corpus could not be properly issued in the *Moore* case.[74] "It is well established by the decisions of this court that the office of a writ of habeas corpus cannot be employed to review irregularities or alleged erroneous rulings made during the trial, however serious," and it could "only be invoked in cases where the judgments under which the persons are detained [are shown] to be absolutely void for want of jurisdiction in the court that pronounced them, either because such jurisdiction was absent from the beginning, or because it was lost during the course of the proceedings." But in the trial in the *Moore* case, the competent jurisdiction of the trial court was maintained throughout the proceedings.[75]

Utley quoted the sections of the opinion in the *Frank* case that held that if a state supplied a "corrective process," by which alleged violations of federal rights could be fairly and adequately evaluated, the state had afforded criminal defendants due process of law, and the evaluations of the state courts were not ordinarily to be overridden by the federal courts on petition for writs of habeas corpus. Arkansas had supplied such a corrective process by means of a motion for a new trial and review in the state supreme court, he argued, and the supreme court had affirmed the convictions after passing upon the claim that the trial had been unfair.[76] Further, many of the affidavits submitted to the U.S. district court on petition for a writ of habeas corpus had been obtained over a year after the Arkansas Supreme Court had affirmed the convictions. Utley argued,

The affidavits were never before the trial court, nor the Supreme Court on appeal. To sustain appellants' application for a writ of habeas corpus on said affidavits, would open an avenue for every person charged with a crime, to wait until he had exhausted his remedies in the State Courts; then open his masked batteries on the State Courts, by going to the Federal Courts by petition for habeas corpus, and support said petitions by affidavits made long after the case had been determined in the State Courts. We can hardly think that this court, or any court, would give its sanction to such practice. . . . Under such a procedure the State is deprived of searching the conscience of said affiants by way of cross examination. Again we desire to urge that for this Court to reverse the judgment of the United States District Court for the Western Division of the Eastern District of Arkansas would open an avenue for every criminal charged with violating our State laws, to open 'masked batteries' on our State Courts, indefinitely.[77]

The oral argument was presented before the U.S. Supreme Court by Moorfield Storey, U. S. Bratton, and Assistant Arkansas Attorney General Elbert Godwin on January 9, 1923. Under the headline "Arkansans Accused," the *Arkansas Gazette* reported that Moorfield Storey, "a former president of the American Bar Association, today charged the Arkansas courts, newspapers, leading citizens, Rotary Clubs, American Legion and other organizations of Helena with attempting to 'railroad the negroes to death.'" For the first time, the *Gazette* published the allegations of torture contained in the affidavits of the two white special railroad agents. The NAACP issued a press release on the oral argument in which it charged that the Arkansas Supreme Court had "railroaded negro peons to [a] death sentence."[78]

U. S. Bratton reported to Walter White that he felt "very hopeful for a reversal. The indications which I observed from the Court's remarks made me feel that they were convinced of the equity of our plea." Only Justice McReynolds appeared to respond negatively to the arguments of Storey and himself, Bratton said, and Justice Holmes had clearly been favorably disposed. "You do not contend," Holmes had asked counsel for Arkansas, "that if the whole affair was a mere sham, that however regular the proceedings may have been, this Court would be deprived of the right of going into the case and granting relief?" And as Moorfield Storey was reaching the conclusion of his argument, Holmes had asked, "Your contention is that the whole procedure was one dominated by a mob and that the conditions surrounding the trial were such as to render the whole trial a nullity, and that under the decisions of this Court in such cases, we have jurisdiction and it is our duty to give relief?" Chief Justice Taft had also seemed to be favorably disposed, Bratton reported, judging from his behavior when the counsel for Arkansas was disputing the truth of the allegations in the petition for a writ of habeas corpus. The Chief Justice had interrupted him and said, "Yes, but you demurred to the petition, thereby admitting the allegations of the [petition]."[79]

In the limited time allotted to him during the oral argument, Bratton said, he had "endeavored to get a mental picture in the minds of the Court as to the exact conditions in Arkansas. I told the Court that conditions had grown up there that were worse than before the Civil War. . . . I then gave them an insight as to the brutality administered to the prisoners." Bratton related the experience of his son, O. S. Bratton, at the hands of the Phillips County authorities. "I referred to the fact that wholesale murders on the part of the whites were committed by the killing of some 200 innocent negroes," Bratton continued, "and that not a single indictment had been returned; that if the influence of those in control of the Court was such as to prevent an indictment, the same influence was sufficient to indict and condemn the negroes that they had marked for execution." Both he and Storey, Bratton concluded, felt "very sanguine of success."[80]

Herbert Seligmann, the NAACP's director of publicity, had attended the oral argument, and his report confirmed Bratton's reasons for optimism. The "outlook is distinctly encouraging," he said, and the Arkansas counsel had been outclassed in the argument, since he had argued like "he were talking to a petit jury in Phillips County." Summing up the various reports of the oral argument, Walter White reported to Scipio Jones that the "cases lie 'on the laps of the gods,' but we here feel very optimistic as to the decision. I hope we shall not be disappointed."[81]

8 "A Great Achievement in Constitutional Law": Victory and Its Aftermath

The NAACP did not have long to wait. The U.S. Supreme Court announced its decision on February 19, 1923. It had handed the NAACP a major victory in its defense of the Phillips County blacks.[1] Writing for the Court, Justice Holmes was able to incorporate in the majority opinion the views he had expressed in dissent in the *Frank* case eight years earlier.

Holmes began by reciting the petitioners' allegations that the Committee of Seven had promised the execution of the blacks if the community would abstain from lynching them, that torture had been used to secure testimony against the defendants, and that the trials of the defendants had occurred in an atmosphere permeated with the mob spirit. And he noted that the Committee of Seven, the American Legion, the Rotary Club, and the Lions Club of Helena had all referred to the promised execution of the blacks.[2] "In Frank v. Mangum . . . ," Holmes continued,

it was recognized, of course, that if in fact a trial is dominated by a mob, so that there is an actual interference with the course of justice, there is a departure from due process of law; and that 'if the state, supplying no corrective process, carries into execution a judgment of death or imprisonment based upon a verdict thus produced by mob domination, the state deprives the accused of his life or liberty without due process of law.' We assume, in accordance with that case, that the

corrective process supplied by the state may be so adequate that interference by habeas corpus ought not to be allowed. It certainly is true
that mere mistakes of law in the course of a trial are not to be corrected
in that way. But if the case is that the whole proceeding is a mask,—
that counsel, jury, and judge were swept to the fatal end by an irresistible wave of public passion, and that the state courts failed to correct
the wrong,—neither perfection in the machinery for correction nor the
possibility that the trial court and counsel saw no other way of avoiding an immediate outbreak of the mob can prevent this court from
securing to the petitioners their constitutional rights.[3]

In *Moore* v. *Dempsey,* Holmes noted, a motion for a new trial
with many of the same charges subsequently included in the
habeas corpus petition was overruled by the trial court, and the
Arkansas Supreme Court had upheld the trial court's action.
"The supreme court said that the complaint of discrimination
against petitioners by the exclusion of colored men from the
jury came too late," he continued, "and, by way of answer to the
objection that no fair trial could be had in the circumstances,
stated that it could not say 'that this must necessarily have been
the case;' that eminent counsel was appointed to defend the
petitioners, that the trial was had according to law, the jury
correctly charged, and the testimony legally sufficient." The Arkansas Supreme Court had subsequently held, Holmes pointed
out, that the state chancery court lacked jurisdiction to issue
writs of habeas corpus and an injunction in the case.[4] "We shall
not say more concerning the corrective process afforded to petitioners than that it does not seem to us sufficient to allow a
judge of the United States to escape the duty of examining the
facts for himself, when, if true, as alleged, they make the trial
absolutely void," Holmes concluded. "We have confined the
statement to facts admitted by the demurrer. We will not say
that they cannot be met, but it appears to us unavoidable that
the district judge should find whether the facts alleged are true,
and whether they can be explained so far as to leave the state
proceedings undisturbed. Order reversed. The case to stand for
hearing before the District Court."[5]

Justice McReynolds, who had been in the majority in the
Frank case, now found himself in the minority. His dissenting
opinion was joined by Justice Sutherland. The petition for a
writ of habeas corpus in the *Moore* case, McReynolds said, was
supported by affidavits of "these . . . ignorant men whose lives
are at stake," of three other blacks who had pleaded guilty to

murder and of "two white men,—low villains, according to their own admissions." "The matter is one of gravity," Mc-Reynolds continued. "If every man convicted of crime in a state court may thereafter resort to the Federal court, and, by swearing, as advised, that certain allegations of fact tending to impeach his trial are 'true to the best of his knowledge and belief,' and thereby obtain as of right further review, another way has been added to a list already unfortunately long to prevent prompt punishment. The delays incident to enforcement of our criminal laws have become a national scandal and give serious alarm to those who observe. Wrongly to decide the present cause probably will produce very unfortunate consequences."[6]

"In Frank v. Mangum . . . ," McReynolds argued, "after great consideration a majority of the court approved the doctrine which should be applied here. The doctrine is right and wholesome. I cannot agree now to put it aside and substitute the views expressed by the minority of the court in that cause." The record of the trial of the defendants in the *Moore* case disclosed "no irregularity," and in conformity with the doctrine of the *Frank* case, Arkansas had provided a "corrective process" for the defendants through review in the state supreme court. "The state supreme court, as well as the trial court, considered the claims of petitioners, set forth by trusted counsel in the motion for a new trial," McReynolds pointed out. "This court denied a petition for certiorari wherein the facts and circumstances now relied upon were set forth with great detail. Years have passed since they were convicted of this atrocious crime. Certainly they have not been rushed towards the death chair; on the contrary, there has been long delay, and some impatience over the result is not unnatural."[7]

"With all those things before him," McReynolds continued, "I am unable to say that the district judge, acquainted with local conditions, erred when he held the petition for the writ of habeas corpus insufficient. His duty was to consider the whole case and decide whether there appeared to be substantial reason for further proceedings." McReynolds concluded, "Under the disclosed circumstances I cannot agree that the solemn adjudications by courts of a great state, which this court has refused to review, can be successfully impeached by the mere ex parte affidavits made upon information and belief of interested convicts, joined by two white men,—confessedly atrocious criminals. The fact that petitioners are poor and ignorant and black naturally arouses sympathy; but that does not release us from enforcing principles which are essential to the orderly operation of our Federal system."[8]

The NAACP rejoiced in the court's decision, and the Association's board of directors passed a resolution putting "on record their deep sense of gratitude to their President, Moorfield Storey, for his efficient and self-sacrificing efforts in defending the rights of the Negro, for now the third time, before the Supreme Court of the United States. They not only appreciate their financial obligation in Mr. Storey's refusal of all compensation, but much more the spiritual debt to one who expresses so thoroughly in his life and work the objects of this Association."[9]

Walter White wrote to Bratton also expressing "both on behalf of the Association and personally our deep and sincere appreciation for the splendid part played by you in these cases from the very beginning." "It has been a long and toilsome road," White added, "since that day I walked into your office at Little Rock as a representative of the Chicago Daily News and we will always remember with great gratitude how splendidly you have aided in this hard struggle."[10] Bratton replied to White that he did "not feel that I have done anything more than what any good citizen should have done. I have suffered beyond what any man can realize, both financially and otherwise, but if my loss and suffering can be responsible for a revealing of the true conditions and bring about a remedying thereof, then I will feel amply repaid for all my losses. Aside from my own personal feelings on the matter, you must know that I am gratified at the result from the standpoint of simple vindication of my views as to the law and what could be done. For you will recall that I took the position from the outset that their convictions would never stand the test."[11]

Louis Marshall, a well-respected constitutional lawyer, had been president of the American Jewish Committee at the time of the *Frank* case and had served as Leo Frank's principal counsel in his appeal to the Supreme Court. When the Court upheld the denial of a writ of habeas corpus, he had said that "I shall never again be able to feel that reliance upon the courts in respect to the accomplishments of the ends of justice, that I had hitherto entertained." Walter White sent Marshall a copy of the Supreme Court's decision in *Moore* v. *Dempsey,* and in a reply,

Marshall said that the decision was "exceedingly gratifying to me, especially in view of the fact that it has given the Supreme Court an opportunity to adopt the principle for which I contended in Frank v. Mangum . . . , and which was advocated in the dissenting opinion rendered in that case by Justices Holmes and Hughes. The stone the builders rejected has now become the cornerstone of the temple. I regard it as a great achievement in constitutional law. Due process of law now means, not merely a right to be heard before a court, but that it must be before a court that is not paralyzed by mob domination."[12]

He was also gratified, Marshall told White, that "there were but two dissenting Judges, one of them, Mr. Justice McReynolds, having united in the decision in Frank v. Mangum, and Mr. Justice Sutherland being the only one of the Justices who have been added to the court since the decision in the Frank case who did not unite with the newly appointed Judges to the Supreme Court in the adoption of the doctrine for which I contended." Marshall added, "I am sure that Mr. Justice Holmes must feel delighted by this action by the Court. I always regarded the dissent by Justices Holmes and Hughes [in the *Frank* case] as one of the noblest and most courageous of utterances in the history of our judiciary."[13] Marshall enclosed a one-hundred-dollar contribution as a "thank-offering." Walter White expressed the Association's appreciation for the contribution and pointed out that in "preparing for the hearing in the Federal Supreme Court Mr. Storey's main fear was that the Supreme Court decision in the case of Frank vs. Mangum . . . would be a stumbling block that might militate against our success. Just as he expected, the State of Arkansas relied upon the decision in that case to prove its contention that the Supreme Court was without authority to interfere in these cases. It is a matter of great gratification to us not only that the lives of these men were saved but that the Supreme Court reversed itself in effect in contrasting this decision with that in the case of Leo Frank. In view of the splendid fight made by you for Leo Frank, it is very encouraging that we have succeeded in securing this latter decision which cannot but affect greatly similar cases in the future."[14]

Louis Marshall, a New York Republican and an economic conservative, was, however, deeply committed to civil rights. He had not only become a defender of Leo Frank but had also appeared before the Supreme Court in the defense of the rights of a variety of groups, including Japanese aliens and Catholics. The NAACP's success in *Moore v. Dempsey* so impressed Marshall that he became a member of the Association's legal committee, and until his death in 1929, he played important roles as counsel for the NAACP in attacking racially restrictive covenants[15] and the white primary.[16]

The *Moore* decision produced relatively few editorial comments in the national press. There were, for example, no editorial comments on the *Moore* case by such national journals as the *New York Times* or the *Washington Post,* nor were there editorial comments in such leading southern newspapers as the *Atlanta Constitution, Birmingham Age-Herald,* and the *New Orleans Times-Picayune.* The *New Republic,* however, did print most of the Supreme Court's opinion in the case, along with a follow-up editorial.[17]

The *Louisville Courier-Journal* also commented on the case and noted that the "decision constitutes, virtually, the chastening of a State by the Federal Government in a case in which there is reason to believe that the State's courts did not deal fairly with defendants charged with murder. . . . The principle that the Federal Government may constitute itself a reviewer of the decisions of the criminal courts of States, overruling the authority of State courts of last resort, will, if established, constitute a change hardly less than revolutionary." The *St. Louis Post Dispatch* dissented "from the doctrine of Federal interference in state cases, but there is some ground for satisfaction in the action of the United States Supreme Court, which remanded the cases of Negroes convicted of participation in the Elaine (Ark.) riots. The ground for remanding was that the Negroes were not given a fair hearing. Fourteen Negroes and five white persons were killed in the rioting which, by nearly all accounts, was started by the whites. The Arkansas formula seems to consist in hanging the Negroes who escape the bullets."[18]

The *Arkansas Gazette* deplored the decision in an editorial that generally endorsed and liberally quoted from the dissenting opinion of Justice McReynolds. The Supreme Court decision meant, the *Gazette* said, that the "ex-parte statement of ignorant negro convicts is sufficient to overturn the ruling of the highest court in Arkansas. To reach its decision the majority of the Supreme Court of the United States had to reverse the same court's ruling in the Leo Frank case, which came up from Georgia. Unless the court is willing to reverse itself again the next time a criminal case is brought before it by the same procedure, the powers of the state courts will in large measure be nullified and the law's delays, already scandalous, will be multiplied a hundred fold. . . . The Supreme Court has been looked upon as the last bulwark of law and order in the United States, where there is so little law. It is terrifying to contemplate the consequences of the decision in this case."[19] Scipio Jones forwarded the *Gazette's* editorial to Walter White, remarking, the "Gazette has fought us ever since this unfortunate occurrence and is still fighting us, as you will see from reading the editorial."[20] White replied that the editorial was "not too thinly veiled an appeal to the mob" and that he hoped that the convicted blacks would be safe from any attempt to lynch them.[21]

The *Moore* defendants would have a hearing in the U.S. district court. Their counsel would have the opportunity in that hearing to prove that they had been denied due process of law. The lives of these six men were no longer in immediate jeopardy, but while their case was being appealed to the Supreme Court, the group in the *Ware* cases had faced the possibility of retrial for murder in the Lee County Circuit Court at Marianna. These cases had been continued on motion of the prosecution in October 1921 until the April 1922 term of the court, counsel for the defendants agreeing to this continuance. During the April 1922 term of the court, defense counsel filed a petition requesting that the cases be tried. The prosecution again requested a continuance, and the court granted the prosecution's request over the objections of defense counsel. The cases were rescheduled for trial in October of 1922, at which time defense counsel again requested a trial. The prosecution, over objections of the defense, once more requested and received a continuance in the cases.[22]

The constant preparations for the *Ware* group's retrial during this period placed a financial strain on the NAACP. Scipio Jones was convinced that local white counsel needed to be retained for the defendants at a cost of ten thousand dollars; he had raised seven thousand dollars of this amount in Arkansas, primarily through black fraternal organizations, such as the Mosaic Templars of America, but once state officials learned that the Mosaic Templars were contributing to the Phillips County cases, they threatened to revoke the organization's charter, which eliminated that source of funds. When Jones asked the NAACP for financial assistance, the organization, in financial straits at this time, was forced to announce a special appeal for contributions. Despite the hostility toward E. L. McHaney on the part of the NAACP, Walter White wrote McHaney regarding the *Ware* cases, and McHaney told White that he had been informed by the local prosecutor that the cases would not be retried. This of course increased the NAACP's reluctance to contribute more money at this time.[23]

During this period, Ed Ware wrote secretly to Jones from the Lee County jail, describing how he and the others were faring during their long wait for retrial.

this comes in Secret to Let you no How We are. all is not so Well Really non of us isnt Well But Some is Better than others. i My Self seems Like i Have Completely Lost My Health. i Hope this Letter will find you and your family well. also your friends. Listen Mr. Jones if there is any Way that you can give me some Relief now is the time i Wish you Would if you please Sir Because we is Suffering so much . . . Here on this Hard concreet floor. and We is kep so confine and is fed so Bad untill we are Just about Woe out. Please Sir Help us if you can. Because it is not near as good as it is at the Walls [the state penitentiary] Where a man can Walk on the ground and catch some fresh air. I dont Look for No ans. from this But i Will Look for Some Relief all the Boys Joins me in Sending Love. . . .[24]

An Arkansas statute, governing delays in trying persons under indictment for criminal offenses, provided that if a person under indictment had been committed to prison but not tried during the two terms of court following the indictment, "he shall be discharged so far as relates to the offense for which he was committed, unless the delay shall have been on the application of the prisoner." A prisoner was not to be discharged if the judge of the court had failed to hold court during the relevant terms or if there had not been time for the trial. A discharge was also not warranted if there were material evidence important to the prosecution's case which was unavailable, the state had made reasonable attempts to obtain the evidence, and it was likely to be available by the next term of court.[25] At the April 1923 term of the Lee County Circuit Court, Scipio Jones and other counsel filed a motion to discharge all of the defendants from custody under the provisions of this statute. Although the trial had been continued in October of 1921 with the consent of the defense, the motion to discharge noted that the cases had been continued over the objections of the defense at the April and October 1922 terms of the Lee County Circuit Court, and, therefore, that under the provisions of the statute, the defendants were entitled to be discharged from custody.[26] The prosecution opposed the motion, arguing that defense counsel had acquiesced in the continuances and that evidence important to the state's case and then unavailable would be available at the next term of the court. Under the provisions of the statute, the prosecution argued, the cases should be scheduled for the next term of the court to allow time for the state to gather its evidence.[27]

Lee County Circuit Judge E. D. Robertson upheld the prosecution's objections to the motion to discharge the defendants and postponed the cases until the October 1923 term of the court. Whereupon Scipio Jones and the white counsel he had retained appealed Judge Robertson's decision to the Arkansas Supreme Court, which on June 25 reversed Judge Robertson and ordered the discharge of the six men.[28] The supreme court noted that, contrary to the claims of the prosecution, the record indicated that the cases had been continued twice over the objections of defense counsel. As to the allegation that new witnesses could be discovered by the state if a continuance were granted, the court held that these "allegations . . . were the merest drag-net. They did not name a single witness, nor set up any facts to which any witness would testify if the cause were continued. They did not designate any place where a single witness could be found. Taken as a whole, the allegations of the [prosecution's] response were but tantamount to saying to the court, 'There are some witnesses somewhere scattered throughout the State, who, if found, will furnish material evidence for the prosecution, and, if the cause is continued, the State will endeavor to produce them.'"[29] The facts conclusively demonstrated, the court continued, that "the delay in the prosecution was not on account of the failure of the judge to hold any term of the court. . . ." None of the exceptions enumerated in the statute providing for discharge upon failure to try a defendant during two terms of the court following his indictment existed in these cases.[30]

The statute had as its "manifest purpose," the court said, the promotion of "dispatch in the administration of justice," and "it must commend itself to the enlightened judgment of everyone who loves law and order as a wise as well as a humane enactment."

"Justice delayed is justice denied," says Mr. Gladstone. It is highly important to the public weal that those accused of crime shall be brought to a speedy trial in order that, if guilty, public justice may be meted out without delay. This is as powerful a deterrent to the commission of public offenses as is the knowledge that condign punishment will follow when the lawbreaker is overtaken in his crime. [The principle embodied in the statute was] humane and just to the accused, who may be innocent, because it imposes upon the ministers of justice the obligation not to unnecessarily delay the trial of the charge which the State has lodged against him, and to afford him an opportunity to prove his innocence before he has been compelled to endure a prolonged punishment by imprisonment beyond the end of the second term of the court after the term in which he was indicted. [The statute in question had] been a part of our laws ever since the State had an existence [and was] consonant with that provision of our Bill of Rights, art. 2, sec. 10 of the Constitution, which declares that 'in all criminal prosecutions the accused shall enjoy the right to a speedy and public trial,' and also with art. 2, sec. 13, which declares that 'he ought to obtain justice freely, and without purchase, completely, and without denial, *promptly, and without delay*, conformably to the laws.'[31]

"The truth is," the court held, "there was a failure of prosecution, pure and simple, because the State did not demand a trial and bring forward its evidence in support of the charge made in the indictment." The Lee County Circuit Court had misconstrued the law applicable to the case. "We are bound by the court's findings of fact, but not by its conclusion of law. The court erred in its conclusion of law. The law applicable to the facts must be declared, else the appellants will be deprived of the right to a speedy trial, which the framers of our Constitution and the framers of this statute purposed that every person charged with a public offense should have. That every such person has such right, under constitutions and statutes similar to ours, is, so far, proclaimed by the authorities with one voice." "The order of the trial court overruling appellants' application for discharge is therefore reversed," the supreme court concluded, "and an order will be entered here directing the sheriff of Lee County to discharge the appellants from custody."[32]

After almost four years under indictment for murder, twice tried and twice convicted on that charge, the six convicted blacks—Ed Ware, Albert Giles, Joe Cox, John Martin, Alf Banks and Will Wordlow—would be discharged from custody. Although John E. Miller, original prosecutor of the group in the Phillips County Circuit Court, pointed out that they were still subject to reindictment and retrial on the murder charges, he conceded that it would be almost impossible to find witnesses to testify against them at this late date.[33]

When word of the Arkansas Supreme Court's decision reached Marianna on June 25, Lee County Circuit Court Judge E. D. Robertson ordered the county sheriff, A. F. Calloway, to transport the men to Little Rock and to deliver them to the warden of the penitentiary. Sheriff Calloway, accompanied by deputies Frank O'Shields and Henry Slaughter, took the six men by train to Little Rock, arriving at eleven o'clock at night. Scipio Jones and a fellow black attorney, Robert L. Booker, met them at the Little Rock railroad depot, and went with them to the penitentiary.

Night watchman Sam Taylor refused to open the gates and admit the blacks. Warden Hamp Martin was awakened, but he also refused. While the prisoners and Sheriff Calloway and his deputies, plus Scipio Jones and Robert Booker, waited outside for almost an hour, until about 1 a.m., the warden telephoned the secretary of Governor McRae and a penitentiary commissioner. No one appeared to know what to do. Sheriff Calloway told the penitentiary officials that if they "turned down the blacks," he would simply leave them where they were, standing outside the walls of the prison. He and his deputies then shook hands with the night watchman and a newspaper reporter who was on the scene, climbed into a waiting taxi and left, with the six blacks and their lawyers "looking after him in surprise." All six were once again free men.[34]

Ed Ware said he felt "mighty fine." "When I first got in this trouble," he said, "I consulted my God and He told me He would take care of me. I know the good Lord listened to our prayers. I worried a great deal when I first came here, and these other boys did too. After consulting God, we made up our minds that if we would have to die in that chair, we would be ready to meet Jesus. We all know that Jesus took care of us." Ware said the treatment had been best at the penitentiary, and they had been accorded numerous privileges in the Phillips County jail, but they disliked the Lee County jail because they were required to be silent. He said he would probably return to farming, but, not in Phillips County. "I'd plow up all the cotton," he said, "watching and looking around."[35]

In the early morning darkness, Scipio Jones arranged for cars to transport the six men into Little Rock. He found temporary housing for them in the black community. He asked them to remain in Little Rock, since the Arkansas Supreme Court's decision was subject to a petition for a rehearing, and it was possible the state might file such a petition. He assured the state attorney general that he would surrender the men if he were ordered to do so. The state attorney general allowed the period during which petitions for rehearings could be filed to expire, and the court's decision freeing the men became final on July 12. Their long nightmare was over.[36]

Their release reportedly stunned the white citizens of Helena. One lawyer who had assisted in prosecuting them charged that "somebody had blundered." The members of the American Legion were reported to be deeply resentful. Lee County Circuit Court Judge E. D. Robertson defended his handling of the situation after the Arkansas Supreme Court had reversed his decision. He had ordered Sheriff Calloway to take the men to the penitentiary because he feared for their safety. "I do not think there was any danger of trouble from residents of Phillips County, and there has been no display of feeling here against the negroes who were released at Little Rock early today," Robertson said. "But, as a precaution, I ordered Sheriff Calloway to take them and turn them over to the penitentiary authorities. The sheriff carried out his orders exactly. I told him to take the negroes to the penitentiary, and if the warden would not accept them to turn them loose in the warden's presence."[37]

Later Judge Robertson ordered warden Martin to show cause why he should not be held in contempt of court for his refusal to accept custody. Martin responded that Judge Robertson's order requiring him to accept the prisoners was unlawful whereupon Robertson held Martin in contempt and fined him five hundred dollars. Martin appealed the contempt conviction and in January 1924 the Arkansas Supreme Court reversed his conviction. Judge Robertson, the court held, had the power to send individuals to the penitentiary only if they had been convicted of crimes, and since the six had not been convicted of any crime at the time the judge's order was void.[38]

The *Arkansas Gazette* was appalled at the way in which the *Ware* cases had ended, and in an editorial entitled, "The Breakdown of the Law in the Elaine Cases," declared that never "has a more grievous blow been struck at the orderly administration of law in Arkansas than by the astounding ending of the cases of six convicted Elaine rioters. Never before has any one incident so discredited our courts and never before has the public had more just ground for complaints." "Thus we have the unfortunate and unpardonable situation," the *Gazette* continued, "that if these six negroes are guilty of the crime of murder, of which they were twice adjudged guilty, they now go scot free in spite of their guilt. And if they are not guilty of murder they have not been cleared of that charge. They have simply gotten their freedom through the failure of the state to bring them to trial within the period fixed by law." "The proceedings at the gates of the penitentiary on Monday night were of a piece with the outcome of these cases in the courts . . . ," the *Gazette* declared. "In that instant in which they were left standing at night before the gates of the penitentiary, not knowing where to turn because the officers of the law differed as to what should be done with them, these negroes were fit symbols of the failure in the administration of justice that occurred in their cases. They have spent four years in jail and at the end they have been neither convicted nor vindicated of guilt."[39]

The NAACP was, of course, elated. "This is a tremendous victory, after nearly four years of fighting," Walter White wrote Louis Marshall. "I am sure you realize how happy we are, in which happiness I know you join with us."[40] The Association at last sensed that complete victory could ultimately be won. "It is evident, if the State could not muster sufficient evidence to win [the *Ware et al.* cases] that it will hardly proceed further against the six men whose cases are now pending in the Federal Court," Walter White said. "It has been a long and difficult fight against tremendous odds, but we feel sure that now the case will be won."[41]

Scipio Jones was still seeking the freedom of the Phillips County blacks who had been sentenced to prison terms. All of those in prison had been freed by the summer of 1923, except for eight who had been sentenced to twenty-one years in prison.[42]

After its victory in the Supreme Court in *Moore* v. *Dempsey*, the NAACP debated what strategy to follow in the habeas corpus proceeding in the U.S. district court. U. S. Bratton advised the Association that "those who have been pressing the prosecution will not want the real facts developed any more fully than they can avoid," and they would not fight the *Moore* case in the habeas corpus hearing in the U.S. district court. "If that bunch of murderers attempt to go . . . and try out the case," Bratton added, "I want to see to it that all the facts possible are brought out, which will show what a travesty on justice was perpetrated. A record can be made that will absolutely put all decent people of the South to shame and force them to rise up against such conditions."[43]

Moorfield Storey advised the NAACP to move cautiously and not to press for an early hearing in the habeas corpus proceedings. "The authorities are very tired of these cases and want to drop them, and will do it as soon as they can find a good excuse." "They are undoubtedly sensitive to public opinion, and if we push them, they may perhaps fight," Storey said. "They have now no witnesses with which to prove the case, but I have no doubt they can be invented if we force them, and my impression is that it is best to let things slumber until the time is ripe for an abandonment of the prosecution. The recent decision of the Supreme Court [in the *Moore* case] probably has wakened public opinion up in Arkansas, and it will take time for it to subside. Time works in our favor."[44]

Walter White had suggested to Storey that he should go to Arkansas to conduct the habeas corpus proceedings, but Storey emphatically rejected that idea. "So far as trying the case is concerned, it is out of the question for me to go down there and try it in Arkansas," Storey said. "I have always felt that foreign counsel is at a disadvantage in any state . . . , and I think it best that local counsel should deal with local questions." "Moreover," Storey noted, "I am in my seventy-ninth year, and the climate of Arkansas in the summer, together with the journey backward and forward, would very likely use me up for a year at least, and I do not think I am called upon to take that risk. My general opinion is to wait a while for some movement by the other side, and when that is made, deal with it as the occasion permits."[45]

While the NAACP had prevailed in the Supreme Court, the Association was by no means out of the woods. The state could conceivably contest the *Moore* case vigorously in the U.S. district court, and even if the NAACP could convince the federal court that the six blacks had received an unfair trial, the state could still opt to reindict and retry the men for murder. Although Storey correctly pointed out that the state could not produce the witnesses who had testified at the original trial, the issue in the habeas corpus hearing would not be guilt or innocence but whether the men had been denied a fair trial; the burden of proof in the habeas corpus proceeding would be on the NAACP to prove that an unfair trial had occurred. To meet that burden of proof, the testimony of the two white special railroad agents, T. K. Jones and H. F. Smiddy, corroborating the testimony of the use of torture and mob domination, would be crucial. But it was unclear whether Jones and Smiddy would be willing to testify, since they would have to return to Arkansas. They were by no means popular figures in their home state. Nor had their relations with the NAACP been of the best after they had sworn to the affidavits. These affidavits had been secured by McHaney, but at the time both had been promised financial help.

In October 1922, the NAACP had promised to provide one thousand dollars for Jones and Smiddy.[46] Ironically, the top officers of the NAACP did not learn their names from Scipio Jones or E. L. McHaney, and when Jones and Smiddy wrote letters to the Association, expressing dissatisfaction with the amount of financial support, NAACP officers had no idea who they were. Jones apparently registered such a complaint in a letter to James Weldon Johnson in the spring of 1922, but Johnson, unaware of who Jones was, sent his letter on to Arthur B. Spingarn, an NAACP attorney who would become president of the Association in 1939. Johnson could not "imagine what claim Mr. T. K. Jones has against us," he told Spingarn. "I have no recollection at all of our having employed him or authorized anyone else to do so."[47] But Smiddy proved to be the more troublesome. He had quit his job as a special agent for the railroad, had served for a time on the Helena police force and as a deputy sheriff with Phillips County, then was reemployed by a railroad company, but lost his job in September 1921. He turned up in Topeka, Kansas, unemployed and penniless, and appealed to the Topeka branch of the NAACP for help. James H. Guy of the Topeka branch wrote to Walter White. White, who had never heard of Smiddy, told Guy, "I do not know his history nor have [I] heard anything of him throughout the entire history of the Arkansas cases." Later, White wrote back to Guy apologetically. "In Mr. Jones' report to us he stated that 'two white men' had been secured to testify at the trials [of the *Ware et al.* blacks at] the 1922 term of court regarding the exact way in which the trouble in Phillips County started. He did not give us the names of the two witnesses. . . ."[48] In early February 1922, Smiddy wrote to the national office of the NAACP, pointing out that he had been "forced to leave [Arkansas] on account of the affidavit I made for HON Scipio Jones, to suspend the writ of execution of the 12 [Phillips County] Rioters sentenced to be electrocuted on or about Sept. 23, 1921." After he had sworn to the affidavit, Smiddy said, "the Arkansas officers, bent on executing the Negroes, began to make various charges against me for the sole purpose of compelling me to withdraw the affidavit. My life was threatened, and my family was compelled to suffer. I consulted Mr. [Scipio] Jones, and with his consent and being furnished with traveling money I came here."[49] To harass him, Smiddy said, Arkansas officials had caused him to be indicted in the U.S. district court in Helena for extortion. He was then free on a thousand dollar bond pending trial on that charge. The charge was "all simon pure trumppery, and there is no truth whatever in the charge. I am here away from my family and dare not go back. I must have help and advice. Scipio Jones, who was my friend till I helped him out is now neglecting me and my family, and I must have help."[50]

"We want to do something for him if he is going to be of use to us," Walter White wrote Jones, enclosing Smiddy's letter. But Jones, clearly angered by Smiddy's letter, responded to Smiddy that he was "very much surprised at the contents of your letter and regard it as the height of ingratitude on your part." He had only recently visited Smiddy's wife and four children in Memphis, and he had given them fifty dollars. "To date, I think I have contributed to you and your family $670.00, and a like amount to Mr. T. K. Jones." "I can hardly believe that you wrote [that charge that Jones had abandoned him]," Jones said. "I appreciate what you did for my clients, but I did not tell you to make the affidavit, did not promise you any assistance for making it, and was not present when you made it."[51] Jones told Walter White of the contributions he had made to Smiddy and his family. White was "glad to get the information regarding Mr.

Smiddy. I knew at the time I wrote you that you had contributed sums at various times towards his support and I confess that it made me rather angry when he wrote me as he did. I am glad you checked him up so sharply."[52]

In a letter to White on February 15, Smiddy acknowledged that Scipio Jones had "balled me out good and plenty about the letter I wrote you several days ago, [and] I am sorry that he fels that way about it but I was laying hear sick and had no money to help my self and my Wife and Daughter sick in bed at Memphis Tenn., it worried me and I did not know what to say so I wrote you about it, it was not the money I did what I did for the Colored People in the South, I knew the streight of the thing and I wanted to see them come out of it and I did this for them and I dont think I aught to suffer for it, Scipio A. Jones was not Present when I made this affidavit and did not promise me any amount of money to do so, Mr. E. L. McHaney got me to make this affidavit and said that I would be taken care of until I could get on my feet again. . . ."[53] He had lost his job soon after he had sworn to the affidavit, and he had been unable to get another. Since he could "never go back to the South again" and "they told me that I and my Famley would be taken care of," he wanted to move his family to Kansas "for my Wife is worrying herself to death about me and the Four little children we have neither one of the children are big enough to take care of them selves, so you can see I am in A bad shape right now."[54]

"Scipio writes me and says that he has given me the some of $670.00," Smiddy continued, "now I have been out of work for SIX months and how far $670.00 Dollars go with A man that has the Famliy that I have got. . . ." "I'm the Fellow that saved them [the Phillips County blacks] not no one els, I could not get A nother white man down their to make A affidavit to help save them only A man by the Name of T. K. Jones and he did not want to give the streight facks about it until I got right behind him. . . ." He had had to leave Arkansas on the run, Smiddy said, and "they had me arrested in Memphis and had no charges against me so I beat them in that case, now they have A Federal charge against me in Little Rock Ark. which is trumped up on me for making this affidavit for the Boys so they want to get me back down their to kill me and my Statement, so you all take this up with som of your Friends in Washington D.C. and get this dismissed for I am not guilty of the charge any more than you are, now they are going to try to get me back down their but I will go back ded not alive. . . ."[55] "Please help me out of this if their is any chance to [do] so. I am not A bad Fellow at all or no cruck or I have never did no one no harm," Smiddy concluded. "Scipio writes me and tells me that he gave my Wife A check for $50.00 that sure was nice for I was worried about them more than I was about my self, now Mr. White these Fellows have helped me A lettle but I wont ask them for it I have not had any money to get clean clothes with and I am going Hungry ever day I get A dime some time from som of the boys, any thing that you can do for me to relive me A little will be appreciated and I sure need it bad if any one does need it."[56]

The Topeka NAACP branch assured Smiddy it would defend him if Arkansas attempted to extradite him on the federal charge.[57] Jones and McHaney had furnished his bond and were prepared to defend him against the charge if he returned to Arkansas.[58] Smiddy nonetheless continued to complain about his treatment at the hands of Jones and the NAACP. U. S. Bratton, who saw him in Topeka, wrote to Jones that Smiddy "complained that he had not been treated fairly by you. He said that his family was in Memphis without any support, and that he must get them away from there; he indicated that he was not going to go back on anything that he had said, but appealed to me to see what could be done for him."[59] "It is important that he be not permitted to be humiliated and suffer great loss, as a result of his giving you the facts. I think that to permit such would indeed be an outrage, for it is undoubtedly too often true that men who dare to have the courage to stand out for what they know to be right are permitted to be humiliated and suffer severe reverses for that reason." "When I was in New York I talked with [NAACP] Headquarters and received advice that they would put up at least $500.00 towards the expenses of each of these witnesses," Bratton told Jones. "If they do this, it undoubtedly should take care of the expense of moving his family and going a long way toward saving him [from difficulties]. I would be pleased to hear from you, and think that you had better write [Smiddy], for unless he feels that he is being treated right, it is possible he may not be available when you need him."[60] Jones wrote back that he had supported and would continue to support Smiddy and his family. "I had furnished Smiddy and his family with more than $800.00 to date. In fact,

I have taken care of both Smiddy's and Jones' families for about six months and am still contributing to their support."[61]

It must have been clear to the Association that it faced some difficulties if it hoped to rely on the testimony of Smiddy and Jones in the habeas corpus proceeding in the federal court. First of all Smiddy would return to Arkansas only with extreme reluctance and, if Smiddy's word could be taken for it, Jones had been less than enthusiastic in swearing to his affidavit in the first place. Second, Smiddy obviously bore a grudge against Jones and the NAACP for what he saw as their lack of financial support. Smiddy certainly appears to have been far less than an ideal witness from the standpoint of both intelligence and character. Further, the testimony of both H. F. Smiddy and T. K. Jones could be seriously undermined, and the NAACP acutely embarrassed, if it were brought out on cross-examination that both had been receiving financial support from the NAACP and from Scipio Jones.[62]

Besides these potential problems, the NAACP would face potentially even more serious difficulties if the *Moore* case were pushed to a hearing in the U.S. district court, since a close examination of the issues before the Arkansas Supreme Court would indicate that the mob domination issue had been raised in the original appeal to that court only indirectly if at all. No issue of mob domination appeared in the record of the trials of the *Moore* defendants, given the anemic defense offered by their original counsel, but neither was the issue of mob domination directly raised in the motions for new trials filed by Scipio Jones and Colonel Murphy. The motions did say that there was extensive prejudice against the defendants both before and during the trials, but no specific allegation that the trials were actually dominated by a mob had been made.

The motions for new trials claimed that, immediately following the riot, "the excitement of the white residents and citizens of [Phillips] County was intense, and their feelings against the blacks, including the defendants, bitter, active and persistent," and that "while [the *Moore et al.* men were in jail] several hundred white men of [Phillips County] assembled at or near the Court House and jail for the purpose of mobbing them, and were only prevented from doing so as defendants are informed and believe, by the presence of the U.S. soldiers. . . ." At the trials, the motions for new trials further charged, the "excitement and bitterness of feeling among the whites of [Phillips] County against the negroes, especially against defendants, was un-abated, still at the height of intensity" and "this feeling among the whites was co-extensive with the County. . . ." This "excite-ment and feeling against the defendants among the whites of [Phillips] County," the motions for new trials concluded, "was such that it was impossible to obtain any unprejudiced jury of white men to try them and . . . no white jury being fairly dis-posed, would have had the courage to acquit them."[63] These charges would support an argument that a continuance or a change of venue should have been granted because of the im-possibility of securing an unbiased jury, and that a fair trial could not have been obtained because of the pervasive commu-nity prejudice against the defendants. Still, they fell short of claiming that the trials were actually dominated by a mob. All that was before the Arkansas Supreme Court in the original appeal were the motions for new trials and two affidavits, by Will Wordlow and Alf Banks, in which they testified that they had been subjected to torture.[64] The first actual claims of mob domination came in the affidavits of Jones and Smiddy, but those affidavits were not obtained by McHaney until September 1921, well after the Arkansas Supreme Court's consideration of the original appeal.[65] And when the allegations of mob domi-nation in the affidavits of Jones and Smiddy got before the court in the writ of prohibition case against the Pulaski County Chan-cery Court, the supreme court held that under Arkansas proce-dure, such allegations had been raised too late.[66]

On remand from the U.S. Supreme Court, therefore, if the *Moore* case had proceeded to a hearing in the U.S. district court, it appears entirely possible that the NAACP would have lost the case because the issue of mob domination had not been raised at the appropriate time under Arkansas procedure, that is, in the original appeal to the Arkansas Supreme Court. And under the decisions of the U.S. Supreme Court on the habeas corpus jurisdiction of the federal courts, failure of a state criminal de-fendant to raise a federal right at the appropriate time under state procedure resulted in forfeiture of the right; then that right could not be raised later on petition for a federal writ of habeas corpus. In the motion for a new trial, the failure of Leo Frank's attorneys to raise the issue of his absence from the courtroom when the jury returned the verdict in his case had led to the Georgia Supreme Court's refusal to consider that issue, since it had not been raised at the appropriate time under Georgia procedure. The U.S. Supreme Court had upheld the Georgia Supreme Court on this point, ruling that the federal district court had been correct in refusing to hear the issue on petition for a federal writ. Considering the tardiness with which the mob domination issue had been raised in the *Moore* case, the U.S. district court in Arkansas would appear to have been fully justified in refusing to consider that issue if a habeas corpus hearing had been held.[67]

The issue of the use of torture to secure confessions or testimony had, of course, been raised in the habeas corpus proceeding and the torture issue might have been an alternative basis upon which the NAACP could have argued that the defendants had been denied a fair trial. Such an argument would, however, have encountered difficulties similar to those related to the mob domination issue. In the original appeal to the Arkansas Supreme Court, the record contained the affidavits on torture of Wordlow and Banks, but they were two of the six convicted in the *Ware* cases, and their affidavits therefore did not relate directly to the trials of the six other men. Only after the Arkansas Supreme Court had affirmed the *Moore* case convictions did defense counsel get the affidavits of Smiddy and Jones, as well as affidavits of similar torture from Walter Ward and John Jefferson, who had testified against the defendants. In the motions for new trials, Scipio Jones and Colonel Murphy did not make torture a ground for reversing the convictions.[68]

It was, therefore, entirely possible that the U.S. district court might hold that the torture issue had not been adequately raised in the *Moore* case in the Arkansas Supreme Court and that as a consequence, the issue could not be raised in a petition for a federal writ of habeas corpus. But even if the federal court were to consider the torture issue, no decisions of the U.S. Supreme Court had yet held that the use of coerced testimony or confessions in a state criminal trial would violate the Due Process Clause of the Fourteenth Amendment. Indeed, not until 1936 would the Court hold that the use of coerced confessions in state criminal trials violated that clause. And not until 1953 would it hold that issues of coerced confessions could be used to attack a state criminal conviction on petition for a federal writ of habeas corpus.[69]

Moorfield Storey's counsel of caution to the NAACP on proceeding further with the *Moore* case therefore appears to have been fully justified, a counsel of caution reinforced by indications from Arkansas authorities that a plea bargain might be acceptable. Just over a month after the Supreme Court's decision in the *Moore* case, Scipio Jones was in contact with John E. Miller, the former prosecutor in the Phillips County cases, and on March 24, Miller reported to Jones, in a "strictly confidential" letter, on a conference with the current prosecutor in Phillips County. "He is just as anxious as you are to dispose of these cases, and will agree to a plea of guilty of second degree murder, and a sentence of five years dated from the date of the incarceration of these parties in the Penitentiary." "However," Miller added, "before he can negotiate with you about the matter, he will have to obtain the consent of the Phillips County authorities, and he is arranging a date for an early conference with them. After this conference, he will either advise me what he can do, or may negotiate directly with you." In any case, Miller concluded, he would keep in touch with Jones.[70]

Scipio Jones consequently asked Walter White in early April if he thought "it would be advisable to dispose of our twelve cases by accepting short prison sentences for our Elaine clients?" "I have been seriously considering the matter for some time but have not attempted to dispose of the cases in that way and will not do so unless it meets with the approval of the Association," Jones said. "I think it highly probable that the matter may be disposed of in this way and if this course meets with your approval, I will see what can be done and submit to you the terms of compromise before accepting them."[71]

On April 30, Jones had again communicated with the NAACP about a compromise, enclosing the copy of the letter from Miller. Walter White replied on May 1 that since it was possible the *Ware* blacks might be discharged from prison, it might be unwise for Jones and the NAACP even to intimate that they were prepared to compromise the cases.

White had asked Moorfield Storey for his advice, but Storey replied ambiguously. On April 16, Storey had written White that "it would be well to accept some such compromise as Mr. Jones suggested" since the result would be to leave "the State of Arkansas chastened by the decision of the Supreme Court and that we should be vindicated in the public mind, as the abandonment of the real charge on which the men were convicted, by changing the sentence of death to one of brief imprisonment would be a virtual confession by the state that the proceedings were not justified." But on May 7, Storey wrote to White that he would "dislike to have the prisoners plead guilty and take a five years' sentence. They had better lie in jail without plea for a year or two than incur certain imprisonment and discredit all our attempts to save them by pleading guilty."[72] In view of Storey's apparent change of mind, the national office of the NAACP wrote to Scipio Jones that if it could be avoided, the Association would prefer not to compromise by having the defendants plead guilty to second degree murder or to any other crime. The principle at stake, the NAACP said, "is so vital a one and the effect of winning these cases through complete acquittal of the defendants would be so far-reaching, that a compromise at this stage of the fight, after the worst of it has been gone through successfully, is exceedingly distasteful." On the other hand, the NAACP informed Jones, the Association was "not unmindful of the personal interest of the men involved, nor of the conditions obtaining in a state like Arkansas." Since Jones was there on the spot, the Association concluded that the decision on whether to compromise the cases was largely up to him. He was, however, expected to take into consideration both the views of Storey and of the Association in making his decision.[73]

Scipio Jones decided to proceed with the habeas corpus hearing and to pursue the litigation seeking the discharge of the *Ware* men in the Supreme Court of Arkansas. In May 1923, he renewed the petition for a writ of habeas corpus in the U.S. District Court for the Eastern District of Arkansas. He was informed by Judge Jacob Trieber that the habeas corpus hearing would be conducted by U.S. District Judge Arba S. Van Valkenburgh of Kansas City, Missouri, but Judge Van Valkenburgh proved to be reluctant to proceed. He was convinced that Arkansas Governor McRae was going to pardon the men. His opinion was undoubtedly influenced by the Arkansas Supreme Court action of June 26, 1923, freeing the six convicted men. Scipio Jones, for his part, was convinced that Governor McRae would not pardon the *Moore* blacks, and in August he reported to the NAACP that he was trying to find a way to convince Van Valkenburgh to proceed with the habeas corpus hearing.[74]

Jones had urged the NAACP to ask Moorfield Storey to contact

George B. Rose, a white Little Rock attorney, to ask his help. Storey had met Rose in Washington, D.C., and Rose had told him that he felt that Storey had performed a great service for the state of Arkansas, an apparent reference to the successful argument in the Supreme Court. At the NAACP's request, Storey did write Rose, reminding him of his comment. The situation was "in many ways embarrassing," Storey said. "I gather that the authorities of Arkansas will find it hard to reproduce the evidence on which the men who are now held for trial were convicted, and on the other hand, it would be an expensive job to collect the witnesses and prove the allegations in our petition for habeas corpus, which were never denied. Indeed, after the argument [in the Supreme Court] the Attorney-General [of Arkansas] said to me he had been very careful in the various hearings that were had on this matter never to discuss the facts."[75]

"I fancy that the authorities of Arkansas would on the whole be glad to drop these proceedings and let these colored people go," Storey continued in his letter to Rose, "and I wonder whether you, who felt that the State of Arkansas was served by the decision of the Supreme Court, would not be willing to take a hand and see if you cannot bring about some adjustment of the matter which will relieve all parties concerned. I think the men when the verdict has been set aside ought to be discharged, and I think the proceedings against the men who stand under sentence should be dropped, and they also set free." "It seems to me a case where the real people of Arkansas should take a hand, and either through the action of the Governor or otherwise clear the situation." "Perhaps you will be willing to let Mr. Scipio Jones, who has been counsel in Arkansas in these matters, call upon you and discuss the situation. If you are not willing to act as counsel, perhaps you can make some suggestions as to whom he can properly employ. We want a man of courage."[76]

When Storey wrote on May 29 to tell James Weldon Johnson that he had written to Rose, he said he had "always felt that it was going to be hard to prove the allegations in our petition [for a writ of habeas corpus], not because they were not true, but because it would be hard to get the witnesses to come and testify." "If the testimony can be taken by deposition that difficulty would largely disappear, but of course a deposition is not as good as a living witness," Storey continued. "My feeling is that somehow or other the people of Arkansas would like to drop this business, and I think perhaps Mr. Rose can point out how this can be done."[77]

Rose reacted favorably to Storey's suggestion that he attempt to settle the Phillips County cases, and in early July of 1923, he wrote to John E. Miller, the former Phillips County prosecutor that he had no "interest in the prosecution of the Elaine rioters, except as a citizen of the State of Arkansas; but in view of the decision of our [State] Supreme Court turning loose six of them because the State was not able to make a case against them, but was forced to continue these cases from term to term, and in view of the sentiment throughout the country, it seems to me that it would be very unwise to press these cases much further. If there was a conspiracy, the heads of it, the men who ought to be punished to the limit of the law, have escaped from our juris-diction and will not be returned here for trial."[78] At the request of the prison management, Rose told Miller, he had gone to the prison "to make an encouraging talk to the prisoners," and while there he had talked to the Phillips County men and their wives. He became convinced, Rose said, "that if they were guilty, they were simply farm negroes who had been misled and that there was really no malice in them." "I believe," Rose continued, "that it would meet the end of justice if you would accept the plea of guilty of homicide and have them sentenced for three or four years and let the sentence date back to the time of their arrest. This would vindicate the law, and I think would meet the ap-proval of nearly everyone."[79]

"Rightly or wrongly, this matter has been taken up by the Northern press, and the conviction is general throughout the country that the prosecutions are unjustified," Rose continued. "It would make a good impression everywhere if the course I suggested were adopted, and it would do something to stop the emigration of the negroes to the North, which is proving so disastrous to many of our Southern planters. I hope that you will pardon my interfering in a matter which does not concern me directly, but you and I both are citizens of Arkansas, inter-ested in her good name and in her prosperity, and it is only in that capacity that I speak."[80]

John Miller, responding to Rose, noted that he was no longer prosecutor in Phillips County, but he continued to insist that there "is no doubt but that a conspiracy existed, but unfortu-nately, the State was never able to fasten the guilt on the real

Walter F. White, NAACP assistant secretary, who
"passed" as white to investigate the circumstances
of the riot; he later organized the NAACP defense
of the convicted men. *Courtesy of the Library of Congress*

Article by Walter White in the *Chicago
Daily News*, October 18, 1919. *Courtesy of the
Library of Congress*

FINDS NO "MASSACRE PLOT" IN ARKANSAS

Investigator Says Riots Resulted from Attempts to Exploit Negroes.

[The following dispatch gives the result of
an inquiry made by representatives of the
National Association for the Advancement of
Colored People.]

BY WALTER F. WHITE.
Special to The Chicago Daily News.

New York, Oct. 18.—Away from the
state of Arkansas, the scene of severe
fighting during the early days of October,
where passions run high and it is dangerous to life and limb even to attempt
to discuss rationally the rioting and its
causes, one can tell of that section of our
country where thousands of negroes are
held in the bonds of debt-slavery and
peonage of the most flagrant sort.

It is difficult for those who live in
northern states to imagine conditions so
barren of hope and of robbery so flagrant. The attempt of a few negroes to
free themselves and their fellows from
this condition and the resulting attempts
to check such efforts on the part of the
whites resulted in the deaths of at least
twenty-five negroes and five whites—although some give the figures as high as
100 negroes and twenty-five whites.

The world at large was informed that
the negroes had planned a general mas-

Mary White Ovington of New York, prominent white and NAACP board member, active in support of convicted Arkansas
blacks. *Courtesy of the New York Public Library*

James Weldon Johnson, first black
secretary of the NAACP, who directed the
new office during the Arkansas affair. *Courtesy of the New York Public Library*

"Massacring Whites" in Arkansas
By WALTER F. WHITE

Article by Walter
White in *The Nation*,
December 6, 1919.
*Courtesy of the Library
of Congress*

EARLY in October the report was spread broadcast in
this country that Negroes in Phillips County, Arkansas,
had organized to massacre the whites. A group of Negro
farmers, members of the Progressive Farmers and Household Union of America, were charged with having plotted
insurrection, with "night riding," with the intention to
take over the land of the white men after the owners had
been massacred. Investigation has thrown a searching light
upon these stories and has revealed that the Negro farmers
had organized not to massacre, but to protest by peaceful
and legal means against vicious exploitation by unscrupulous landowners and their agents.

On October 1, W. D. Adkins, a special agent of the Missouri Pacific Railroad, in company with Charles Pratt, a
deputy sheriff, and a Negro trusty were driving past a
Negro church near Hoop Spur, a small community in Phillips County. According to Pratt, persons in the church
fired without cause on the party, killing Adkins and wound-
ing Pratt. According to testimony of persons in the church,
however, Adkins and Pratt fired into the church, apparently
to frighten the Negroes gathered. The fire was returned
with the casualties noted. Whatever the facts may be, this
incident started four days of rioting. Negroes were disarmed and arrested, while their arms were given to whites
who hastened to the community from Mississippi, Arkansas,
and Tennessee; Federal troops were called from Camp Pike;
Negroes who had taken refuge in the canebrakes were
hunted down and killed; and the final death roll showed five
whites and twenty-five Negroes killed, although some place
the Negro fatalities as high as one hundred.

According to the facts gathered on the scene, the purpose
and plan of the organization was as follows: The Progressive Farmers and Household Union of America came into
being in order to combat a system of exploitation known as
"share-cropping," which has served for half a century as a
convenient means of gaining wealth by many whites without the inconvenient necessity of working. This system will
be described later. Organized at Winchester, Drew County,
the articles of incorporation were drawn by Williamson and
Williamson of Monticello, white men and ex-slaveholders.
These articles were filed in due legal form with the county
clerk at Winchester, the county seat. Branches or lodges
were to be formed in other communities, and it was hoped
that the movement would spread to all parts of the South,
as the economic exploitation pictured below existed in
all of them. The Farmers Union was in the form of a fraternal organization or secret order because the State tax
for such an organization is much lower than for any other
and because the veil of secrecy with passwords and grips

and insignia appealed to the untutored minds of most of
the members. Each male member was to pay $1.50 and each
female fifty cents. The money thus collected was to go into
a common fund to be used to employ a lawyer to make a
test in court of cases where Negroes were unable to secure
settlements.

A careful examination of the literature of the organization does not reveal the "dastardly" plot which has been
charged. The organization was declared to be for the purpose of "advancing the intellectual, material, moral, spiritual,
and financial interests of the Negro race." Applicants for
membership had to answer under oath such questions as
"Do you believe in God?" "Do you attend church?" "Do
you believe in courts?" and "Will you defend this Government and her Constitution at all times?" There is nothing
in any of the literature seen or published which indicates
any other motive than that of aspiring towards the securing
of relief from exploitation.

A "Committee of Seven" composed of white citizens of
Helena held hearings for the purpose of determining the
facts in the case. At least two members of that committee are plantation owners themselves. According to two
sources of information, when suspects were brought before
this committee they were seated in a chair charged with electricity. If the Negroes did not talk as freely as the Committee wished, the current was turned on until they did so.
This committee has declared that it secured many confessions from Negro suspects, but so far as could be learned
none of the details of these confessions has been published.

The cause of the Phillips County trouble, according to
Governor Charles H. Brough, was the circulation of what he
considers incendiary Negro publications like *The Crisis*, the
official organ of the National Association for the Advancement of Colored People. Having been a professor of economics for seventeen years before becoming Governor, it
is incredible that he is ignorant of the exploitation of Negroes in his State. It is also reasonable to believe that
Governor Brough should know that no publication would
have much chance of creating unrest and discontent among
contented, justly treated people. A further fact for consideration is that 78.6 per cent. of the population of Phillips County is Negro—the actual figures being: white, 7,176;
colored, 26,354. With the whites outnumbered almost four
to one, it appears that the fatalities would have been differ-
ently proportioned if a well-planned murder plot had existed among the Negroes.

Now, as to the facts regarding the share-cropping system
which caused the alleged "massacre." Theoretically, under
the system the owner furnishes the land, the share-cropper

Colonel George Murphy, former Confederate officer and Little Rock attorney, who defended the convicted blacks. He died during the first trial. *Courtesy of the Arkansas History Commission*

Scipio Africanus Jones, ex-slave and prominent black Little Rock attorney, who led the defense of the convicted men after Colonel Murphy's death. *Arkansas Democrat. Courtesy of the Library of Congress*

E. L. McHaney, member of the law firm of Murphy, McHaney & Dunaway, white defense attorneys in the riot cases. *Courtesy of the Arkansas History Commission*

George B. Rose, white Little Rock attorney, who worked to gain release of the convicted blacks. *Courtesy of the Library of Congress*

NEW FORM OF LYNCH-MURDER

Arkansas Trying to Beat Georgia's Vile Record.

The Truth of the Elaine Riots—Arkansas Worse Than Turkey Was—Prompt Action Necessary

More than eleven colored men have been condemned to die because of the riot at Elaine, Ark. In addition to this about forty others have been sentenced to serve long terms in the penitentiary. This nation should demand a stay of sentence in all of these "convictions" until an impartial and just tribunal passes upon the whole matter from beginning to the end. The court that sentenced those colored men was composed of the murderers that began the riot. From information of a reliable character it has been established that the Elaine riot grew out of an attempt of southern white planters to take the farm products of colored men and sell them at the highest market prices—the white men to give the colored men whatever they chose. Colored men banded together to protect themselves. But this organizing was made a pretext by white assassins to form a mob and butcher them! When the blacks held their own, U. S. soldiers were pressed into service to cow and disarm them while white villians went armed and killed them as fast as they were disarmed. Now this Arkansas court, composed of the bloodiest assassins of the world, finished the work left undone by the mob. Not a white brute has been tried, nor has there been a warrant sworn out for the mob that is known to all. Arkansas is worse than Turkey of past years! If this bloody carnage of human beings is allowed to go through, it means Negroes in Arkansas are doomed to slavery, death, peonage and pogroms that the world will shudder at. Civilized America should protest! There must be some way to save our courts from the infamy of southern outlaws. Every judge and court officer connected with that Elaine travesty, should be imprisoned and their infamous decree set aside.

Let black men everywhere raise money and send petitions to Congress, calling upon it to act at once by for-

Dr. Wm. A. Byrd

bidding the execution of those condemned men until an investigation is made and the truth is given to the world. America, take notice, you must either establish law in the South —in Arkansas, or there will be bloodshed such as the Civil War will not approach. The day that white villians in southern skins can kill and brutalize colored people without giving account for it has passed. Germany and the Germans are and were gentlemen of the finest type compared with the vicious villians of Elaine, Arkansas. Colored people let us stand as never before for our life and liberties.

(Rev.) Wm. A. Byrd.

Editorial in the black paper, *The Cleveland Gazette*, November 15, 1919.
Courtesy of the Library of Congress

Moorfield Storey, Boston aristocrat and law-yer, who, as NAACP president, presented the case to the U.S. Supreme Court in 1923. *Courtesy of the New York Public Library*

News Summary
See Page 2

THE BOSTON HERALD

CLOUDY—RAIN
BOSTON AND VICINITY—Cloudy
and rain today. Fair and warmer to-
morrow.
NORTHERN NEW ENGLAND—Fair.
Cloudy and cooler tomorrow.
Full report on page 8.

VOL. CLXVI, NO. 117   FRIDAY MORNING, OCTOBER 25, 1929—SIXTY-FOUR PAGES   ••••   TWO CENTS

FAMOUS BOSTON LAWYER DEAD

Moorfield Storey Cham-pioned Negroes and Was Noted Biographer

Moorfield Storey, former president of the American Bar Association and one of the most eminent lawyers of the nation, died last night at his home in Lincoln after an illness of several months duration. He was 84 years old. The news of his death came as a dis-tinct shock to his many friends, most of whom had not known of his serious illness.

The funeral services will be Sunday afternoon, at 3 o'clock at King's Chapel, when the representatives of various bus-inesses and professions, the nation, state and city will unite to pay last tribute to

Storey's obituary in *The Boston Herald*, October 25, 1929. *Courtesy of the Library of Congress*

Justice Charles Evans Hughes, whose dissent with Justice Oliver Wendell Holmes in the Leo Frank case set the precedent for the NAACP victory in the Arkansas cases. *Courtesy of the Library of Congress*

UTLEY REPLIES TO PROPAGANDA IN RIOTERS' APPEAL

Says "Society for Advancement of Colored People" Doing Negroes More Harm Than Good.

Attorney General Utley, in a statement issued Wednesday morning, in answer to press dispatches from Washington that the trials of the Elaine negroes, whose appeals are pending before the United States Supreme Court, had not been fair and that practically every agency in Helena had fought to convict the accused men, said that the propaganda being waged in the Capital city would cause his department no concern.

Mr. Utley stated that the facts in the case had been decided by the trial courts and recited that every appellate court had upheld the lower court's decision. His statement follows:

"This department is not worried at the efforts of the supporters of the Elaine rioters to carry on a campaign of propaganda at Washington while the cases are pending before the United States Supreme Court. We have no sort of fear that the court will be influenced by this.

(*Left*) *Arkansas Democrat*, January 3, 1923. *Courtesy of the Library of Congress*

(*Below*) *Arkansas Democrat*, January 10, 1923. *Courtesy of the Library of Congress*

ELAINE CASES BEFORE HIGH COURT NEXT WEEK

Attorney General Preparing Record in Cases of Rioters Facing Death.

Cases of Frank Moore, Ed Hicks, J. E. Knox, Ed Coleman and Paul Moore, negroes, sentenced to death for their part in the Elaine race riot of 1919, will be considered in the United States Supreme Court next Wednesday, according to J. S. Utley, attorney general, who Wednesday was working on the records, in an effort to complete the state's side for presentation.

The negroes are in custody at the "walls" in Little Rock, appeal from their sentences of death having been taken to the federal courts by E. L. McHaney, their attorney, last year.

Members of the U.S. Supreme Court, whose 1923 decision, citing the threat of violence as a barrier to justice in the Arkansas case, was a landmark of due process. (Rear) Justices Pierce Butler, Louis Brandeis, George Sutherland, Edward T. Stanford. (Front) Justices Willis Van Devanter, Joseph McKenna, Chief Justice William Howard Taft, Oliver Wendell Holmes, James C. McReynolds. Justice Holmes wrote the decision in *Moore v. Dempsey;* Justices Sutherland and McReynolds dissented. *Courtesy of the Library of Congress*

leaders of this movement, on account of the fact that they escaped from the jurisdiction of our court. It is true that the particular parties to whom you refer . . . were simply farm negroes, but some of these negroes had a very active part in committing the outrages that were committed. The prosecutions were entirely justified and I regret very much that I was unable, while I was Prosecuting Attorney, to effectively reach the parties who were the leaders of the trouble." Miller nevertheless reported to Rose that he had "information to the effect that there will be no further prosecution in the Elaine cases." He acknowledged that "if I had any other connection with the matter, I should consider very favorably the suggestions made in your letter."[81]

The obvious mellowing of Miller's attitude toward the Phillips County defendants indicated that a compromise was probably within reach in the case, but the officers of the NAACP continued an internal debate regarding what the Association should do. James Weldon Johnson wrote Walter White in August 1923 that it appeared that the NAACP would have to leave the final decision as to how to proceed further in the *Moore* case up to Scipio Jones, and he pointed out that "our great difficulty in these cases is that the burden of proof is upon us [as far as the habeas corpus proceeding was concerned]." On the other hand, Johnson said, he would personally prefer to pursue the cases legally to the end without compromise. "Even if we lost them and the men were sentenced or executed it would not hurt our record in the fight at all," Johnson said. "The reflection would be entirely upon the state of Arkansas and people would know that if the six men who have been released were innocent, that the six men executed were also innocent."[82]

"On the other hand, of course," Johnson continued, "the lives and liberty of the six men cannot be disregarded. Still, if there is sufficient influential sentiment in Arkansas to indicate that the men will be pardoned, it would be undoubtedly the wiser course to have them plead guilty. If they plead guilty and were pardoned, the public would understand instantly that it was merely a step to save the face of the state of Arkansas."[83]

In April 1923 the Association sought further legal advice from Herbert K. Stockton, a New York attorney. Stockton agreed with Storey's ultimate judgment that the NAACP would be well advised to compromise the *Moore* case and that it should not press the habeas corpus proceedings in the U.S. district court. "Mr.

Justice McReynolds' dissenting opinion [in *Moore* v. *Dempsey*], with its barely concealed animus," Stockton believed, "is indication enough of what violent prejudice would color the proceedings in the United States District Court, and still more in the State Court on a re-trial of the accused Negroes." The NAACP would have a difficult time proving its case in the habeas corpus proceeding, Stockton predicted, because H. F. Smiddy and T. K. Jones, "through whose affidavits the Supreme Court was able to reverse the lower Court as to hearing the writs, would be so intimidated that they could not be produced as witnesses, or if they were they would try to modify their testimony in favor of the State, in fear of being lynched themselves." And, if after the habeas corpus hearing, the district court ruled against the NAACP and the *Moore* defendants and dismissed the writ of habeas corpus, he continued, "I do not think the Supreme Court would reverse it. . . ." Even if the district court ruled in favor of the *Moore* group, and ordered their release on habeas corpus, they could be retried by the state, and Stockton argued that "the State officials, guided by the majority opinion of the Supreme Court, would shape the prosecution so as to give full effect to the mob vindictiveness without making the proceedings obnoxious to Supreme Court review." Should the *Moore* blacks be successful in the habeas corpus proceeding, and be retried by the state and acquitted, "which I should not expect," he said, "there would be grave danger that all the negroes released by the Courts would be lynched by the mob."[84]

While he favored compromising the *Moore* case through a plea bargain because of these considerations, Stockton warned the NAACP that a plea bargain agreed to by the local prosecutor and defense counsel would not be legally enforceable, and that the judge sentencing the defendants upon a plea to a lesser charge than murder would not be bound by the bargain. "It is essential, therefore," he emphasized, "that such of the accused as plead guilty under the gentlemen's agreement with the District Attorney, *plead guilty to such offense as carries a maximum penalty within the contemplation of the accused in making the plea*," so that even if the sentencing judge ignored the plea bargain, he could not sentence the defendants to prison for more than a specified number of years. In any case, Stockton concluded, it was "important to work this matter out so as to save the lives and restore the liberty of these unjustly accused Negroes, while at the same time keeping intact the very great moral victory which has been won."[85]

While the NAACP was considering such advice, Jones had established contact with the prosecuting attorney in Phillips County and was able, through this attorney, to obtain a petition asking Governor McRae to grant clemency to the *Moore* blacks that was signed by the members of the Committee of Seven, the mayor of Helena, the Phillips County sheriff, and other county officials and citizens.

The undersigned members of the Committee of Seven, and other citizens interested, who were appointed by Governor Brough to look after the prosecution of the Elaine negroes, following the riots of 1919, have been informed that the attorney for the six Elaine negroes now in the penitentiary at Little Rock, under sentence of death, [is] willing to abandon any further defense of these negroes, provided their sentences are commuted to second degree murder, and their terms fixed at 12 years in the penitentiary. In view of the fact that the other six negroes who were equally guilty have escaped all punishment, and that the further prosecution of these negroes would entail on our people a large expense and considering all the conditions, we hereby petition you to commute the sentences of these negroes to a term of 12 years each in the penitentiary.[86]

After securing this petition, Jones telegraphed the NAACP national office on November 2 to report that, upon payment of a thousand dollars to the Phillips County attorney involved in the negotiations, "punishment [for the *Moore* defendants] will be fixed at twelve years with satisfactory assurance sentence will terminate [in] less than a year." Jones asked for the advice of the national office, but they insisted upon more details. Jones telephoned to explain that "he felt it was best to give this lawyer $1,000 to present the petition for commutation of sentence since he felt confident that after the men had served one year they would be liberated." Johnson told Jones that "even with those facts a decision could not be made hastily and that it would be necessary for him to present the facts in full."[87]

However, Jones obviously felt that the iron was hot, and without waiting for the NAACP's authorization, he accepted the compromise, advising the Association by telegram on November 3 that he had agreed to the "proposition and commutation granted this afternoon." Arkansas Governor McRae thus announced on November 3 that he was commuting the death sentences of the blacks in the *Moore* cases to twelve years in prison.

He told the press that he took this action in response to the petition submitted to him by the Committee of Seven and other Phillips County officials and citizens.[88]

Walter White had informed Storey of the compromise Jones had been offered and had sought Storey's advice on the matter, but by the time Storey could respond, Jones had presented the NAACP with a *fait accompli*. Storey nevertheless approved Jones' action, acknowledging that he had "recognized the difficulty after this lapse of time of reproducing to the judge in the federal court the conditions which existed when these men were convicted. Our principal witnesses, the two white men, would have been difficult to get again, and I suppose they would be very reluctant to come within the jurisdiction of the court for fear of what might happen to them." "If [the men] can now get off with a few more months' imprisonment, I think we have accomplished our purpose," Storey continued. "The wild statements of a plotted insurrection have been disproved, and I fancy that all respectable people in Arkansas are ashamed of what took place. Our responsibility in the matter is really non-existent, since Mr. Jones, the counsel of these people, has himself accepted the proposition without waiting for our advice." Storey assured White, "I am very much pleased with the result of the campaign, which seemed so desperate when we went in to defend these unfortunate people, and you will allow me to say that I think the credit for the result is mainly due to you. I congratulate you on the success of your efforts."[89]

The long and complex legal battle to save the lives of the Phillips County blacks thus came to an end, and all that remained was the question of when the men would become eligible for parole or be otherwise released from prison. In December 1924, a little more than a year after the compromise had been reached, Governor McRae granted indefinite furloughs to the eight men who were serving twenty-one-year prison sentences in connection with the Phillips County riot, but it was reported that he had decided against commuting the sentences of the men in the *Moore* cases.[90]

In an interview with Governor McRae in January 1925, Scipio Jones presented the case for releasing these men. "Just completed presentation of our matters," Jones telegraphed Walter White on January 13, "anticipate favorable results by tomorrow." McRae's term of office ended in mid-January, but as one of his last acts before leaving office, on January 13, the governor granted indefinite furloughs to the six men in the *Moore* cases. McRae had received a petition signed by citizens and officials of Phillips County urging him to free the men; the good "behavior of the negroes, who have been model prisoners since their sentence," he added, "also was considered in the grant."[91]

"After five years' effort, which has taken him into the county, state and federal courts," the *Arkansas Gazette* reported, "Scipio Jones, negro attorney, armed with the governor's proclamation, will report at the gates of the Cummins State farm this morning [January 14] and obtain the release of five of the negroes. He will then return to Little Rock and report at the penitentiary 'walls' where Paul Hall is incarcerated and secure his freedom." The coffins constructed for their burial when the sentence of execution seemed assured were still in the penitentiary, the *Gazette* said, and the coffins served "as a symbol of the case which has gained widespread publicity and has been watched with interest in all parts of the country."[92]

On January 14, 1925, Frank Moore, J. E. Knox, Ed and Frank Hicks, Ed Coleman, and Paul Hall once again became free men. When Scipio Jones wired the national office of the NAACP on January 13 announcing that the men were to be freed,[93] the staff of the Association was so excited that Walter White forgot to acknowledge Jones's telegram until almost three weeks later. "When your telegrams . . . came," White finally wrote Jones, "all of us here at the office were so overjoyed at the ending of the Arkansas Cases in such a glorious victory and I, myself, was so excited over it, that I had the fine intention of sending you a congratulatory telegram at once. I find that I have neglected to do so." The NAACP would soon be holding a national conference in Denver, White said, and Jones would have to speak at the conference and "let our members from all over the country see the man who has made such a brave and brilliant fight in Arkansas."[94] In early March, Jones received more formal recognition of his efforts in the Phillips County cases when the NAACP board of directors expressed "the Association's indebtedness to you for the splendid manner in which you conducted the Arkansas Cases." He had "rendered a service not only to the men whose lives were saved and who were freed from prison," the board said, "but . . . you benefitted all America."[95]

The joy of the NAACP over this final victory in the Phillips

County cases was matched by the reaction of the black community throughout the country.[96] Reverend J. R. Marshall of Philadelphia probably reflected the reaction of the black community generally in his letter to the NAACP. "It was like a thunder bolt from a clear sky," Marshall wrote the Association. "Had it not been for the masterly work done by the Association, long before this, those innocent men would have answered the roll call in judgment. . . . For the justice of the colored race, you are doing more than all the other organizations combined. Ask for what you wish from this day on."[97]

Walter White reported the conclusion of the defense effort to Louis Marshall, noting that the release of the *Moore* blacks "completes the case in which sixty-seven men were sentenced to long prison terms ranging from twenty years to life imprisonment and the twelve to death." "We not only saved the lives of the twelve but have now freed them and all the others," White proudly concluded. "Among the very first, I wanted to share this good news with you." The NAACP, White might have added, had also succeeded in *Moore* v. *Dempsey* in obtaining the Supreme Court's reversal of *Frank* v. *Mangum*. And it was undoubtedly with this accomplishment in mind that Louis Marshall thanked White for his "thoughtfulness in informing me of the splendid result in the Arkansas cases." "It is," Marshall said, "a record of which any association may be proud."[98]

⑨ The NAACP and the Phillips County Cases: An Overview

The decision of the United States Supreme Court in *Moore* v. *Dempsey* had an important impact upon federal habeas corpus law. It also became a milestone in the modern interpretation of the Due Process Clause of the Fourteenth Amendment in relation to the conduct of state criminal trials. The *Moore* case was the first of a series of decisions in this century to liberalize the rules determining whether a state conviction may be collaterally attacked via the federal writ of habeas corpus because of alleged violations of the federal constitutional rights of the defendant. The Court in *Moore* rejected the rule of extreme comity adhered to in *Frank* v. *Mangum*, a rule that had made state appellate court determinations of whether federal rights had been violated well-nigh conclusive.[1] "Instead of being merely a secondary alternative to the state court channel of litigation," one commentator has said of the effect of the *Moore* decision, "federal habeas corpus was thereby recognized as an available sequel. A case which had completely run the state channel could then be taken into federal court for independent reexamination of the federal contentions previously passed upon by the state courts."[2]

Some commentators, however, have argued that the *Moore* case did not reverse the decision in the *Frank* case, that the Supreme Court was consistent in both cases. Those holding this view maintain that the Court merely found the corrective process supplied by the appellate review of the *Moore* case in Arkansas to be inadequate, while the corrective process furnished by Georgia in the *Frank* case had been found to be adequate. "Though the opinion is admittedly far from clear," one commentator has said, "all *Moore* v. *Dempsey* may be saying, is that a conclusory and out-of-hand rejection by a state of a claim of violation of federal right, without any process of inquiry being afforded at all, cannot insulate the merits of the question from the habeas corpus court: if the state's findings are to 'count', they must be reasoned findings rationally reached through fair procedures. So viewed, the case is entirely consistent with *Frank*."[3]

Justice John Marshall Harlan, writing in dissent in 1963, supported this interpretation of the *Moore* decision. What "the Court appears to have held [in *Moore*]," he said, "was that the state appellate court's perfunctory treatment of the question of mob domination, amounting to nothing more than reliance on the presumptive validity of the trial, was not in fact acceptable corrective process and federal habeas would therefore lie to consider the merits of the claim."[4] Harlan was speaking for only three members of the Court; the majority held that the *Frank* decision "was substantially repudiated in Moore v. Dempsey. . . . It was settled in Moore, the Court continued, restoring what evidently had been the assumption until Frank . . . that the state courts' view of the merits was not entitled to conclusive weight. We have not deviated from that position."[5]

Certainly, Justice McReynolds, in dissent in the *Moore* case, felt that the Court was repudiating the decision in *Frank* v. *Mangum*. "In Frank v. Mangum . . . , after great consideration a majority of this court approved the doctrine which should be applied here," McReynolds said. "The doctrine is right and wholesome. I cannot agree now to put it aside and substitute the views expressed by the minority of the court in that cause."[6] A close examination of the proceedings in the *Moore* case leads to the conclusion that McReynolds was correct in charging that the Court was abandoning the principles of the *Frank* decision. Storey's argument in the Supreme Court to the contrary notwithstanding, the appellate review available in the *Moore* case in the Arkansas Supreme Court was fully adequate to supply a corrective process for the remedying of any federal rights that had been violated. Although technically the Arkansas Supreme

Court was limited in its review of criminal cases to the correction of errors of law, the errors of law subject to review by the court included erroneous overrulings of motions for new trials. And motions for new trials were to be granted in Arkansas when the substantial rights of defendants had been violated or when a fair trial had been denied. The state supreme court was further authorized to review all errors prejudicial to a defendant in a capital case, even if the errors had not been excepted to at the trial, if the errors were incorporated in a motion for a new trial. The appellate review available in the Arkansas Supreme Court in the *Moore* case could not therefore be said to have failed to provide the corrective process contemplated by the *Frank* case.[7]

In his dissent in *Frank* v. *Mangum*, Justice Holmes had also said that mob domination of a trial was so fundamental a denial of due process that it would cause loss of jurisdiction in the trial court, and that if a petition for a federal writ of habeas corpus "discloses facts that amount to a loss of jurisdiction in the trial court, jurisdiction could not be restored by any decision above."[8] No matter how liberal the appellate review afforded to a defendant convicted at such a trial, Holmes appeared to be saying, that corrective process would not be sufficient to overcome the loss of jurisdiction in the trial court and the resulting invalidity of the conviction under due process. In his majority opinion in *Moore* v. *Dempsey*, Holmes reiterated this point by saying that "if the case is that the whole proceeding is a mask,— that counsel, jury, and judge were swept to the fatal end by an irresistible wave of public passion, and that the state courts failed to correct the wrong,—*neither perfection in the machinery for correction* nor the possibility that the trial court and counsel saw no other way of avoiding an immediate outbreak of the mob can prevent this court from securing to the petitioners their constitutional rights."[9] (Emphasis added.)

To the majority of the Court in the *Moore* case, the fact that the State of Arkansas had provided a corrective process to the *Moore* defendants comparable to that afforded Leo Frank by the State of Georgia was not a sufficient ground for the U.S. district court to refuse to hold a hearing on the allegations of mob domination. Indeed, according to Holmes' language, even "perfection" in the corrective process afforded by state appellate review could not overcome the invalidity of a criminal conviction at a trial dominated by a mob, since such a trial was simply void under due process. Without pointing to any inadequacies in the corrective process afforded the *Moore* defendants by Arkansas, and without indicating how that corrective process differed from that provided by Georgia in the *Frank* case, Holmes held in *Moore* that the corrective process "does not seem to us sufficient to allow a judge of the United States to escape the duty of examining the facts for himself, when, if true, as alleged, they make the trial absolutely void."[10]

If a mob-dominated trial is absolutely void, it would appear that the only adequate corrective process for a conviction obtained at such a trial would be a reversal of the conviction. And, as Holmes seems plainly to have indicated in the *Moore* case, if a reversal of such a conviction has not been provided by the state appellate courts, the conviction could be properly attacked on petition for a writ of habeas corpus in the federal courts. One commentator correctly concluded that Justice Holmes in the *Moore* case "held that perfection of the machinery of corrective process is not sufficient to satisfy the federal right of 'due process. . . .' According to him, to furnish due process the state courts must correct the wrong. In short, the statement of Mr. Justice Holmes in the minority opinion in *Frank* v. *Mangum* became the view of the majority in *Moore* v. *Dempsey*."[11]

The immediate effect of the Court's liberalization of the availability of the federal writ of habeas corpus in the *Moore* case was minimal, since the requirements imposed upon state criminal trials by the Due Process Clause of the Fourteenth Amendment were rather slight in 1923, and violations of due process in state criminal trials where no mob domination existed were therefore largely nonexistent. Under the then prevailing interpretation of the Due Process Clause by the Supreme Court, the states were required to furnish defendants a fair trial and a trial that was mob dominated was not fair under due process standards, but the Court had repeatedly refused to hold that due process guaranteed specific procedural rights to criminal defendants in addition to the general right to a fair trial. The Court had held, for example, that the Due Process Clause did not guarantee to state criminal defendants the right to an indictment by a grand jury,[12] the right to trial by jury,[13] the right to confront and cross-examine adverse witnesses,[14] or the right against compulsory self-incrimination.[15]

Moore v. *Dempsey* constituted a major turning point in the development of modern standards of due process, the Court ruling that the Due Process Clause was not necessarily satisfied by a trial conducted according to the usual modes of proceeding and with the opportunity for a defendant to obtain appellate review of his conviction. In *Moore*, the Court began to look behind the procedural formalities of state criminal trials to ask whether, in fact, the defendant had received a fair trial at which there had been an adequate opportunity to be heard. In this case, it had concluded that a mob-dominated trial violated this elementary due process right to a fair hearing in so fundamental a way that reversal of the resultant conviction was the only appropriate remedy.

Once the Court had begun to scrutinize state criminal proceedings more closely to determine whether a fair trial had in fact been had under the Due Process Clause, it determined that other elements were essential to a fair trial besides the absence of mob domination of the proceedings. In *Powell* v. *Alabama*, decided in 1932, the Court held that the trial and conviction of ignorant black youths for the capital offense of rape without effective representation by counsel on their behalf (the Scottsboro incident) denied the right to a fair trial mandated by the Due Process Clause. "What, then, does a hearing include?" the Court asked in that opinion. "Historically and in practice, in our own country at least, it has always included the right to the aid of counsel when desired and provided by the party asserting the right. The right to be heard would be, in many cases, of little avail if it did not comprehend the right to be heard by counsel." Due process therefore required, the Court held, that the states appoint counsel for indigent defendants in capital cases, and even in non-capital cases if the lack of counsel would result in an unfair trial for a defendant.[16]

In *Mooney* v. *Holohan*, decided in 1935, the Court similarly held that the knowing use of perjured testimony by the prosecution to convict a defendant denied the right to a fair trial required by the Due Process Clause. The requirements of due process, the Court said, "cannot be deemed to be satisfied by mere notice and hearing if a State has contrived a conviction through the pretense of a trial which in truth is but used as a means of depriving a defendant of liberty through a deliberate deception of court and jury by the presentation of testimony known to be perjured. Such a contrivance by a State to procure the conviction and imprisonment of a defendant is as inconsistent with the rudimentary demands of justice as is the obtaining of a like result by intimidation."[17]

During the following year, the Court, in *Brown* v. *Mississippi*, held that the right to a fair trial in a state criminal proceeding had been violated by the use of confessions obtained from the black defendants through the use of brutal physical torture. The *Brown* case, appropriately enough, was appealed to the Court under the sponsorship of the NAACP.[18] Chief Justice Hughes cited *Moore* v. *Dempsey* in his opinion for a unanimous Court reversing the murder convictions of the defendants. The use of a coerced confession to convict a defendant violated the Due Process Clause, Hughes said, since it "made the whole proceeding a mere pretence of a trial and rendered the conviction and sentence wholly void."[19]

Just thirteen years, then, after its decision in *Moore* v. *Dempsey*, the Court had held not only that the Due Process Clause was violated by mob domination of a criminal trial but also that a fair trial required the appointment of counsel for indigent defendants in all capital cases and in some non-capital cases and that the use of perjured testimony by the prosecution or of confessions that had been obtained through the use of coercion invalidated convictions. During the 1940s and 1950s, the Court added to the list of procedural rights essential to a fair trial. Among other decisions, it held that the procurement of evidence against a defendant by methods that "shock the conscience," such as pumping a suspect's stomach, violates due process, as does the failure to provide a defendant with adequate notice and a public trial.[20]

Until the 1960s, the Supreme Court approached the review of state criminal convictions from the standpoint of whether the defendant had been afforded a fair trial. And while the Court significantly increased the number of procedural elements essential to a fair trial beginning with *Moore* v. *Dempsey* and continuing through the 1950s, it consistently refused to hold that the specific procedural rights in the Bill of Rights applied in state criminal trials until 1961, at which time it held that the Fourth Amendment prohibition of unreasonable searches and seizures fully applied to state criminal proceedings.[21] The Court had abandoned its previous reluctance to apply the criminal procedure provisions of the Bill of Rights to the states via the Due Process Clause. During the next eight years, the Court held applicable to the states—via the Due Process Clause—the Cruel and Unusual Punishment Clause of the Eighth Amendment,[22] the Self-Incrimination[23] and Double Jeopardy[24] Clauses of the Fifth Amendment; and the Speedy Trial,[25] Jury Trial,[26] Confrontation,[27] Compulsory Process,[28] and Assistance of Counsel Clauses[29] of the Sixth Amendment. By 1969 almost all of the criminal procedure protections of the Bill of Rights had been held to be required in state criminal proceedings under the Due Process Clause of the Fourteenth Amendment.[30]

What had begun in *Moore* v. *Dempsey,* as a discrete ruling that a conviction at a trial dominated by a mob was void under the Due Process Clause, had become by 1970 a requirement that most of the criminal procedure provisions of the Bill of Rights had to be observed by the states in their conduct of criminal trials. This expansion of the meaning of the Due Process Clause begun in the *Moore* case made the federal writ of habeas corpus increasingly important as a means of vindicating federal rights, since the number of such rights applicable in state criminal proceedings constantly grew from 1923 to the 1970s, while, in a parallel development, the Supreme Court was liberalizing the rules governing the availability of the writ of habeas corpus to state prisoners.[31]

Although the use of the federal writ of habeas corpus as a means of attacking a state criminal conviction was relatively rare at the time of the decision of the *Moore* case, 541 petitions for writs of habeas corpus were filed by state prisoners in the federal courts in 1952; 1,020 in 1961; and 9,419 in 1981.[32] This growing resort to federal writs of habeas corpus by state prisoners led to serious criticism from state judges, and as early as 1952 the Conference of State Chief Justices, complaining about the habeas jurisdiction of the federal courts, argued that orderly "procedure under our dual system of government should require that a final judgment of a state's highest court be subject to review or reversal only by the Supreme Court of the United States," and not by U.S. district courts in habeas corpus proceedings.[33] Congress considered proposals during the 1950s to restrict the habeas corpus jurisdiction of the federal courts, but in the end these proposals were rejected.[34] During the 1970s the Burger Court did hold that issues relating to whether a state court had improperly failed to exclude evidence that was the product of an unreasonable search and seizure could not be raised on petition for a writ of habeas corpus in the federal courts if the state had provided a full and fair opportunity for the litigation of such issues.[35] The federal writ of habeas corpus nevertheless remains an important means by which most of the expanded list of procedural rights applicable to state criminal trials under the Fourteenth Amendment could be vindicated.

In *Moore* v. *Dempsey,* therefore, not only had the NAACP won an important legal case, but it had also established what came to be regarded as milestones both in the modern development of the Due Process Clause of the Fourteenth Amendment and in the law governing the writ of habeas corpus in the federal courts. "In retrospect," one commentator has said, "it is fitting that the case which gave birth to the modern aspect of due process also worked a procedural revolution in one of the primary remedies for vindicating rights guaranteed by the fourteenth amendment."[36]

The Phillips County episode also marked a milestone for the NAACP as an organization, since the Association had never before undertaken litigation as complex and as protracted as that in the *Moore* and *Ware* cases. The NAACP was ultimately to become nationally known for its litigation efforts on behalf of blacks in the U.S. Supreme Court, especially with its victory over public school segregation in *Brown* v. *Board of Education* in 1954,[37] but before the Phillips County cases, it had played an important role in Supreme Court litigation on only two occasions. The Association had participated in *Guinn* v. *United States* in 1915,[38] by filing an *amicus curiae* brief attacking Oklahoma's use of a grandfather clause to disfranchise blacks, and the organization had successfully attacked residential segregation in a case it sponsored to the Court in 1917, *Buchanan* v. *Warley.*[39]

The NAACP's participation in the Phillips County cases contributed to its growing fund of experience in the conduct of constitutional litigation as a means of attacking the injustice and discrimination practiced against blacks. These cases also contributed to the NAACP's viability as an organization. The Association had overcome a crisis in its finances and in its leadership during the course of their litigation.[40] Still, the Phillips County cases revealed weaknesses in the NAACP's capacity to conduct constitutional litigation effectively, weaknesses that would cause the organization future problems and that would have to be corrected before it could achieve a high level of performance as a litigating group. The first such weakness was the lack of the effective organization required in conducting constitutional cases. The availability of Moorfield Storey to represent the NAACP with great ability at the appellate court level obscured the fact that the Association was dependent upon the ad hoc retention of local counsel, of varying levels of character and competence, to conduct its litigation at crucial stages in the lower courts. And as its experience with E. L. McHaney demonstrated, dependence upon local counsel who were not committed to, or who might even be hostile to, the NAACP's goals could prove to be well-nigh disastrous.

Nor was this problem peculiar to the Phillips County cases. This became clear in the Association's experience in the Scottsboro litigation during the 1930s. The NAACP at first retained an attorney to defend the nine black youths convicted of the capital crime of rape in Alabama, but that man proved to be an incompetent lawyer as well as an alcoholic.[41] The Association later retained one of the best criminal lawyers in Birmingham, yet the attorney refused to challenge racial discrimination in the selection of the juries in the cases or to appeal the cases beyond the Alabama Supreme Court.[42] The NAACP's actions proved futile; the Communist Party–controlled International Labor Defense won control of the Scottsboro litigation, forcing the NAACP and its counsel out of the cases.[43]

The NAACP involved in the Phillips County and Scottsboro cases was not the smoothly functioning litigating group that it would become in the 1950s. The problems the NAACP faced in those early cases would not be overcome until the Association developed a network of dependable and committed attorneys across the country and a strengthened organizational capacity for the planning and direction of litigation. Both goals would slowly be reached by the Association. Its capacity for the effective conduct of constitutional litigation was considerably enhanced by the services, first, of Charles H. Houston; then, of Thurgood Marshall as special counsel and by the establishment of the NAACP Legal Defense and Education Fund in 1939. But the weaknesses revealed in the Phillips County cases were neither easily nor quickly overcome.[44]

Another problem that surfaced during the Phillips County litigation was NAACP condescension toward, and arm's-length treatment of, less well educated blacks and those who were not members of the Association. This attitude surfaced early in the cases when Walter White described Robert Hill in his *Chicago Daily News* article as being "an ignorant, illiterate country farm hand, without brains enough to engineer" an insurrection against the whites. And James Weldon Johnson displayed a similar attitude when he suggested that even if the condemned blacks were executed, the NAACP would not be harmed as an organization. There had been suggestions that the men in the *Ware* cases might undertake speaking engagements in Arkansas after their release, but Johnson vetoed the idea, pointing out that the "men are uneducated if not illiterate and nobody could tell what they would say."[45]

An attitude of condescension and suspicion was also evident in the NAACP's reaction to the involvement of local Arkansas blacks through the Citizens Defense Fund Commission. John Shillady initially disparaged this group.[46] The Association also greeted the participation of Scipio Jones and other black lawyers in the cases with suspicion. This attitude toward the local blacks undoubtedly contributed to the conflicts that ultimately occurred between the Association and the CDFC.

Fortunately, such attitudes did not seriously affect the NAACP's ultimate success in the Phillips County litigation. But during the 1930s, similar postures did contribute to a disaster for the Association in the Scottsboro cases. The NAACP sought to represent the nine Scottsboro defendants, but failed initially even to contact the parents of the boys, all minors who could not make the final selection of the attorneys to represent them. And when the International Labor Defense persuaded most of the parents to allow it to control the defense of their sons, Walter White commented publicly that it "should be remembered that the boys and their parents are humble folk and have had few opportunities for knowledge. They have been confused by the conflicting statements made to them." William Pickens, an NAACP field secretary, said privately that some of the parents were "the densest and dumbest animals it has yet been my privilege to meet." The ILD, of course, took full advantage of such attitudes in wresting the control of the Scottsboro litigation from the NAACP.[47] After their dismissive and patronizing behavior toward the parents of the Scottsboro boys had succeeded in helping the ILD seize control of the litigation, the NAACP in desperation asked Clarence Darrow and Arthur Garfield Hays to represent them and the Scottsboro defendants. But the ILD, which had authorization from the parents of the defendants to represent them, insisted that Darrow and Hays repudiate the NAACP and accept direction from the ILD in their conduct of the litigation, and both men withdrew from the cases. The episode not only portrayed the NAACP as inept but also was embarrassing to Darrow and Hays. It led to serious criticism of the Association.[48]

No one, however, could deny that the Association had won a notable victory in the Phillips County cases, despite a situation that had appeared hopeless at the conclusion of the trials in November 1919. The NAACP victory was undoubtedly achieved in large measure as a result of the courage and ability of Walter White in his capacity as assistant secretary of the Association. James Weldon Johnson had reported to the NAACP board of directors in July 1923 that the "handling of the Arkansas cases at the National Office has been almost entirely in the hands of Mr. White who has performed the work with a great deal of intelligence and skill."[49]

White had been appointed assistant secretary of the Association in January 1918, less than a year before the riot occurred, and he cut his teeth as an NAACP officer in handling the Phillips County cases in the national office. When James Weldon Johnson resigned the office of executive secretary of the NAACP in 1931, Walter White was selected as his successor. "The reputation White acquired in these years [during the Phillips County litigation]," the historian of the NAACP has said, "undoubtedly led to his selection as Johnson's successor as secretary of the Association."[50] White served as secretary of the NAACP until his death in 1955, having lived to witness the Association's great victory in the school desegregation cases in 1954.

Moorfield Storey continued to serve as president of the NAACP until his death on October 24, 1929. On the occasion of Storey's death, the board of directors of the NAACP adopted a resolution praising his services to the Association. "At the time of the Arkansas massacre of October, 1919, when upwards of two hundred Negro men, women and children were slaughtered by mobs because they had dared to attempt to organize against vicious economic exploitation," the resolution read, "it was Mr. Storey who wrote the brief and argued the cases, in the United States Supreme Court, of the six Negro peons sentenced to death in connection with the Arkansas cases. The great victory won by Mr. Storey which freed these six men and six others also sentenced to death, and sixty-seven who had been sentenced to long prison terms, is rightly regarded as one of the greatest steps toward assurance of a fair trial to persons accused of crime that has ever been won. The decision of the United States Supreme Court in these cases serves to assure a fair and impartial trial free from mob domination, to white men as well as black."[51]

In addition to securing the freedom of the defendants, Storey and the NAACP had hoped that the litigation in the Phillips County cases would expose the peonage conditions in eastern Arkansas and serve to improve the economic lot of the blacks in that region of the country. As James Weldon Johnson said at the outset of the litigation, "while the lives of the twelve men under sentence of death are very important, and we are very anxious to save them, we are making an equal effort for the correction of the evils which brought on the conflict . . . , not only in Arkansas, but in all other southern states where the system of exploitation exists."[52] The NAACP, however, did not accomplish this larger purpose in the Phillips County cases; the economic status of the tenant farmers and sharecroppers in eastern Arkansas continued to be deplorable. By the 1930s eastern Arkansas blacks, some of whom had been members of the Progressive Farmers Union in 1919, were joining with white sharecroppers and tenant farmers in organizing the Southern Tenant Farmers Union (STFU) under socialist auspices to protest their economic condition. And like the Progressive Farmers Union, the STFU was met with violence, intimidation, and suppression by the planters of the region.[53]

Although some Phillips County blacks survived the riot of 1919 to join the STFU in the 1930s, the twelve men who had been condemned to death in the riot's aftermath went their separate ways after their release from prison. In response to inquiries from the NAACP, in 1936 Scipio Jones reported that of the twelve, nine were still living, "one in Little Rock, and one in Crittendon County, this state, and two live in Chicago, the others' whereabouts is unknown."[54]

Other participants in the Phillips County cases did not follow the defendants into obscurity. E. L. McHaney was elected to the Arkansas House of Representatives and represented Pulaski County (Little Rock) from 1921 to 1923. In 1927 McHaney was appointed to the Arkansas Supreme Court. He served as a judge on that court until his death in May 1948.[55]

McHaney was appointed to the state supreme court by Governor John E. Martineau, who as Chancellor of the Pulaski County Chancery Court had prevented the execution of the *Moore* blacks in 1921 by issuing writs of habeas corpus and an injunction. Martineau ran for governor in 1924 as an anti–Ku Klux Klan candidate, but was defeated in the Democratic primary. In 1926, however, in one "of the most bitter campaigns in Arkansas history," Martineau defeated incumbent Governor Tom J. Terral in the primary and was elected governor.[56] When devastating floods struck Arkansas in 1927 as a result of the overflowing of the Mississippi River, Martineau's handling of the relief efforts for the flood victims brought him into close contact with Herbert Hoover, then Secretary of Commerce in the Coolidge administration. As a consequence, Hoover recommended Martineau to President Coolidge for an appointment as U.S. district judge for the Eastern District of Arkansas, and with the support of U.S. Senator from Arkansas Joseph T. Robinson, Martineau's brother-in-law, Martineau was appointed to the federal bench in March 1928. He served as U.S. district judge until his death in March 1937. Ironically, in one of the last cases Judge Martineau presided over, a city marshal was accused of violating federal antipeonage statutes in the employment of black laborers on his plantation in Earle, Arkansas.[57]

E. M. Allen left Phillips County after the 1919 riot and later became president of the National Surety Company in New York City. Questioned in 1960 about the Phillips County trouble, Allen still clung to the version of the riot that had been endorsed by the Committee of Seven. He had owned the townsite at Elaine at the time of the trouble, Allen said, and "I bent over backwards to obtain the true facts and to present them in an unbiased fashion, as I was gravely concerned over the future welfare of Elaine following the disturbance." Allen insisted that the principal object of Robert Hill in organizing the Progressive Farmers Union had been to defraud the blacks who joined the union. "No one knows how much money Hill picked up fleecing the Negro members of these [union] lodges," he said. "Some Negroes in Elaine raised a purse of $300 to defray the expense of extraditing him from Kansas. Gov. Allen of Kansas told me he had to refuse for fear of mob violence. He was right, but the violence would have been committed by the Negroes Hill had robbed, not by the whites."[58]

John E. Miller, the prosecuting attorney in the trials following the Phillips County trouble, was elected to the U.S. House of Representatives in 1931 and served as a congressman until 1937. In the summer of 1937, U.S. Senator Joseph T. Robinson, the majority leader of the Senate, died, and a special election to fill his seat was held. The Democratic State Committee nominated Governor Carl E. Baily to replace Robinson, but Miller announced as an independent candidate for the Senate seat. Running as an anti–New Dealer, Miller defeated Baily by a margin of 3 to 2, the first time in the post-Reconstruction history of the state that a nominee of the Democratic Party for a state or national office had been defeated.[59] After serving for four years in the U.S. Senate, Miller was nominated by President Franklin Roosevelt as U.S. district court judge for the Western District of Arkansas, and the Senate confirmed the appointment in January 1941.[60] Miller served as a U.S. district judge in Arkansas until his retirement in February 1967.[61] During his service as a federal judge, Miller was involved in the implementation of the Supreme Court's school desegregation decisions in the 1950s. He was one of several southern federal district judges who were reluctant and dilatory in their enforcement of those decisions. Speaking to a county bar association in Arkansas after the Supreme Court ordered desegregation of the public schools, Judge Miller criticized "some of the appellate courts" for an "inclination . . . to arrogate unto themselves the power to declare for us certain standards contrary to the mores . . . which have existed for centuries in this country." Some of Miller's rulings from the federal bench in Arkansas contributed to the crisis over the desegregation of the public schools in Little Rock in the late 1950s. He retired from the federal bench in 1967 and died in January 1981.[62]

Miller had remained convinced that he had been fully justified in prosecuting the Phillips County blacks. Interviewed about the riot in 1965, he expressed doubt that there had been a long-standing conspiracy among the blacks in the county to engage in an insurrection against the whites, but maintained that the blacks had been agitated over what they felt were real grievances and had used arms to protect the secrecy of the Progressive Farmers Union. Thus their prosecution was justified.[63]

Scipio Africanus Jones, the man who won freedom for all of the Phillips County defendants, received effusive praise from the NAACP and the Little Rock black press after his victory. "Mr. Jones went down to Helena and took charge of that case when it was a tangled mess after the defendants had been beaten into making damaging statements," the Little Rock *Arkansas Survey* said. "He went down there and gathered the data for his case when Helena was a seething cauldron of Hate; when the least indiscretion meant death. . . . For four years he travelled and investigated and studied and plead until the 13th of January when Governor McRae opened the prison gates to the last of the alleged rioters. And during the four years [Scipio Jones] has maintained his poise. At all times he has conducted his case so as to retain the friendship and the help of the good people of the state. All hail . . . Jones. Praise him for his knowledge of law, his nerve, his patience and his sagacity. [He] will receive little glory, but it is the great state of Arkansas which is the real beneficiary of his service."[64]

The victory in the Phillips County cases was the apex of Scipio Jones's legal career, but he was later elected as a special judge of the Chancery Court of Pulaski County and played a role in attacking both the Arkansas grandfather clause, which had disfranchised blacks, and racial discrimination in the selection of juries in the state. He was instrumental in obtaining legislative appropriations to pay out-of-state tuition for black students who sought professional education but were barred from Arkansas professional schools.[65] A life-long Republican, Scipio Jones was active in the Arkansas Republican Party and strongly resisted attempts by white Republicans to exclude blacks from participation. In 1928 and in 1940, he was elected as a delegate to the Republican national conventions.[66]

Scipio Jones died at his home in Little Rock on March 28, 1943, at the age of eighty. Funeral services were held at the Bethel A.M.E. Church, where he had been a member for fifty years, and many governmental and political leaders, including some old enemies, attended the services. In recognition of the status he had achieved in the community, the all-white school board of North Little Rock named the black high school in Jones's memory. Born a slave, and compelled to live all his life in a racially segregated society, Scipio Africanus Jones had fought the good fight to change that society.[67]

A Note on Sources

For the documentation herein, I have relied substantially upon the materials available in the NAACP Papers, which are located in the Manuscript Division of the Library of Congress. These materials are organized into sections designated by a letter and a number, and in citing them, I have used this designation.

Unfortunately, a large portion of the NAACP Papers relating to the Phillips County riot were lost, but, earlier, Arthur I. Waskow had made verbatim, typewritten transcriptions of much of this material in preparing his book *From Race Riot to Sit-In, 1919 and the 1960s* (Garden City, N.Y.: Doubleday & Co., 1966). These notes were deposited in the Wisconsin State Historical Society together with Waskow's notes on materials in the National Archives relevant to the Phillips County trouble. The notes are Accession M76–358 in the Wisconsin State Historical Society. My references to them in the footnotes are designated by the words "Waskow Papers," or "NA, Waskow Papers," if the notes relate to National Archives materials.

I have also used materials from the Kansas State Historical Society's Department of Archives and the American Civil Liberties Union Archives at Princeton University. References to materials from these sources are designated "DA-KSHA" and "ACLU Archives."

Finally, I have relied upon the briefs and record filed in the U.S. Supreme Court in *Moore* v. *Dempsey*, 261 U.S. 86 (1923), which are located in the Law Library of the Library of Congress.

Chapter Notes

Preface

1. *Moore* v. *Dempsey*, 261 U.S. 86 (1923). My work on the nationalization of the Bill of Rights was published as *The Supreme Court and the Second Bill of Rights* (Madison: University of Wisconsin Press, 1981).
2. *Gitlow* v. *New York*, 268 U.S. 652 (1925).

Introduction

1. See David Fellman, *The Defendant's Rights Today* (Madison: University of Wisconsin Press, 1976), 17–18.
2. Cortner, *Supreme Court*, 177–278.
3. *Moore* v. *Dempsey*, 261 U.S. 86 (1923).
4. *Frank* v. *Mangum*, 237 U.S. 809 (1915). On the *Frank* case, see Leonard Dinnerstein, *The Leo Frank Case* (New York: Columbia University Press, 1968).
5. *Moore* v. *Dempsey*, 91.
6. NAACP Press Release, Jan. 14, 1925, NAACP Papers, D-44.
7. On the NAACP's participation in voting rights cases, see Clement E. Vose, *Constitutional Change* (Lexington, Mass.: Lexington Books, 1972), chaps. 2 and 12; on the NAACP's housing litigation, see Vose, *Caucasians Only* (Berkeley: University of California Press, 1959); and on the school desegregation cases, see Richard Kluger, *Simple Justice* (New York: Knopf, 1976).

1. Autumn 1919: The Phillips County Riot

1. On the Red Scare generally, see Julian F. Jaffe, *Crusade Against Radicalism: New York during the Red Scare, 1914–24* (Port Washington, N.Y.: Kennikat Press, 1972); for the impact of the Red Scare on civil liberties, see Zechariah Chafee, Jr., *Free Speech in the United States*

(Cambridge, Mass.: Harvard University Press, 1954), and Paul L. Murphy, *The Meaning of Freedom of Speech* (Westport, Conn.: Greenwood, 1972). On the Red Scare in Arkansas, see Joey McCarty, "The Red Scare in Arkansas: A Southern State and National Hysteria," *Arkansas Historical Quarterly* 37 (1978): 264–77.

2. See Arthur I. Waskow, *From Race Riot to Sit-In, 1919 and the 1960s* (Garden City, N.Y.: Doubleday, 1966), and Charles Flint Kellogg, *NAACP: A History of the National Association for the Advancement of Colored People* (Baltimore: The Johns Hopkins University Press, 1967), chap. 10, "Lynching and Mob Violence," 209–46.

3. Fourteenth Census, III, p. 96 (Washington, D.C.: Government Printing Office, 1922). For a description of the founding and early history of Helena, see Ted R. Worley, "Helena on the Mississippi," *Arkansas Historical Quarterly* 12 (1954): 1–15.

4. *Arkansas Gazette*, Oct. 4, 1919, p. 1; Oct. 3, 1919, p. 18; J. W. Butts and Dorothy James, "The Underlying Causes of the Elaine Riot of 1919," *Arkansas Historical Quarterly* 20 (1961): 95–104. This article by two lifelong residents of Phillips County strongly defends the official version of the Elaine riot. With their assertion that "all those accused of complicity in the Elaine riot were given fair trials" (p. 103), the authors raise serious doubts as to the accuracy and objectivity of their findings. This article was apparently published in response to an earlier article supportive of the black, or NAACP, version of the Elaine riot. See O. A. Rogers, Jr., "The Elaine Race Riots of 1919," *Arkansas Historical Quarterly* 19 (1960): 142–50.

Arthur I. Waskow, in his *From Race Riot to Sit-In*, states that the Committee of Seven which later investigated the Elaine riot was "formally appointed by Governor Brough, but in reality it had grown out of the earlier secret committee of Phillips County whites to investigate rumors of an uprising" (p. 132).

5. *Arkansas Gazette*, Oct. 2, 1919, pp. 1, 16.

6. Ibid.

7. Ibid., Oct. 2, 1919, p. 1; Oct. 3, 1919, p. 1. Reports of fighting in Elaine, and that the bodies of fifteen slain blacks were in the streets, were apparently false. See Butts and James, "Underlying Causes," p. 95.

8. *Arkansas Gazette*, Oct. 3, 1919, pp. 1, 18.

9. Ibid., Oct. 4, 1919, p. 1.

10. Ibid., Oct. 2, 1919, p. 1.

11. Ibid., Oct. 3, 1919, p. 1.

12. Ibid.

13. Ibid.

14. Charles W. Crawford, "From Classroom to State Capitol: Charles H. Brough and the Campaign of 1916," *Arkansas Historical Quarterly* 21 (1962): 213–30. See also William Foy Lisenby, "Brough, Baptists, and Bombast: The Election of 1928," *Arkansas Historical Quarterly* 32 (1973): 120–31; and Ralph W. Widener, Jr., "Charles Hillman Brough," *Arkansas Historical Quarterly* 34 (1975): 99–121.

15. Telegram, W. S. Kirby, U.S. Senator, to Army Chief of Staff, Oct. 2, 1919, memorandum, n.d., War Dept. Mss; and memorandum from

Col. Isaac C. Jenks, Infantry, Third Division, to Commanding General, Camp Pike, Oct. 14, 1919, War Dept. Mss., NA, Waskow Papers.

16. Memorandum from Col. Isaac C. Jenks to Commanding General Camp Pike, Oct. 14, 1919, War Dept. Mss., NA, Waskow Papers.

17. *Arkansas Gazette*, Oct. 4, 1919, p. 1.

18. Ibid., Oct. 3, 1919, p. 1; Oct. 4, 1919, p. 1. The soldier who was killed was Corporal Luther Earles; the wounded soldiers were Sergeant Kervile V. Gay and Andrew Seson.

19. Ibid., Oct. 5, 1919, p. 1.

20. Ibid., Oct. 4, 1919, p. 1.

21. Ibid.

22. Ibid., Oct. 21, 1919, p. 3.

23. Ibid., Oct. 6, 1919, p. 1.

24. Memorandum from Lt. Col. Jesse Gaston to Commanding General, Camp Pike, Oct. 5, 1919, War Dept. Mss., NA, Waskow Papers.

25. S. D. Sturgis, Major General, Commanding Camp Pike, to Adjutant General, Oct. 28, 1919, War Dept. Mss., NA, Waskow Papers.

26. O. S. Bratton to U. S. Bratton, Nov. 5, 1919, Waskow Papers.

27. *Arkansas Gazette*, Oct. 12, 1919, p. 1.

28. Ibid., Oct. 8, 1919, p. 1.

29. Ibid., Oct. 6, 1919, pp. 1, 3.

30. Record, *Moore* v. *Dempsey*, pp. 12–14. On E. M. Allen, see Waskow, *From Race Riot to Sit-In*, 137; and Butts and James, "Underlying Causes," 99, n. 19.

31. Record, *Moore* v. *Dempsey*, pp. 12–14; see also *Arkansas Gazette*, Oct. 7, 1919, pp. 1, 3.

32. *Arkansas Gazette*, Oct. 5, 1919, p. 25; Oct. 6, 1919, p. 3; Nov. 10, 1919, p. 1.

33. Ibid., Oct. 5, 1919, p. 1; Powell was misidentified in this story as "V. B." Powell; see ibid., Oct. 6, 1919, p. 3.

34. There were false reports of Hill's arrest in York, Alabama, and Clarendon, Arkansas, during this period. See ibid., Oct. 12, 1919, p. 1; Oct. 17, 1919, p. 1.

35. Ibid., Oct. 5, 1919, p. 1.

36. Ibid., Oct. 8, 1919, p. 1.

37. Ibid., Oct. 6, 1919, p. 1.

38. Ibid., Oct. 9, 1919, p. 1.

39. Ibid., Oct. 10, 1919, p. 1.

40. Ibid., Oct. 30, 1919, p. 1; Nov. 1, 1919, p. 5.

41. Ibid., Nov. 2, 1919, p. 1.

42. Ibid., Nov. 3, 1919, p. 1.

43. Ibid., Oct. 31, 1919, p. 1.

44. In *Strauder* v. *West Virginia*, 100 U.S. 303 (1880), the Supreme Court held that state discrimination against blacks in the selection of juries violated the Equal Protection Clause of the Fourteenth Amendment. White southern lawyers defending black defendants rarely raised the issue, however, since to do so would involve questioning the system of racial segregation.

45. *Arkansas Gazette*, Nov. 3, 1919, pp. 1, 3. The record of the *Moore* trial is summarized in the Record, *Moore* v. *Dempsey*, pp. 1–30.

46. *Arkansas Gazette,* Nov. 5, 1919, p. 1.
47. Ibid., Nov. 12, 1919, p. 1.
48. Ibid., Nov. 18, 1919, p. 1.
49. Ibid., Nov. 20, 1919, p. 11.
50. Ibid., Nov. 6, 1919, p. 1; Nov. 7, 1919, p. 1; Nov. 8, 1919, p. 1; Nov. 21, 1919, p. 9. The total number of blacks convicted in the aftermath of the Phillips County trouble varies in the contemporary press accounts and in the subsequent tally by the NAACP. On Nov. 21, 1919 (p. 9), the *Arkansas Gazette* reported the number to be 92, but on Nov. 22, 1919 (p. 1), it published it as 75. A. C. Millar, a Methodist minister, reported in a *Gazette* article on Nov. 14, 1919 (p. 6) that a total of 65 convictions had been obtained. The NAACP rather consistently stated that 67 blacks were sentenced to prison terms and 12 were sentenced to death, bringing the total to 79. See Walter White to Louis Marshall, Jan. 14, 1925; Memo on Arkansas Cases, n.d., NAACP Papers, D-44.
51. *Arkansas Gazette,* Nov. 8, 1919, p. 1.
52. Ibid., Nov. 23, 1919, p. 24.
53. Ibid., Nov. 22, 1919, p. 1.
54. Ibid., Oct. 3, 1919, p. 6, editorial, "The Phillips County Trouble."
55. Ibid., Oct. 5, 1919, pt. 2, p. 4, editorial, "The Trouble in Phillips County."
56. Ibid.
57. Ibid., Nov. 14, 1919, p. 6, editorial, "An Injustice to Arkansas."
58. Ibid., Oct. 7, 1919, p. 6, editorial, "The Law and No Mob." See also ibid., Nov. 13, 1919, p. 6, editorial, "Lynching versus Legal Trial."
59. Ibid., Oct. 8, 1919, p. 6, editorial, "Work for Negro Leaders."
60. Ibid.
61. Ibid. The *Gazette* attributed the anti-South propaganda principally to a black newspaper published in Chicago, without naming the offending paper. It was undoubtedly the *Chicago Defender,* a leading black newspaper of this period.
62. *Arkansas Gazette,* Oct. 3, 1919, pp. 1, 18.
63. Ibid., Oct. 4, 1919, p. 2.
64. Ibid., Oct. 19, 1919, p. 6.
65. Ibid., Oct. 4, 1919, p. 2.
66. Ibid., Nov. 5, 1919, p. 8.
67. Ibid., Jan. 18, 1920, p. 1.
68. Ibid., Nov. 14, 1919, p. 6.
69. Ibid.
70. Ibid.
71. Ibid. On Millar, see Thomas Rothrock, "Dr. Alexander Copeland Millar," *Arkansas Historical Quarterly* 22 (1963): 215–23.
72. *Arkansas Gazette,* Nov. 14, 1919, p. 6.
73. NAACP Press Release, Jan. 14, 1925, NAACP Papers, D-44.

2. Walter White's Longest Train Ride: The NAACP Reacts

1. *St. Louis Argus,* Nov. 7, 1919, Waskow Papers. John Shillady immediately replied to this editorial, pointing out that upon hearing of

the "Arkansas outbreak the NAACP did send a man to Arkansas who made a thorough investigation of the trouble." (John R. Shillady to J. E. Mitchell, *St. Louis Argus*, Nov. 12, 1919, Waskow Papers).

2. Kellogg, *NAACP*, 136.
3. Ibid., pp. 240–41.
4. Financial Statement of August 31, 1920, NAACP Papers, A-15. This statement reported that for the first time since October 1919, the NAACP had a balance in its favor during August 1920. The balance totaled $153.45.
5. Walter White, *A Man Called White: The Autobiography of Walter White* (New York: Viking, 1948), 46–47.
6. Walter White to John Shillady, Oct. 7, 1919, Waskow Papers.
7. Kellogg, *NAACP*, p. 135.
8. Walter White to Dr. Charles E. Bentley, Oct. 24, 1919; see also Walter White to Charles H. Dennis, Managing Editor, *Chicago Daily News*, Oct. 9, 1919, Waskow Papers.
9. White, *A Man Called White*, 49–50; Mary White Ovington, *Portraits in Color* (Freeport, N.Y.: Books for Libraries Press, 1927), 143.
10. White, *A Man Called White*, 51.
11. U. S. Bratton to Frank Burke, Assistant of Division and Chief of Bureau of Investigation, Dept. of Justice, Nov. 6, 1919, Waskow Papers.
12. Ibid.
13. Ibid.
14. Ibid.
15. Walter White to C. P. Dam, Jan. 12, 1920, NAACP Papers, C-338.
16. Walter White to Mrs. Alma T. Weiss, Nov. 5, 1919, NAACP Papers, C-5.
17. *Chicago Daily News*, Oct. 18, 1919, in Waskow Papers. In this article, White misidentified Robert L. Hill as "William Hill." The allegation that Hill was illiterate was also incorrect.
18. *Pittsburgh Dispatch*, Oct. 24, 1919; *Boston Chronicle*, Nov. 1, 1919; *Buffalo Express*, Oct. 14, 1919, Waskow Papers. Walter White to Carey B. Lewis, *Chicago Defender*, Nov. 5, 1919, NAACP Papers, C-5.
19. Walter White to Alvin Johnson, *New Republic*, Nov. 11, 1919, NAACP Papers, C-5; Waskow, *From Race Riot to Sit-In*, 149; Walter White, "'Massacring Whites' in Arkansas," *The Nation*, Dec. 6, 1919, 715–16.
20. Walter White, "The Race Conflict in Arkansas," *Survey* 43 (1919): 233–34.
21. Report of the Secretary for the Feb. 1920 Meeting of the Board of Directors, NAACP Papers, A-15; Waskow, *From Race Riot to Sit-In*, 149, reports that ultimately 5,000 copies of the *The Nation* article were distributed by the NAACP.
22. White, "'Massacring Whites' in Arkansas," 715–1o.
23. White, "Race Conflict in Arkansas," 233–34.
24. NAACP Press Release, Jan. 14, 1925, NAACP Papers, D-44. See also Memo, "Arkansas Cases," n.d., NAACP Papers, D-44, which states that 250 men, women, and children were killed by white mobs. George Washington Davis of Pine City, Arkansas, grand secretary of the Pythian and Masonic Lodges, stated that 103 members of these black

lodges were killed in the riot. Davis appears to be an unreliable source, however, since he also claimed 250 whites were killed, a patently inaccurate assertion (Statement of George Washington Davis of Pine County, Ark., Nov. 30, 1920, Waskow Papers). In his oral argument before the U.S. Supreme Court in *Moore* v. *Dempsey*, U. S. Bratton told the Court that "some 200 innocent negroes" had been killed in the riot (See U. S. Bratton to Walter White, Jan. 11, 1923, Waskow Papers). In 1929 the NAACP reiterated its belief that "upwards of two hundred Negro men, women and children were slaughtered by mobs because they had dared to attempt to organize against vicious economic exploitation" (Resolution on the Death of Moorfield Storey, Oct. 28, 1929, NAACP Papers, C-75).

25. Walter White to James H. Guy, Jan. 31, 1920, NAACP Papers, G-73.
26. Kellogg, *NAACP*, p. 136; see Francis L. Broderick, *W.E.B. Du Bois: Negro Leader in Time of Crisis* (Stanford: Stanford University Press, 1959).
27. "The Real Causes of Two Race Riots," *Crisis*, Dec. 1919, 56–62.
28. Ibid., p. 60. The *Crisis* referred to the brothers as "Johnston," while the *Arkansas Gazette* used "Johnson." I have followed the latter spelling herein. See *Arkansas Gazette*, Oct. 3, 1919, pp. 1, 18; Oct. 4, 1919, pp. 1, 4.
29. "Real Causes of Two Race Riots," 60–62.
30. *Arkansas Gazette*, Oct. 14, 1919, p. 16.
31. Ibid., Nov. 4, 1919, p. 14.
32. Ibid., Feb. 22, 1920, p. 8.
33. Ibid., Oct. 19, 1919, pt. 2, p. 4, editorial, "Setting a Community Right before the Country."
34. Ibid., Oct. 12, 1919, p. 1.
35. Ibid., Oct. 14, 1919, p. 6.
36. Mark A. DeWolfe Howe, *Portrait of an Independent; Moorfield Storey, 1845–1929* (Boston: Houghton Mifflin, 1932), 254. For a good recent biography of Storey, see William B. Hixson, Jr., *Moorfield Storey and the Abolitionist Tradition* (New York: Oxford University Press, 1972).
37. *Guinn* v. *United States*, 238 U.S. 357 (1915); *Buchanan* v. *Warley*, 245 U.S. 60 (1917); for other early NAACP cases, see Kellogg, *NAACP*, 57–65.
38. *Arkansas Gazette*, Oct. 19, 1919, pt. 2, p. 4.
39. Ibid., Nov. 14, 1919, p. 6, editorial, "An Injustice to Arkansas."
40. William Aery to E. M. Allen, Nov. 11, 1919, Waskow Papers.
41. *Arkansas Gazette*, Nov. 23, 1919, p. 19.
42. Ibid.
43. Ibid.
44. Ibid., Nov. 25, 1919, p. 6. Walter White to William Anthony Aery, Nov. 28, 1919, Waskow Papers. Aery replied on Dec. 8, 1919, that he understood "very clearly why it seems advisable at this time that Mr. Bratton's testimony should remain, as far as possible, secret." William Anthony Aery to Walter White, Dec. 8, 1919, NAACP Papers, C–5.
45. Minutes of the Board of Directors, April 12, 1920, NAACP Papers,

A-1; Monroe N. Work to John Shillady, April 7, 1920; John Shillady to Monroe N. Work, April 10, 1920, Waskow Papers.

46. *Arkansas Gazette*, Nov. 23, 1919, p. 19.
47. Monroe N. Work, Tuskegee Institute, "A Report on the Elaine Riots," marked as received April 8, 1920, "not to be published," Waskow Papers.
48. White, *A Man Called White*, 52.
49. Nov. 19, 1919, *Cong. Rec.*, 66th Cong., 1st sess., 8818–21. Caraway also inserted into the *Congressional Record* a story from the New York *World* of Nov. 16, 1919, which supported the official version of the riot.
50. Kellogg, *NAACP*, 136.

3. A Glimmer of Hope: The Organization of a Legal Defense

1. Minutes of the Board of Directors, Nov. 10, 1919, NAACP Papers, A-15.
2. Chronological List of Events in Arkansas Riot Cases, n.d., Waskow Papers.
3. Mary White Ovington to Edith Wharton Dallas, Dec. 9, 1919, Waskow Papers; Mary White Ovington to Mr. William English Walling, Nov. 12, 1919, NAACP Papers, A-17.
4. O. S. Bratton to U. S. Bratton, Nov. 5, 1919, Waskow Papers.
5. Ibid.
6. Ibid.
7. Ibid. *Arkansas Gazette*, Oct. 5, 1919, p. 1.
8. *Arkansas Gazette*, Oct. 12, 1919, p. 1.
9. U. S. Bratton to Sheriff Kitchens and the Committee of Seven, Oct. 15, 1919, Waskow Papers.
10. Ibid.
11. O. S. Bratton to U. S. Bratton, Nov. 5, 1919, Waskow Papers. See also *Arkansas Gazette*, Nov. 1, 1919, p. 5.
12. *Arkansas Gazette*, Oct. 31, 1919, p. 1; Nov. 4, 1919, p. 7. Casey fled to Kansas following the riot, but was arrested there in late October. He voluntarily returned to Phillips County, waiving extradition. See the *Arkansas Gazette*, Oct. 28, 1919, p. 1.
13. Guy G. Bratton to U. S. Bratton, Nov. 9, 1919, Waskow Papers. The barratry charge against the Brattons and Casey was nol-prossed at the November 1920 term of the Phillips County Circuit Court. See Butts and James, "Underlying Causes," 103–4.
14. Minutes of the Board of Directors, Nov. 10, 1919, NAACP Papers, A-15.
15. Kellogg, NAACP, 237. The Curtis Resolution was Senate Resolution 189, 66th Cong., 1st Sess.
16. Walter White to Senator Charles Curtis, Nov. 7, 1919, NAACP Papers, C-241; Memo Regarding Activities of Nov. 1, 1919, Walter White, Waskow Papers. Senator Knute Nelson was chairman, while Senators Thomas Walsh and W. P. Dillingham were members, of the Senate Judiciary Committee which had jurisdiction over the Curtis

Resolution. Senator Frank Kellogg was a prominent Republican from Minnesota.

17. James Weldon Johnson to Senator Charles Curtis, Dec. 16, 1919; James Weldon Johnson to Senator Charles Curtis, Dec. 30, 1919, NAACP Papers, C-241.
18. See the *Arkansas Gazette,* Jan. 15, 1920, p. 12; Jan. 18, 1920, p. 1.
19. Minutes of the Anti-Lynching Committee held at the residence of Mr. Moorfield Storey, Boston, Nov. 14, 1919, NAACP Papers, C-338.
20. *Arkansas Gazette,* Oct. 12, 1920, p. 6.
21. John Shillady to Monroe N. Work, April 10, 1920, Waskow Papers.
22. Report to the Members of the Board of Directors, Nov. 21, 1919, NAACP Papers, A-15.
23. Minutes of the Board of Directors, Nov. 24, 1919, NAACP Papers, A-1.
24. James Weldon Johnson to Robert R. Church, Dec. 2, 1919, Waskow Papers.
25. Mary White Ovington to Edith Wharton Dallas, Dec. 9, 1919, Waskow Papers.
26. Walter White to George Nevels, Dec. 31, 1919, NAACP Papers, C-5.
27. James Weldon Johnson to William C. Graves, Secretary of Mr. Julius Rosenwald, Dec. 23, 1919, NAACP Papers, C-66.
28. James Weldon Johnson to William C. Graves, Dec. 29, 1919, NAACP Papers, C-66.
29. James Weldon Johnson to William C. Graves, Dec. 20, 1920, NAACP Papers, C-66.
30. Minutes of the Board of Directors, NAACP Papers, A-1.
31. C. L. Stewart to the *Crisis,* Dec. 22, 1920, NAACP Papers, C-155.
32. *Arkansas Gazette,* Oct. 3, 1919, p. 3.
33. Ibid., Oct. 9, 1919, p. 1.
34. Ibid., Oct. 13, 1919, p. 10.
35. Ibid., Oct. 19, 1919, p. 2.
36. Ibid., Oct. 19, 1919, p. 6.
37. Ibid., Nov. 20, 1919, p. 24.
38. Ibid., Nov. 21, 1919, p. 9; Nov. 22, 1919, p. 1.
39. Ibid., Nov. 24, 1919, p. 2.
40. Ibid., Nov. 25, 1919, p. 8.
41. Ibid.
42. J. M. Cox to William Pickens, Feb. 13, 1920, Waskow Papers.
43. *Arkansas Gazette,* Nov. 25, 1919, p. 8.
44. Organization Statement of Citizens Defense Fund Commission, Little Rock, Ark., n.d., Waskow Papers.
45. Thomas J. Price to Walter White, Nov. 26, 1919, Waskow Papers.
46. Walter White to Thomas J. Price, Dec. 1, 1919; James Weldon Johnson to Robert R. Church, Dec. 12, 1919, Waskow Papers.
47. James Weldon Johnson to Robert R. Church, Dec. 12, 1919, Waskow Papers.
48. U. S. Bratton to the NAACP, n.d., Waskow Papers.
49. Work, "Report on the Elaine Riots."
50. Report of J. H. McConico, Secretary of the Citizens Defense Fund Commission, April 7, 1920, Waskow Papers.

51. Ibid.
52. See the *Crisis*, Feb. 1921, 164–65; April 1921, p. 254; Nov. 1922, 10–11.
53. Walter White to Scipio A. Jones, March 8, 1921, Waskow Papers.
54. Organization Statement of Citizens Defense Fund Commission, Little Rock, Ark., n.d.; Walter White to Scipio A. Jones, March 8, 1921, Waskow Papers. Although Waskow, in his *From Race Riot to Sit-In*, p. 157, states that the NAACP did not make public its role in the defense of the Phillips County blacks until March 1921, the Association had in fact publicly acknowledged its participation in December 1920. See the *Crisis*, Dec. 1920, 65.
55. John Shillady to Monroe N. Work, April 10, 1920, Waskow Papers.
56. Monroe N. Work to John Shillady, April 19, 1920, Waskow Papers.
57. Tom Dillard, "Scipio A. Jones," *Arkansas Historical Quarterly* 31 (1972): 201–19. See also Ovington, *Portraits in Color*, 92–103.
58. Kellogg, *NAACP*, 63.
59. Monroe N. Work to John Shillady, April 19, 1920, Waskow Papers.
60. *Arkansas Gazette*, Dec. 11, 1919, p. 9.
61. Guy Bratton to U. S. Bratton, Nov. 9, 1919; Nov. 16, 1919, Waskow Papers.
62. John Shillady to Hugh T. Fisher, May 11, 1920, Waskow Papers.
63. U. S. Bratton to John Shillady, Feb. 12, 1920, NAACP Papers, D-44.
64. Mary White Ovington to Archibald H. Grimke, Dec. 4, 1919, Waskow Papers.

4. The Hill Extradition Fight

1. *Topeka State Journal*, Jan. 22, 1920, p. 6; *Arkansas Gazette*, Jan. 22, 1920, p. 13.
2. Hill claimed, however, that the proper name of the union was Farmers and Labors Household Union of America. See Robert Hill to U. S. Bratton, Dec. 4, 1919, Waskow Papers.
3. Ibid.
4. Robert Hill to the NAACP, Nov. 26, 1919, Waskow Papers.
5. *Topeka State Journal*, March 22, 1920, pp. 1, 2.
6. Robert Hill to the NAACP, Nov. 26, 1919, Waskow Papers.
7. Robert Hill to U. S. Bratton, Dec. 4, 1919, Waskow Papers.
8. Ibid.
9. Robert Hill to the NAACP, Nov. 26, 1919, Waskow Papers.
10. Robert Hill to Thomas Price, n.d., Waskow Papers.
11. Walter White to Thomas Price, Oct. 31, 1919, Waskow Papers.
12. The address Hill gave in his letter to Price was Boley, Oklahoma. See Robert Hill to Thomas Price, n.d., Waskow Papers.
13. *Arkansas Gazette*, Dec. 1, 1919, p. 1.
14. *Topeka State Journal*, Jan. 22, 1920, p. 6.
15. *Arkansas Gazette*, Jan. 25, 1920, p. 1.
16. *Topeka State Journal*, Jan. 24, 1920, p. 1; *Arkansas Gazette*, Jan. 23, 1920, p. 1.
17. *Arkansas Gazette*, Jan. 26, 1920, p. 1.

18. James H. Guy, Report on Hill Case, Oct. 12, 1920, NAACP Papers, G-73.
19. Ibid.
20. James Weldon Johnson to Robert R. Church, Dec. 2, 1919, Waskow Papers.
21. Report of the Secretary for Feb. 1920 Meeting of the Board of Directors, NAACP Papers, A-15.
22. John Shillady to Hugh Fisher, Jan. 23, 1920, Waskow Papers.
23. Hugh Fisher to John Shillady, April 23, 1920, NAACP Papers, D-42.
24. *Topeka State Journal*, Jan. 24, 1920, p. 1.
25. Hugh Fisher to John Shillady, Jan. 26, 1920, Waskow Papers.
26. *Topeka State Journal*, Jan. 27, 1920, p. 1. The Supreme Court's decision was *Kentucky* v. *Dennison*, 24 How. 66 (1861).
27. *Arkansas Gazette*, Jan. 29, 1920, p. 9.
28. Ibid., Jan. 30, 1920, p. 1.
29. Ibid., Feb. 3, 1920, p. 9.
30. *Crisis*, March 1920, 235; *Chicago Defender*, Feb. 14, 1920, p. 13.
31. *Arkansas Gazette*, Feb. 7, 1920, p. 9.
32. Ibid., Feb. 29, 1920, p. 6.
33. Ibid., March 26, 1920, p. 6.
34. Hugh Fisher to Walter White, Feb. 3, 1920, Waskow Papers.
35. Hugh Fisher to John Shillady, Feb. 3, 1920, Waskow Papers.
36. John Shillady to NAACP Branches, Feb. 6, 1920; see also John Shillady to Hugh Fisher, Feb. 6, 1920, Waskow Papers.
37. William Pickens to J. M. Cox, Feb. 6, 1920, Waskow Papers.
38. J. M. Cox to William Pickens, Feb. 13, 1920, Waskow Papers.
39. Ibid.
40. Ibid.
41. For further discussion on this point, see Richard C. Cortner, *A "Scottsboro" Case in Mississippi: The Supreme Court and Brown v. Mississippi* (Jackson: University Press of Mississippi, 1986), chap. 3.
42. William Pickens to J. A. Booker, Feb. 24, 1920, Waskow Papers.
43. William Pickens to James Monroe Cox, Feb. 24, 1920, Waskow Papers.
44. James A. Booker to William Pickens, Feb. 20, 1920, Waskow Papers.
45. U. S. Bratton to John Shillady, Feb. 25, 1920, Waskow Papers.
46. *Arkansas Gazette*, June 9, 1920, p. 5.
47. Ibid., March 12, 1920, p. 1.
48. See Record, *Moore* v. *Dempsey*, Affidavit of Alf Banks, Jr., Dec. 20, 1919; Affidavit of William Wordlow, Dec. 20, 1919, pp. 38–40.
49. Hugh Fisher to Walter White, Jan. 31, 1920, Waskow Papers.
50. Hugh Fisher to John Shillady, Jan. 27, 1920, Waskow Papers.
51. U. S. Bratton to John Shillady, Feb. 6, 1920, Waskow Papers.
52. Hugh Fisher to John Shillady, Feb. 13, 1920, Waskow Papers.
53. U. S. Bratton to John Shillady, Feb. 12, 1920, NAACP Papers, D-44.
54. John Shillady to Hugh Fisher, Feb. 16, 1920, Waskow Papers.
55. James Weldon Johnson to John Shillady, Feb. 16, 1920, Waskow Papers.
56. Hugh Fisher to John Shillady, Feb. 21, 1920, Waskow Papers.

57. *Arkansas Gazette*, March 16, 1920, p. 4.
58. *Topeka State Journal*, March 22, 1920, p. 1.
59. *Arkansas Gazette*, March 23, 1920, p. 1; Hugh Fisher to John Shillady, March 23, 1920, Waskow Papers.
60. *Topeka State Journal*, March 22, 1920, p. 1.
61. Hugh Fisher to John Shillady, March 24, 1920, Waskow Papers.
62. Hugh Fisher to John Shillady, March 23, 1920, Waskow Papers.
63. *Arkansas Gazette*, March 24, 1920, p. 1.
64. Hugh Fisher to John Shillady, March 23, 1920, Waskow Papers; *Topeka State Journal*, March 23, 1920, p. 1; *Arkansas Gazette*, March 24, 1920, p. 1.
65. *Topeka State Journal*, March 23, 1920, p. 1.
66. John Shillady to Gov. Allen, March 27, 1920, Waskow Papers.
67. Hugh Fisher to John Shillady, March 24, 1920, Waskow Papers.
68. *Topeka State Journal*, March 23, 1920, p. 1.
69. Ibid.
70. *Arkansas Gazette*, March 30, 1920, p. 1.
71. Ibid.
72. Ibid., March 25, 1920, p. 6, editorial, "Thwarting the Courts."
73. Ibid., March 25, 1920, p. 1.
74. Ibid.
75. John Shillady to Hugh Fisher, March 29, 1920, Waskow Papers.
76. Hugh Fisher to John Shillady, April 1, 1920, Waskow Papers.
77. Anonymous, to Gov. Allen, March 24, 1920, DA-KSHS; Gov. Allen to Ben Freeman, April 1, 1920, DA-KSHS.
78. *Arkansas Gazette*, April 16, 1920, p. 1.
79. Hugh Fisher to John Shillady, April 23, 1920, NAACP Papers, D-42.
80. *Arkansas Gazette*, April 20, 1920, p. 1; April 21, 1920, p. 1.
81. Ibid., April 21, 1920, p. 1; *Crisis*, June 1920, 90.
82. *Arkansas Gazette*, April 22, 1920, p. 6, editorial, "How They Helped Allen."
83. *Topeka State Journal*, March 23, 1920, p. 1.
84. Hugh Fisher to John Shillady, March 24, 1920, Waskow Papers.
85. *Arkansas Gazette*, April 10, 1920, p. 1.
86. Ibid.
87. Hugh Fisher to John Shillady, April 10, 1920, Waskow Papers.
88. Hugh Fisher to John Shillady, April 14, 1920, Waskow Papers.
89. Ibid.
90. John Shillady to Hugh Fisher, April 17, 1920, Waskow Papers.
91. *Arkansas Gazette*, April 11, 1920, p. 4.
92. Hugh Fisher to John Shillady, April 23, 1920, NAACP Papers, D-42.
93. Ibid.
94. *Arkansas Gazette*, Oct. 8, 1920, p. 8; Hugh Fisher to John Shillady, June 19, 1920, Waskow Papers.
95. *Arkansas Gazette*, June 15, 1920, p. 6.
96. Robert Hill to Governor Henry J. Allen, April 19, 1920, DA-KSHS.
97. Hugh Fisher to John Shillady, June 19, 1920, Waskow Papers.
98. Hugh Fisher to John Shillady, July 12, 1920, NAACP Papers, D-42.
99. Kellogg, *NAACP*, 216.

100. Hugh Fisher to John Shillady, May 6, 1920, Waskow Papers.
101. U. S. Bratton to John Shillady, May 11, 1920, Waskow Papers.
102. Affidavits of A. M. Thomas, James H. Guy, and Hugh T. Fisher, May 13, 1920, Waskow Papers.
103. Walter White to James Weldon Johnson, May 24, 1920, Waskow Papers.
104. Ibid.
105. *Arkansas Gazette*, Oct. 8, 1920, p. 8.
106. Hugh Fisher to James Weldon Johnson, Oct. 18, 1920, Waskow Papers; *Arkansas Gazette*, Oct. 13, 1920, p. 1; Memo on Hill Case, Oct. 3, 1929, NAACP Papers, C-196.
107. Hugh Fisher to John Shillady, April 23, 1920, NAACP Papers, D-42.
108. John Shillady to Hugh Fisher, April 28, 1920, NAACP Papers, D-42.
109. James H. Guy, Report on Hill Case, Oct. 12, 1920, NAACP Papers, G-73.
110. E. M. Allen to Governor Henry J. Allen, April 23, 1920, DA-KSHS.
111. E. M. Allen to Governor Henry J. Allen, May 9, 1920, DA-KSHS.
112. E. M. Allen to Governor Henry J. Allen, May 18, 1920, DA-KSHS.
113. Robert Hill to the NAACP, June 30, 1921, NAACP Papers, G-73.
114. James Weldon Johnson to Robert Hill, July 8, 1921, NAACP Papers, G-73. In 1927 Hill was convicted in the U.S. district court in Topeka for filing a false affidavit regarding a veteran's death benefits claim, but this conviction was reversed by the U.S. Court of Appeals for the Tenth Circuit in 1931. See *Hill* v. *United States*, 54 F.2d 599 (10th Cir., 1931).

5. Victory and Defeat: The Phillips County Cases in the State Courts

1. Record, *Moore* v. *Dempsey*, 261 U.S. 86 (1923), 35–37.
2. Ibid.
3. Chronological List of Events in Arkansas Riot Cases, n.d.; Mary White Ovington to Archibald Grimke, Dec. 4, 1919, Waskow Papers.
4. The substance appears to have been formaldehyde. See Affidavit of T. K. Jones, Sept. 19, 1921, Record, *Moore* v. *Dempsey*, 89.
5. Memo, U. S. Bratton to Mary White Ovington, Dec. 6, 1919, Waskow Papers.
6. U. S. Bratton was quoted in Mary White Ovington to Archibald H. Grimke, Dec. 4, 1919, Waskow Papers.
7. Affidavit of Alf Banks, Jr., Dec. 20, 1919, Record, *Moore* v. *Dempsey*, 38–39.
8. Affidavit of William Wordlow, Dec. 20, 1919, Record, *Moore* v. *Dempsey*, 39–40.
9. Record, *Moore* v. *Dempsey*, 33; see also, *Arkansas Gazette*, Dec. 20, 1919, p. 16; Dec. 21, 1919, p. 2.
10. *Arkansas Gazette*, Dec. 23, 1919, p. 9; Jan. 10, 1920, p. 12.
11. Ibid., March 23, 1920, p. 7.
12. Ibid., March 21, 1920, p. 10.
13. *Banks* v. *State*, 143 Ark. 154, 155–56 (1920).
14. Ibid., 157–58.

15. *Hicks* v. *State*, 143 Ark. 158, 160 (1920).
16. Ibid., 160–62.
17. Ibid., 162.
18. Ibid., 163.
19. Ibid., 163–64.
20. Ibid., 164.
21. U. S. Bratton to Walter White, Oct. 15, 1920, Waskow Papers. For a discussion of the development of the exhaustion of state remedies requirement with regard to the availability of the federal writ of habeas corpus to state prisoners, see William F. Duker, *A Constitutional History of Habeas Corpus* (Westport, Conn.: Greenwood Press, 1980), 203–10.
22. E. L. McHaney to Arthur B. Spingarn, June 18, 1920, NAACP Papers, D-44.
23. Walter White to C. P. Dam, Jan. 12, 1920, NAACP Papers, C-338.
24. *Arkansas Gazette*, April 3, 1920, p. 7.
25. Ibid., April 27, 1920, p. 6.
26. Quoted in ibid., April 28, 1920, p. 5.
27. Ibid.
28. Ibid., May 6, 1920, p. 16; May 7, 1920, p. 9; May 19, 1920, p. 7.
29. Ibid., May 4, 1920, p. 1.
30. *Ware* v. *State*, 146 Ark. 321, 324–25 (1920).
31. U. S. Bratton to John Shillady, Aug. 15, 1920, Waskow Papers.
32. *Arkansas Gazette*, May 4, 1920, p. 1.
33. *Ware* v. *State*, 326–27.
34. Mary White Ovington, *Portraits in Color*, 98–99; *Arkansas Gazette*, May 7, 1920, p. 1; May 8, 1920, p. 1.
35. *Arkansas Gazette*, May 4, 1920, p. 1; May 6, 1920, p. 1; May 8, 1920, p. 1; May 9, 1920, p. 12; May 11, 1920, p. 3; May 12, 1920, p. 1.
36. Ibid., May 12, 1920, p. 1.
37. Ibid., May 16, 1920, p. 3.
38. Ibid., May 17, 1920, p. 3.
39. Ibid., May 19, 1920, p. 3.
40. Ibid., June 20, 1920, p. 5.
41. *Moore* v. *Arkansas*, 254 U.S. 630 (1920).
42. Mary White Ovington, *Portraits in Color*, p. 99.
43. *Arkansas Gazette*, Oct. 13, 1920, p. 6, editorial, "G. W. Murphy."
44. *Arkansas Democrat*, Oct. 12, 1920, p. 6, editorial, "Colonel Murphy Gone."
45. Murphy, McHaney & Dunaway to Arthur B. Spingarn, Oct. 18, 1920, Waskow Papers.
46. E. L. McHaney to Arthur B. Spingarn, June 18, 1920, NAACP Papers, D-44.
47. Ibid.
48. U. S. Bratton to John Shillady, Aug. 15, 1920, Waskow Papers.
49. Conference of NAACP Executives, July 7, 1920, NAACP Papers, C-6; Report of the Secretary, Sept. 1920, NAACP Papers, A-15.
50. Walter White to James Weldon Johnson, Oct. 17, 1920, Waskow Papers.

51. U. S. Bratton to Walter White, Oct. 15, 1920, Waskow Papers.
52. Walter White to J. H. McConico, Oct. 26, 1920, Waskow Papers.
53. J. H. McConico to Walter White, Nov. 4, 1920, Waskow Papers.
54. Record, *Moore* v. *Dempsey*, 76–77; *Arkansas Gazette*, Nov. 4, 1920, p. 7.
55. Record, *Moore* v. *Dempsey*, 77.
56. Minutes of the Board of Directors, Nov. 6, 1920, NAACP Papers, A-12; *New York Call*, Nov. 21, 1920, Vol. 14, ACLU Archives.
57. Record, *Moore* v. *Dempsey*, 78.
58. Ibid., 71.
59. Ibid.
60. *Arkansas Gazette*, Nov. 16, 1920, p. 11.
61. Ibid.
62. Ibid. This was signed by Herbert Thompson; T. H. Faulkner, Jr.; J. B. Lambert; and L. J. Wilkes, Jr.
63. Ibid., Nov. 16, 1920, p. 1.
64. Ibid.
65. Copy of Dec. 1, 1920, Statement to Evening Paper, by S. A. Jones, Waskow Papers.
66. Similar criticism apparently was published in Arkansas, however, since Brough appears to have been responding to it in the *Arkansas Gazette*, Nov. 18, 1920, p. 1.
67. *Arkansas Democrat*, Nov. 17, 1920, p. 6, editorial, "Why Rush These Cases."
68. *Arkansas Gazette*, Nov. 17, 1920, p. 7, editorial, "Now for More Misrepresentation."
69. Ibid.
70. Ibid., Nov. 18, 1920, p. 1; Nov. 30, 1920, p. 7.
71. Ibid., Nov. 30, 1920, p. 7.
72. *Ware* v. *State*, 146 Ark. 321 (1920).
73. Ibid., 327.
74. Ibid., 328–29.
75. Ibid., 327.
76. Ibid., 334.
77. Ibid., 335.
78. Ibid., 336–37.
79. *Crisis*, Jan. 1921, 119; Feb. 1921, 164.
80. *Arkansas Democrat*, Dec. 6, 1920, p. 9.
81. *Arkansas Lawyer* 7 (1973), 33; "From Classroom to State Capitol," 220.
82. *Arkansas Gazette*, June 6, 1920, p. 16.
83. Record, *Moore* v. *Dempsey*, p. 75.

6. The Genesis of *Moore* v. *Dempsey*

1. *Crisis*, Feb. 1921, 164–65; April 1921, 254; Memo of Expenses, Arkansas Riot Cases, n.d., NAACP Papers, C-196.
2. J. H. McConico to Editor of the *Crisis*, March 2, 1921, Waskow Papers.

3. Organization Statement of Citizens Defense Fund Commission, Little Rock, Ark., March 2, 1921, Waskow Papers.
4. Walter White to Scipio Jones, March 8, 1921, Waskow Papers.
5. *Crisis,* April 1921, p. 254.
6. J. H. McConico to John Shillady, June 10, 1920, Waskow Papers.
7. Walter White to Bishop C. S. Smith, Dec. 22, 1922, NAACP Papers, C-155.
8. *Arkansas Gazette,* May 10, 1921, p. 12.
9. Report of the Secretary, Aug., 1921, NAACP Papers, A-15; Walter White to Moorfield Storey, June 22, 1921, NAACP Papers, C-76; *Arkansas Gazette,* June 21, 1921, p. 1.
10. *Arkansas Gazette,* May 14, 1921, p. 7.
11. Ibid., June 2, 1921, p. 1; June 3, 1921, p. 1.
12. *Arkansas Democrat,* June 7, 1921, p. 1.
13. Ibid., June 8, 1921, p. 1.
14. *Arkansas Gazette,* June 8, 1921, p. 5.
15. *Arkansas Democrat,* June 8, 1921, p. 1.
16. Robert T. Kerlin to James Weldon Johnson, May 8, 1921, Waskow Papers.
17. Robert T. Kerlin to Walter White, May 19, 1921, Waskow Papers.
18. Walter White to Robert T. Kerlin, May 21, 1921, Waskow Papers.
19. Letter of Robert T. Kerlin to Governor McRae, Waskow Papers; the letter is also quoted in part in Waskow, *From Race Riot to Sit-In,* 161–62.
20. Ibid.
21. *Arkansas Democrat,* June 9, 1921, pp. 1, 9.
22. Ibid.
23. Robert T. Kerlin to Walter White, June 17, 1921, Waskow Papers.
24. Walter White to Scipio Jones, June 20, 1921, Waskow Papers.
25. Mary White Ovington to the NAACP Branches, Oct. 8, 1921, NAACP Papers, C-155.
26. *Arkansas Gazette,* June 9, 1921, pp. 1, 3.
27. Ibid. See also *Arkansas Democrat,* June 8, 1921, p. 1; June 9, 1921, p. 3.
28. Quoted in the *Arkansas Gazette,* June 9, 1921, p. 3.
29. Ibid.
30. Ibid.
31. Ibid.
32. Ibid.
33. *Arkansas Democrat,* June 9, 1921, p. 3.
34. *Arkansas Gazette,* June 2, 1921, p. 1.
35. Record, *Moore* v. *Dempsey,* 9; *Arkansas Gazette,* June 9, 1921, p. 1. The *Arkansas Democrat* published the petitions for writs of habeas corpus filed in the chancery court, which were essentially the same as the petitions subsequently filed in the U.S. district court in *Moore* v. *Dempsey.* See *Arkansas Democrat,* June 9, 1921, pp. 3–11.
36. Record, *Moore* v. *Dempsey,* 9; *State* v. *Martineau,* 149 Ark. 237 (1921).
37. Record, *Moore* v. *Dempsey,* 9.

38. *Arkansas Democrat*, June 10, 1921, p. 1.
39. Ibid., June 11, 1921, p. 4, editorial, "Sanity Wins in Elaine Cases."
40. Ibid.
41. Ibid.
42. *Arkansas Gazette*, June 13, 1921, p. 4. The *Arkansas Democrat* published the petitions for writs of habeas corpus on June 9, 1921, pp. 3–11.
43. *Arkansas Democrat*, June 12, 1921, p. 1.
44. *Arkansas Gazette*, June 14, 1921, p. 1.
45. *State* v. *Martineau*, 244.
46. Ibid., 246–48.
47. Ibid., 249.
48. Walter White to Scipio Jones, June 21, 1921, NAACP Papers, C-76.
49. Walter White to Moorfield Storey, June 21, 1921, NAACP Papers, C-76.
50. Scipio Jones is quoted in Walter White to Moorfield Storey, June 22, 1921, NAACP Papers, C-76.
51. *Arkansas Gazette*, June 21, 1921, p. 1; Record, *Moore* v. *Dempsey*, 9.
52. *Arkansas Gazette*, June 14, 1921, p. 1.
53. Ibid.
54. Ibid., June 15, 1921, p. 5.
55. Ibid., June 21, 1921, p. 1; June 24, 1921, p. 1.
56. Ibid., June 25, 1921, p. 1.
57. Ibid., June 25, 1921, p. 1; June 26, 1921, p. 1.
58. *Phillips County* v. *Arkansas State Penitentiary*, 156 Ark. 604 (1923); Ark. Acts 1923, No. 708, p. 628; J. S. Waterman and E. E. Overton, "The Aftermath of *Moore* v. *Dempsey*," *Arkansas Law Review* 6 (1951): 1–7.
59. E. L. McHaney to Mary White Ovington, Aug. 30, 1921, Waskow Papers.
60. Ibid.
61. In a letter to Walter White on Feb. 15, 1922, H. F. Smiddy confirmed that E. L. McHaney had secured the affidavits and promised that Smiddy would "be taken care of." See also Scipio Jones to H. F. Smiddy, Feb. 9, 1922, NAACP Papers, D-42.
62. Affidavit of T. K. Jones, Sept. 19, 1921, Record, *Moore* v. *Dempsey*, 86.
63. Ibid., 87–88.
64. Ibid., 88–89.
65. Ibid., 89.
66. Ibid., 89–90.
67. Ibid., 90.
68. Affidavit of H. F. Smiddy, Sept. 21, 1921, Record, *Moore* v. *Dempsey*, 92, 95.
69. Ibid., 95, 99.
70. Ibid., 96–97.
71. Record, *Moore* v. *Dempsey*, p. 9; the petition for a writ of certiorari was ultimately dismissed by the Supreme Court on motion of Scipio Jones on October 17, 1921. See *Martineau* v. *Arkansas*, 257 U.S. 665 (1921); *Arkansas Gazette*, Sept. 22, 1921, p. 1.

72. *Arkansas Gazette*, Sept. 22, 1921, p. 1.
73. *Fay* v. *Noia*, 372 U.S. 391, 401–2 (1963).
74. See Duker, *Constitutional History of Habeas Corpus*, 181–211.
75. Ibid. Judiciary Act of Feb. 5, 1867, 14 Stat. 385–86.
76. Record, *Moore* v. *Dempsey*, 1–4. There were apparently two petitions for writs of habeas corpus filed in the *Moore* cases, one on behalf
of Frank Moore, Ed Hicks, J. E. Knox, Ed Coleman, and Paul Hall;
and the other on behalf of Frank Hicks. This was undoubtedly due to
the fact that Frank Hicks had been tried separately for having actually fired the shots that had killed Clinton Lee, while the other five
men were tried together as accessories in the murder of Lee. For
some reason, however, in the record in *Moore* v. *Dempsey* filed in the
U.S. Supreme Court, only the petition on behalf of Moore, Hicks,
Knox, Coleman, and Hall, with the supporting affidavits, was
printed. The record in the *Moore* case also reproduced the record that
had been filed in the U.S. Supreme Court when the Arkansas Supreme Court's original decision affirming the convictions of these five
men had been appealed via a petition for a writ of certiorari.
    The record in the *Moore* case thus left the impression that only five
individuals were involved in the petition for a writ of habeas corpus,
that Frank Hicks was not included. Counsel for Arkansas and for the
Moore defendants, however, stipulated that the *Moore* case could be
presented to the U.S. Supreme Court on the basis of the record of the
proceedings affecting Moore, Ed Hicks, Knox, Coleman, and Hall,
"and that the record in the Frank Hicks case need not be printed."
They also stipulated that the case of Frank Hicks would be consoli-
dated with the cases of the other five men and the cases would be
submitted to the Supreme Court together (See Record, *Moore* v.
Dempsey, 106). This stipulation was apparently overlooked by the
Supreme Court when it reviewed the *Moore* case, since the Court's
opinion incorrectly stated that only five men were involved in the
case. See *Moore* v. *Dempsey*, 261 U.S. 85, 87 (1923); see also Waterman
and Overton, "Aftermath of *Moore* v. *Dempsey*," 7, 55 (1951).
77. Record, *Moore* v. *Dempsey*, 3.
78. Ibid., 5.
79. Ibid., 5–6.
80. Ibid., 10.
81. Ibid., 15–18; 38–40.
82. Ibid., 86–99.
83. Ibid., 11–14; 76–78.

7. Moorfield Storey's Appeal: *Moore* v. *Dempsey* in the Supreme Court

1. *Arkansas Gazette*, Sept, 23, 1921, p. 1.
2. Ibid., Sept. 27, 1921, p. 5; Sept. 28, 1921, p. 5.
3. Record, *Moore* v. *Dempsey*, 261 U.S. 86 (1923), p. 101.
4. In his opinion in *Moore* v. *Dempsey*, Justice Holmes said that the
"case stated by the petition is as follows, and it will be understood
that while we put it in narrative form, we are not affirming the facts

to be as stated, but only what we must take them to be, as they are admitted by the demurrer. . . ."

5. Record, *Moore* v. *Dempsey*, 101–2; *Arkansas Gazette*, Sept. 27, 1921, p. 5; Sept. 28, 1921, p. 5.

6. E. L. McHaney to Mary White Ovington, Aug. 30, 1921, Waskow Papers.

7. Minutes of the Board of Directors, Sept. 12, 1921, NAACP Papers, A-15.

8. James Weldon Johnson to E. L. McHaney, Sept. 15, 1921, Waskow Papers.

9. Murphy, McHaney & Dunaway to the NAACP, Sept. 16, 1921, Waskow Papers.

10. James Weldon Johnson to Murphy, McHaney & Dunaway, Sept. 17, 1921, Waskow Papers.

11. *Arkansas Gazette*, Oct. 10, 1921, p. 2.

12. Walter White to Edward Lasher, Oct. 14, 1922, NAACP Papers, C-155.

13. Mary White Ovington to Mrs. Marianna G. Brubaker, Oct. 25, 1921, NAACP Papers, C-155.

14. Report of the Secretary, Oct. 6, 1921; Nov. 10, 1921, NAACP Papers, A-15.

15. Minutes of the Board of Directors, March 14, 1921, NAACP Papers, A-1-2.

16. *Arkansas Gazette*, Oct. 11, 1921, p. 2.

17. Report of the Secretary, Nov. 10, 1921, NAACP Papers, A-15.

18. Ibid.

19. Ibid.

20. Mary White Ovington to Moorfield Storey, Oct. 24, 1921, NAACP Papers, C-70.

21. Moorfield Storey to Walter White, Oct. 25, 1921, NAACP Papers, C-75–77.

22. Ibid.

23. Walter White to Moorfield Storey, Oct. 26, 1921, NAACP Papers, C–76.

24. James Weldon Johnson to Moorfield Storey, Nov. 2, 1921, Waskow Papers.

25. Moorfield Storey to James Weldon Johnson, Nov. 3, 1921, NAACP Papers, C-75–77.

26. Ibid.

27. Moorfield Storey to James Weldon Johnson, July 12, 1922, NAACP Papers, C-75–77.

28. Moorfield Storey to Mary White Ovington, Nov. 13, 1922, Waskow Papers.

29. Walter White to Moorfield Storey, Nov. 15, 1922, Waskow Papers.

30. Moorfield Storey to Walter White, Nov. 16, 1922, Waskow Papers.

31. *Frank* v. *Mangum*, 237 U.S. 309 (1915).

32. *Ex parte Frank*, 235 U.S. 694 (1914). See also Harry Golden, *A Little Girl Is Dead* (New York: Avon Books, 1967), 105–6. For an excellent scholarly account of the *Frank* case, see Dinnerstein, *The Leo Frank Case.*

33. There was an additional allegation in the habeas corpus petition that the Georgia courts, in refusing to follow past decisions in ruling upon Frank's absence when the verdict was announced, had violated the *ex post facto* prohibition in the Constitution. This clearly unmeritorious contention will not be discussed here.

34. *Frank* v. *Mangum*, 237 U.S. 309 (1915).

35. Ibid., 328.

36. Ibid., 331.

37. Ibid., 326.

38. Ibid.

39. Ibid., 335.

40. Ibid., 327, 329.

41. Ibid., 336.

42. Ibid., 340.

43. Ibid., 343.

44. Ibid., 345.

45. Duker, *Constitutional History of Habeas Corpus*, 203–10. In *Fay* v. *Noia*, 372 U.S. 391 (1963), the Supreme Court eliminated the requirement of an appeal to that court as a part of the exhaustion of state remedies requirement.

46. *Hicks* v. *State*, 143 Ark. 158, 162 (1920).

47. Ibid., 160.

48. See Duker, *Constitutional History of Habeas Corpus*, 210–11.

49. 237 U.S. 309, 347.

50. Ibid., 347–48.

51. Ibid., 348–49.

52. Ibid., 345–50.

53. See Dinnerstein, *The Leo Frank Case*, 139–47.

54. See, for example, *Adkins* v. *Children's Hospital*, 261 U.S. 525 (1923); and *Wolff Packing Co.* v. *Court of Industrial Relations*, 262 U.S. 522 (1923).

55. Scipio Jones to Walter White, Nov. 25, 1922, Waskow Papers.

56. Walter White to Moorfield Storey, Dec. 4, 1922, NAACP Papers, C-76.

57. Walter White to Scipio Jones, Dec. 4, 1922; Scipio Jones to Walter White, Dec. 6, 1922, Waskow Papers; Walter White to Moorfield Storey, Dec. 7, 1922, NAACP Papers, C-76.

58. Scipio Jones to Walter White, Dec. 21, 1922, Waskow Papers.

59. Moorfield Storey to Walter White, Dec. 18, 1922, NAACP Papers, C-75–77.

60. Walter White to Moorfield Storey, Dec. 26, 1922, NAACP Papers, C-76.

61. U. S. Bratton to Walter White, Nov. 28, 1922; see also Walter White to U. S. Bratton, Dec. 7, 1922, Waskow Papers.

62. Brief for the Appellants, *Moore* v. *Dempsey*, 261 U.S. 86 (1923), 29.

63. Ibid., 29–30.

64. Ibid., 30.

65. Ibid., 39–40.

66. Ibid., 33.

67. Ibid., 37.

68. Ibid., 37–38.
69. Ibid., 38.
70. Abstract and Brief for the Appellee, *Moore* v. *Dempsey*, 261 U.S. 86 (1923), 1–55.
71. Ibid., 56–57.
72. Ibid., 60–61.
73. Ibid., 75.
74. Ibid., 63–64, 77–90.
75. Ibid., 61.
76. Ibid., 72–73.
77. Ibid., 91–92.
78. Quoted in *Arkansas Gazette*, Jan. 10, 1923, p. 1.
79. U. S. Bratton to Walter White, Jan. 11, 1923, Waskow Papers.
80. Ibid.
81. Walter White to Scipio Jones, Jan. 12, 1923, Waskow Papers. Seligmann's report is summarized by White in this letter to Jones.

8. "A Great Achievement in Constitutional Law": Victory and Its Aftermath

1. *Moore* v. *Dempsey*, 261 U.S. 86 (1923).
2. Ibid., 87–90.
3. Ibid., 91.
4. Ibid., 91–92.
5. Ibid., 92.
6. Ibid., 92–93.
7. Ibid., 93–101.
8. Ibid., 101–2.
9. Minutes of the Board of Directors, Feb. 24, 1923, NAACP Papers, A-15.
10. Walter White to U. S. Bratton, Feb. 23, 1923, Waskow Papers.
11. U. S. Bratton to Walter White, Feb. 26, 1923, Waskow Papers.
12. Dinnerstein, *The Leo Frank Case*, 113, Louis Marshall to Walter White, March 12, 1923, NAACP Papers, D-44. The sentence that ends as "the cornerstone of the temple" in the above letter appears in the original to have read "the chief of the corner." Walter White in his *A Man Called White*, p. 53, quotes Marshall as having said "cornerstone of the temple," and I have used that version of Marshall's comment herein, as it more clearly conveys his meaning.
13. Louis Marshall to Walter White, March 12, 1923, NAACP Papers, D-44.
14. Walter White to Louis Marshall, March 13, 1923, NAACP Papers, D-44.
15. Restrictive covenants: *Corrigan* v. *Buckley*, 299 F. 899 (D.C. Cir., 1924), appeal dismissed, 271 U.S. 323 (1926).
16. The white primary: *Nixon* v. *Herndon*, 273 U.S. 536 (1927); White, *A Man Called White*, 53; Kellogg, *NAACP*, 245; Memo, Arkansas Cases, Oct. 4, 1929, NAACP Papers, C-196.
17. See the *New Republic*, March 14, 1923, "Due Process of Law in Ar-

kansas," 55–57; March 21, 1923, "Legal Lynching and the Constitution," 84–85.

18. These editorials were reprinted in the *Crisis*, April 1923, 279.
19. *Arkansas Gazette*, Feb. 21, 1923, p. 6, editorial, "The Decision in the Elaine Cases."
20. Scipio Jones to Walter White, Feb. 23, 1923, Waskow Papers.
21. Walter White to Scipio Jones, Feb. 26, 1923, Waskow Papers.
22. *Ware* v. *State*, 159 Ark. 540, 544 (1923); *Arkansas Gazette*, April 17, 1923, p. 12; April 21, 1923, p. 1.
23. Report of the Secretary, Oct. 5, 1922; Nov. 8, 1922, NAACP Papers, A-15. See Walter White to Arthur B. Spingarn, July 8, 1922, NAACP Papers, C-76.
24. Ed Ware to Scipio Jones, Feb. 12, 1923, Waskow Papers.
25. The statute is quoted in *Ware* v. *State*, 159 Ark. 540, 550–51 (1923).
26. *Arkansas Gazette*, April 17, 1923, p. 12; April 21, 1923, p. 1.
27. See *Ware* v. *State*, 546–47.
28. *Ware* v. *State*.
29. Ibid., 557–58.
30. Ibid., 558–60.
31. Ibid., 553–54.
32. Ibid., 560. Judges Jesse C. Hart and Thomas H. Humphreys dissented on the ground that the defendants had acquiesced in the continuances.
33. *Arkansas Gazette*, June 26, 1923, p. 1.
34. Ibid., June 26, 1923, p. 1.
35. Ibid.
36. Ibid., June 27, 1923, p. 1; July 13, 1923, p. 5.
37. Ibid., June 27, 1923, p. 1.
38. *Martin* v. *State*, 162 Ark. 282 (1924).
39. *Arkansas Gazette*, June 27, 1923, p. 7, editorial, "The Breakdown of the Law in the Elaine Cases."
40. Walter White to Louis Marshall, June 25, 1923, NAACP Papers, C–76.
41. Walter White, Open Letter to the NAACP Contributors, June 26, 1923, NAACP Papers, D-44.
42. Report of the Secretary, Aug. 24, 1923, NAACP Papers, A-15.
43. U. S. Bratton to Walter White, Feb. 26, 1923, Waskow Papers.
44. Report of the Secretary, May 9, 1923, quoting a letter from Storey dated May 7, 1923, NAACP Papers, A-15.
45. Ibid.
46. Memorandum from Walter White to James Weldon Johnson, March 30, 1922, NAACP Papers, G-12.
47. James Weldon Johnson to Arthur B. Spingarn, June 9, 1920, NAACP Papers, C-6.
48. Record, *Moore* v. *Dempsey*, 91; James H. Guy to NAACP, Nov. 25, 1921; Walter White to James H. Guy, Nov. 28, 1921; Walter White to James H. Guy, Dec. 5, 1921, NAACP Papers, D-42.
49. H. F. Smiddy to NAACP, Feb. 3, 1922, NAACP Papers, D-42.
50. Ibid.

51. Walter White to Scipio Jones, Feb. 6, 1922; Scipio Jones to H. F. Smiddy, Feb. 9, 1922, NAACP Papers, D-42.
52. Walter White to Scipio Jones, Feb. 17, 1922, NAACP Papers, D-42.
53. H. F. Smiddy to Walter White, Feb. 15, 1922, NAACP Papers, D-42.
54. Ibid.
55. Ibid.
56. Ibid.
57. Report of the Secretary, Dec. 6, 1921, NAACP Papers, A-15; James H. Guy to Scipio Jones, Dec., 1921, NAACP Papers, D-42.
58. Walter White to U. S. Bratton, March 24, 1922, NAACP Papers, G-12.
59. U. S. Bratton to Scipio Jones, March 20, 1922, NAACP Papers, G-12.
60. Ibid.
61. Scipio Jones to Walter White, March 31, 1922, NAACP Papers, G-12.
62. Report of the Secretary, Dec. 6, 1921, NAACP Papers, A-15. It is interesting to note that in discussing Smiddy and Jones, this report states that Scipio Jones had written the NAACP that both men were with the party of whites that had fired into the church at Hoop Spur. In their sworn affidavits, however, neither Smiddy nor Jones admitted to having been with a group that had attacked the black church at Hoop Spur.
63. Record, *Moore* v. *Dempsey*, 57–58. It is possible to determine the substance of the original appeal to the Arkansas Supreme Court because the record on appeal to the U.S. Supreme Court in *Moore* v. *Dempsey* incorporated the record in *Hicks* v. *State*, 143 Ark. 158 (1920) originally filed in the U.S. Supreme Court on petition for a writ of certiorari seeking review of the decision in that state appeal.
64. Record, *Moore* v. *Dempsey*, 60–62.
65. Ibid., 90, 98.
66. *State* v. *Martineau*, 149 Ark. 237, 248–49 (1921).
67. *Frank* v. *Mangum*, 237 U.S. 309, 338–43 (1915).
68. Record, *Moore* v. *Dempsey*, 57–60. The affidavits of Walter Ward and John Jefferson were not obtained until May of 1921; see Record, *Moore* v. *Dempsey*, 15–19. The decision of the Arkansas Supreme Court in the *Moore* cases occurred on March 29, 1920.
69. *Brown* v. *Mississippi*, 297 U.S. 278 (1936), was the first occasion on which the Supreme Court reversed a criminal conviction because confessions used as evidence against the defendants had been coerced. The Court did not recognize coerced confessions as valid bases for attacking state criminal convictions on petition for federal writs of habeas corpus until *Brown* v. *Allen*, 344 U.S. 343 (1953).
70. John E. Miller to Scipio Jones, March 24, 1923, Waskow Papers.
71. Scipio Jones to Walter White, April 2, 1923, NAACP Papers, A-15.
72. Report of the Secretary, May 9, 1923, quoting letters from Moorfield Storey on April 16, 1923, and May 7, 1923, NAACP Papers, A-15.
73. Ibid.
74. Report of the Secretary, June 7, 1923; Aug. 24, 1923, NAACP Papers, A-15.

75. Report of the Secretary, June 7, 1923, quoting a letter from Moorfield Storey to George B. Rose, NAACP Papers, A-15.
76. Ibid.
77. Moorfield Storey to James Weldon Johnson, May 29, 1923, Waskow Papers.
78. George B. Rose to John E. Miller, July 2, 1923, Waskow Papers.
79. Ibid.
80. Ibid.
81. John E. Miller to George B. Rose, July 3, 1923, Waskow Papers.
82. James Weldon Johnson to Walter White, Aug. 3, 1923, Waskow Papers.
83. Ibid.
84. Herbert K. Stockton to Robert W. Bagnell, April 18, 1923, Waskow Papers.
85. Ibid.
86. Quoted in *Arkansas Gazette*, Nov. 4, 1923, p. 1.
87. Minutes of the Board of Directors, Nov. 12, 1923, NAACP Papers, A-15.
88. Ibid. See also, *Arkansas Gazette*, Nov. 4, 1923, p. 1; Nov. 6, 1923, p. 5.
89. Minutes of the Board of Directors, Nov. 12, 1923, NAACP Papers, A-15.
90. *Arkansas Gazette*, Dec. 20, 1924, p. 1. The eight twenty-one-year men were: Will Barnes, Sikes Fox, John Ratliff, Gilmore Jenkins, Sam Wilson, Charles Jones, Ed Mitchell, and Will Perkins.
91. Scipio Jones to Walter White, Jan. 13, 1925, NAACP Papers, D-44; *Arkansas Gazette*, Jan. 14, 1925, p. 1.
92. *Arkansas Gazette*, Jan. 14, 1925, p. 1.
93. Scipio Jones to Walter White, Jan. 13, 1925, NAACP Papers, D-44.
94. Walter White to Scipio Jones, Feb. 3, 1925, NAACP Papers, D-44.
95. Walter White to Scipio Jones, March 7, 1925, NAACP Papers, D-44.
96. See clippings from the *Dallas Express*, Jan. 24, 1925; *South West American*, Jan. 14, 1925; *Arkansas Survey*, Jan. 17, 1925, NAACP Papers, D-44.
97. J. R. Marshall to NAACP, NAACP Papers, D-44.
98. Walter White to Louis Marshall, Jan. 14, 1925; Louis Marshall to Walter White, Jan. 15, 1925, NAACP Papers, D-44.

9. The NAACP and the Phillips County Cases: An Overview

1. See David Fellman, *The Defendant's Rights Today* (Madison: University of Wisconsin Press, 1976), p. 17.
2. Curtis R. Reitz, "Federal Habeas Corpus: Impact of an Abortive State Proceeding," *Harvard Law Review* 74 (1961): 1315, 1329. See also, Henry M. Hart, Jr., "Foreword: The Supreme Court 1958 Term," *Harvard Law Review*, 73 (1959): 84, 105.
3. Paul M. Bator, "Finality in Criminal Law and Federal Habeas Corpus for State Prisoners," *Harvard Law Review*, 76 (1963): 441, 489. For a

similar view, see Duker, *Constitutional History of Habeas Corpus,*
253–54.

4. *Fay* v. *Noia,* 372 U.S. 391, 457–58 (1963).
5. Ibid., 421 (1963).
6. *Moore* v. *Dempsey,* 261 U.S. 86, 93 (1923).
7. See J. S. Waterman and E. E. Overton, "Federal Habeas Corpus Statutes and *Moore* v. *Dempsey,*" *Arkansas Law Review,* 6 (1951): 8, 14
(1951).
8. 237 U.S. 309, 348 (1915).
9. 261 U.S. 86, 91 (1923).
10. Ibid., 92.
11. Waterman and Overton, "Habeas Corpus and *Moore* v. *Dempsey,*" p.
15. See also *Fay* v. *Noia,* 421, note 30.
12. Grand jury indictment: *Hurtado* v. *California,* 110 U.S. 516 (1884).
13. Trial by jury: *Maxwell* v. *Dow,* 176 U.S. 581 (1900).
14. Right to cross-examine: *West* v. *Louisiana,* 194 U.S. 258 (1904).
15. Self-incrimination: *Twining* v. *New Jersey,* 211 U.S. 78 (1908).
16. *Powell* v. *Alabama,* 287 U.S. 45, 68–69 (1932). For an excellent account of the Scottsboro cases, including *Powell* v. *Alabama,* see Dan
T. Carter, *Scottsboro* (Baton Rouge: Louisiana State University Press,
1969). The Court's ruling in *Powell* v. *Alabama* was subsequently interpreted to require the appointment of counsel for indigent defendants in serious, non-capital state cases only where the lack of counsel
would result in an unfair trial for the defendant. See *Betts* v. *Brady,*
316 U.S. 455 (1942). In *Gideon* v. *Wainwright,* 372 U.S. 355 (1963),
however, the Court held that the Assistance of Counsel Clause of the
Sixth Amendment applied to the states via the Due Process Clause
of the Fourteenth Amendment, and that under the Sixth and Fourteenth Amendments, indigent defendants in serious state criminal
cases were entitled to appointed counsel. And a "serious" criminal
case was held to be one in which there was a potential loss of liberty
at stake for the defendant in *Argersinger* v. *Hamlin,* 407 U.S. 25 (1972).
17. *Mooney* v. *Holohan,* 294 U.S. 103, 112 (1935). For a detailed analysis
of the protracted proceedings in the *Mooney* case, see Richard H.
Frost, *The Mooney Case* (Stanford: Stanford University Press, 1968).
18. See the *Crisis,* March 1935, 79; Major Developments in Legal Defense, Nov. 11, 1935; Memorandum from Mr. Wilkens on Cases for
the Board Report, Feb. 4, 1936; Memorandum to Miss Randolph on
Cases for the Board Report, April 9, 1936; Digest of Outstanding
Cases handled by the NAACP during 1935, April 14, 1936, NAACP
Papers, D-12.
19. *Brown* v. *Mississippi,* 297 U.S. 278, 286 (1936).
20. *Rochin* v. *California,* 342 U.S. 165 (1952); *In re Oliver,* 333 U.S. 257
(1948). In *Wolf* v. *Colorado,* 338 U.S. 25 (1949), the Court held that an
unreasonable search and seizure by state officers violated the Due
Process Clause, but it refused to require the state courts to exclude
illegally seized evidence until *Mapp* v. *Ohio,* 367 U.S. 643 (1961). For
additional due process requirements, see Fellman, *Defendant's Rights
Today,* p. 145.

21. *Mapp* v. *Ohio*, 367 U.S. 643 (1961).
22. *Robinson* v. *California*, 370 U.S. 660 (1962).
23. *Malloy* v. *Hogan*, 378 U.S. 1 (1964).
24. *Benton* v. *Maryland*, 395 U.S. 784 (1969).
25. *Klopfer* v. *North Carolina*, 386 U.S. 213 (1967).
26. *Duncan* v. *Louisiana*, 391 U.S. 145 (1968).
27. *Pointer* v. *Texas*, 380 U.S. 400 (1965).
28. *Washington* v. *Texas*, 388 U.S. 14 (1967).
29. *Gideon* v. *Wainwright*, 372 U.S. 335 (1963).
30. For a fuller discussion of this nationalization of the criminal procedure provisions of the Bill of Rights, see Cortner, *Supreme Court
and Second Bill of Rights*, especially chaps. 5–9.
31. See, for example, *Brown* v. *Allen*, 344 U.S. 443 (1953); and *Fay* v.
Noia, 372 U.S. 391 (1963).
32. See Fellman, *Defendant's Rights Today*, p. 149; and C. Herman
Pritchett, *Constitutional Law of the Federal System* (Englewood Cliffs,
N.J.: Prentice-Hall, 1984), p. 145.
33. "Report of the Committee on Habeas Corpus of the Conference of
State Chief Justices," *State Government*, 26 (1953): 241–45.
34. See Louis H. Pollack, "Proposals to Curtail Federal Habeas Corpus
to State Prisoners: Collateral Attack on the Great Writ," *Yale Law
Journal*, 66 (1956): 50–66; see also, Melvin E. Beverly, "Federal-State
Conflicts in the Field of Habeas Corpus," *California Law Review*, 41
(1953); 483–98; Walter V. Shaefer, "Federalism and State Criminal
Procedure," *Harvard Law Review*, 70 (1956): 1–19. In 1966 Congress
did amend the habeas corpus law to require that federal judges defer
to the decisions of state courts on factual matters absent a substantial reason for questioning the correctness of the state court's decision.
35. *Stone* v. *Powell*, 428 U.S. 465 (1976). For some erosions of *Fay* v.
Noia, 372 U.S. 391 (1963), see *Estelle* v. *Williams*, 425 U.S. 501 (1976),
and *Francis* v. *Henderson*, 425 U.S. 536 (1976).
36. Reitz, "Federal Habeas Corpus," 1329.
37. 347 U.S. 483 (1954).
38. 238 U.S. 347 (1915).
39. 245 U.S. 60 (1917); see also Kellogg, *NAACP*, 186–87; 205–6; Vose,
Constitutional Change, 31–46.
40. White, *A Man Called White*, 47, 52.
41. Carter, *Scottsboro*, 19.
42. Ibid., 71–75.
43. Ibid., 94–103.
44. See Vose, *Caucasians Only*, 30–49; Vose, *Constitutional Change*,
287–326.
45. *Chicago Daily News*, Oct. 18, 1919, Waskow Papers; James Weldon
Johnson to Walter White, Aug. 3, 1923, Waskow Papers.
46. John Shillady to Monroe N. Work, April 10, 1920, Waskow Papers.
47. Quotes from Carter, *Scottsboro*, 56–72, 90.
48. Ibid., 97–103. Roger Baldwin of the American Civil Liberties Union
was especially critical of the NAACP's role in the Darrow-Hays-ILD

episode; see Vol. 557, ACLU Archives, Roger Baldwin to Walter White, March 7, 1932; Roger Baldwin to Arthur Garfield Hays, March 7, 1932; Walter White to Roger Baldwin, March 9, 1932; Roger Baldwin to Walter White, March 15, 1932; Walter White to Roger Baldwin, May 31, 1932.

49. Report of the Secretary, July 9, 1923, NAACP Papers, A-15.

50. Kellogg, *NAACP*, 244.

51. Resolution on the Death of Mr. Moorfield Storey, Oct. 28, 1929, NAACP Papers, C-75. See also, Hixson, *Moorfield Storey and the Abolitionist Tradition*, 190.

52. James Weldon Johnson to William C. Graves, Dec. 29, 1919, NAACP Papers, C-66.

53. See H. L. Mitchell, "The Founding and Early History of the Southern Tenant Farmers Union," *Arkansas Historical Quarterly* 32 (1973): 342–69; Jerold S. Auerbach, "Southern Tenant Farmers: Socialist Critics of the New Deal," *Arkansas Historical Quarterly* 27 (1968): 113–31; Mary White Ovington, *And The Walls Came Tumbling Down* (New York: Harcourt, Brace, 1947), 163.

54. Scipio Jones to William Pickens, Oct. 22, 1936, NAACP Papers, D-7.

55. *Arkansas Law Review,* 2 (1947–48): 341 *Arkansas Lawyer,* 6 (1952): 79.

56. *New York Times,* Aug. 9, 1926, p. 4; Charles C. Alexander, "Defeat, Decline, Disintegration: The Ku Klux Klan in Arkansas, 1924 and After," *Arkansas Historical Quarterly* 22 (1963): 311–31.

57. *New York Times,* March 3, 1928, p. 10; March 7, 1937, Sec. 2, p. 8.

58. J. W. Butts and Dorothy Jones, "The Underlying Causes of the Elaine Riot of 1919," *Arkansas Historical Society* 20 (1961): 99, n. 19; 101–2.

59. *New York Times,* Oct. 19, 1937, p. 1.

60. Ibid., Feb. 1, 1941, p. 20.

61. 261 F.Supp. xv.

62. Jack Peltason, *Fifty-Eight Lonely Men* (New York: Harcourt, Brace & World, 1961), 75–76, 196–201; 633 F.2d xxi.

63. Waskow, *From Race Riot to Sit-In,* 333, n. 3.

64. Quoted in Tom Dillard, "Scipio A. Jones," *Arkansas Historical Quarterly* 31 (1972): 208.

65. Ibid., p. 213. See also Guerdon D. Nichols, "Breaking the Color Barrier at the University of Arkansas," *Arkansas Historical Quarterly* 27 (1968): 5–6.

66. Dillard, "Scipio A. Jones," 214–18. See also Tom Dillard, "To the Back of the Elephant: Racial Conflict in the Arkansas Republican Party," *Arkansas Historical Quarterly* 33 (1974): 12–13.

67. Dillard, "Scipio A. Jones," 218–19. In his article, Dillard asserts (p. 207) that Scipio Jones wrote the brief for *Moore* v. *Dempsey* in the U.S. Supreme Court, citing "The Arkansas Peons," by Scipio Jones published in the *Crisis,* Dec. 1921, 72–76, and Jan. 1922, 115–17. "The Arkansas Peons" is in fact a reprinting of the petition for a writ of habeas corpus in the *Moore* case, not the brief. The brief filed in the U.S. Supreme Court in *Moore* v. *Dempsey* was written by Moorfield Storey.

Index

Hoover, Herbert, 197
Horner, E. C., 13, 98
House of Representatives, U.S., 37
housing rights, 3
Houston, Charles H., 193
Hughes, Charles Evans, 143, 145, 190
Humphreys, Thomas H., 104

Indianapolis race riots of 1919, 5
Industrial Workers of the World
    (IWW), 5, 40, 68
International Labor Defense (ILD),
    193, 194–195

Jackson, J. M.:
    Bratton protected by, 40, 41–42
    counsel appointed by, 16
    death sentences given by, 17, 18
    Freeman warrant issued by, 91
    jury motions denied by, 92, 93
    on Kerlin's letter, 111–112
    new trial motions denied by, 86, 89,
        92
    in third *Ware* cases series, 108
    venue change and, 92, 108
Japanese aliens, 159
Jefferson, John, 17, 113, 129, 174
Jenks, Isaac C., 11
Johnson, D. A. E., 31
    Lilly allegedly killed by, 9
    Millar on, 22
    in Phillips County riot, 9
Johnson, James Weldon, 82
    Allen's meeting with, 69
    background of, 25
    on clemency petition and fee, 181
    on compromise in *Moore* cases, 179
    defense funds raised by, 45
    in Hill extradition fight, 58
    Jones and, 168
    in McHaney fee dispute, 132–133
    Murphy investigated by, 44
    on NAACP secrecy, 49–50
    on peonage system, 196
    Price and, 49
    resignation of, 195
    Storey and, 135–136
    uneducated blacks and, 194
    on White, 195
Johnson, Louis, 9
Jones, Adolphus, 51
Jones, Scipio Africanus, 46–47
    background of, 51–52
    black press on, 199

on Bratton, 146–147
on Brough's clemency denial, 100
CDFC payments to, 50
certiorari petition filed by, 125
as Chancery Court judge, 199
as chief counsel, 97
clemency petition secured by, 181–
    182
death of, 199–200
on defendants after release, 196–
    197
defense planned by, 48
demurrer filed by, 78–79
discharge motion filed by, 161–162
District Court petition filed by,
    125–126, 127–130
in *Ed Ware* cases retrial, 90–91
error petition filed by, 119–120
on *Frank Moore* ruling, 105
funds raised by, 160–161
on *Gazette's Moore* report, 160
in grandfather clause case, 199
habeas corpus petitions filed by,
    115–116, 176
in hostile environment, 92
jury issue and, 92, 93
after McHaney's resignation, 133
McRae's meeting with, 182–183
Miller's letter to, 175
NAACP and, 48–50
new trial motions filed by, 84–85
in prisoner discharge, 164, 165
prison term defendants and, 166
Robertson's decision appealed by,
    162
in short prison sentence strategy,
    175, 176
Smiddy and, 168, 169–172
Supreme Court appeal filed by, 134
in third *Ware* cases series, 108
torture charges filed by, 85, 113
Ware and, 161
Jones, T. K., 122–124, 129
    mob domination issue in testimony
        of, 173
    NAACP and, 168–169, 172
    Stockton on, 180
Judiciary Act of 1789, 126
juries:
    in *Ed Ware* cases, 86–87, 92, 93, 103
    in *Frank Moore* cases, 87–88, 128,
        142–143
    habeas corpus and, 142–143
    right to trial by, 188

240   Index

About the Author

Richard C. Cortner is professor of political science at the University of Arizona. This is his eighth book on questions of law; others are *Modern Constitutional Law, The Jones and Laughlin Case,* and *The Apportionment Cases.* He is a graduate of the University of Oklahoma (B.A. 1956) and the University of Wisconsin (Ph.D. 1961) and was a member of the faculty of the University of Tennessee until joining the University of Arizona in 1966. He has been a Woodrow Wilson Fellow and chairman of the Edward S. Corwin award committee of the American Political Science Association. His home is in Tucson, Arizona.

About the Book

This book was composed on the Mergenthaler 202 in Aster by Graphic Composition, Inc. of Athens, Georgia, and designed and produced by Kachergis Book Design of Pittsboro, North Carolina.